11/19/27.

500

G E Lundy
550 Harvard
ave N W

Canton
Ohio

JULIUS CAESAR &
,THE GRANDEUR,
THAT WAS ROME

JULIUS CAESAR
from the bust in the British Museum

JULIUS CAESAR & ᛌTHE GRANDEURᛌ THAT WAS ROME
BY VICTOR THADDEUS

ILLUSTRATIONS BY W. D. WHITE

BRENTANO'S ᛌ 1927 ᛌ NEW YORK

To

ELIZABETH HOPE ROSS

FOREWORD

Ancient Rome still evokes conceptions of grandeur. The popular imagination still sees the Eternal City as eternal in the cultural sense. Was it not once the center of world-civilization? And its fall one of history's greatest tragedies?

But how great actually was Rome? Have its admirers been too inclined to view it only from the Roman viewpoint? Have they, in their veneration for the stately Roman toga, failed to penetrate very deeply into the hearts and intellects of the men who wore it? Is the word grandeur applied to Rome as misplaced as it would be applied to a huge and gaudy side-show?

We see the hundred-per cent Romans brawling drunkenly in their Forum—hurling execrations at one another in their senate-house—lying on the cushions of their litters caressing with obscene fingers their boy-favorites—gloating sadistically, in their amphitheatres and circuses, over the butchery of unhappy gladiators and starved wild animals. They are fat heavy-jowled men with greedy cruel eyes. To make the picture perfect all they need is big cigars.

Now Cæsar takes the stage. He is lean and bald, and amorous, and subject to fits of epilepsy. Sword in one hand, the incendiary torch of Roman civilization in the other, he strides across Gaul, his thin-lipped mouth twisted into a smile as the eagles of his legions scream false promises to the natives.

And his shadow, the shadow of brute force made more brutal by human cunning, comes streaming down the centuries. But legend has chosen to whitewash this shadow as it has chosen to whitewash the tawdry walls of Rome, so that it is Cæsar, the far-seeing statesman, rather than Cæsar the bandit-adventurer, who is in the habit of stepping forward immaculate to take curtain calls as one of history's heroes and supermen.

CONTENTS

ILLUSTRATIONS

JULIUS CAESAR &
'THE GRANDEUR'
THAT WAS ROME

The Youth

I

THE Rome into which Cæsar was born was a city of several hundred thousand inhabitants that lived on the loot from conquered provinces. To the Romans it was the capital of the world.

The free population of the Italian peninsula numbered six millions; there were thirteen million slaves living within the same area. Six centuries had passed since the legendary founding of the city by Romulus, supposed to have been suckled by a wolf, and four since the expulsion of the last king, Tarquin the Proud.

Rome was now an aristocratic republic, its government democratic in form, but for all practical purposes completely in the control of an oligarchy of three hundred senators. These had gradually usurped to themselves the supreme power. While the will of the people was in theory sovereign, the Senate actually legislated with little or no regard for the wishes of the plebeians as expressed in the popular assemblies. It held the keys to the state treasure chest kept in the temple of Saturn, and reserved for its own members the farming of the revenues from the provinces. It had arrogated to its own uses the public lands, and reached out through rural Italy until the fertile and prosperous countryside where small farmers had once made a living was converted almost entirely into the spacious senatorial estates.

Rome itself, while viewed by its burgesses as the metropolis around which the unimportant remainder of the universe rotated with respectful awe, had remained a village in everything but size. The town could not be compared with the magnificent Egyptian city of Alexandria, with its broad clean streets, numerous public squares, large university and great library of seven hundred thousand volumes; or with vanished Carthage. It rose and fell among its seven hills beside the Tiber, a shapeless jumble of narrow crooked alleys, littered with rubbish, and small brick and wooden houses, in all stages of dilapidation, crowded together with no attempt at order or design. Splendid military highways, like the Appian Road, approached the city gates from north, south, east and west, but within all was evil-smelling confusion.

The streets, full of holes and ruts, had large dirty pots placed along them at intervals, to serve as public comfort stations—this was a concession of the fullers, or laundrymen, who, soap as a cleanser being unknown to the Romans, made use of urine to wash their clothes with. The sewers, where they existed, were for the greater part of the year choked with dead bodies, flung here by the professional assassins, of whom every Roman politician of consequence had his private band, as a regular part of a household consisting of an army of cooks, and Greek boy-favorites, several physicians, half a dozen buffoons and dancers, a poet, a memoir-writer, and a philosopher. The buildings, like the streets, had very little stone in their construction, but were in the main crazy unsanitary tenements, with rotting foundations, and walls a crumbling patchwork of unbaked brick and wood honeycombed with rat-holes. There was only one small wooden bridge over the Tiber, and annually this river overflowed its banks, flooding the streets along the waterfront.

Scattered through this unhealthy settlement, where malaria flourished, on the higher and more salubrious points, were the palaces of the wealthy, decorated with marble columns plundered from Grecian temples. They were isolated instances of magnificence in architecture, the really splendid homes of the Roman millionaires lying outside the city in the Campagna, or along the Bay of Naples at Baiae and Terracina. The city had only one important public square—the Forum; originally a swamp, poorly filled-in, it had become the focus of the town's political and financial activities; here, in enclosures resembling cattle-pens, the people voted at election time, here, from the rostra, to the sides of which the political faction that had fought its way to power nailed the heads of its conquered rivals, drunken orators harangued the mob, here were the city's leading bankers' shops, temples, bazaars, and brothels.

The Forum touched the base of the Capitoline Hill, upon the summit of which was situated the gaudy temple to Jupiter Optimus Maximus where returning generals offered up thanks to the gods for their victories; as the triumphal procession began to mount the hill, the captured Barbarian chiefs, who, amid the jeers of the populace, had been led in chains ahead of the general's chariot, would be taken aside and strangled in a dungeon at the foot of the Capitol, their corpses being then thrown down a long flight of steps into the Forum, to lie here exposed to public view until dragged away by one of the packs of half-wild dogs that roamed the city. In the Forum were also staged the gladiatorial combats and prizefights; the latter had been developed to a stage where they were almost as deadly as the former, the cestus worn by the boxers, a fingerless glove made of thongs of leather tied around the hand and arm as high as the elbow, being covered with knots and nails, and loaded with lead and iron, in order to make the blows more powerful— the gloves were usually referred to jocularly as "limb-breakers," they often caused death, and, when they did not kill, so disfigured the fighters that their battered-in heads resembled sieves.

The city playground was the Campus Martius lying beside the Tiber just outside the walls of Rome; this was a level plain large enough for chariot races and wild-beast shows; here the youths of Rome initiated themselves in warlike and athletic exercises, fighting posts with swords in a manner similar to modern bayonet practice, mounting and dismounting from wooden horses, wrestling, spear-throwing, and swimming in the Tiber. For special occasions small wooden amphitheatres were erected in the crowded city, but they were only of temporary construction. Nor had the first stone theatre yet been built.

And, in the same way that Rome, despite the spoils from the provinces that streamed into it, had remained a shapeless conglomeration of flimsy habitations peopled mainly by vicious idlers, with no manufactures worth speaking of, so as a commercial city it was equally backward; no ships of any size could come up the Tiber, at the mouth of which, sanded up and neglected, was the port of Ostia, off which it was not unusual for a fleet of pirate vessels, ostensibly operated by Barbarian enemies, but actually subsidized by some clique of Roman senators, to lie in wait for the transmarine trade.

In Rome, all eyes were fixed on the golden goal of Success. There was one sure road by which this might be reached— *Graft.*

The oligarchy of senators ruling the Republic was open to any proposition that appeared a paying one. For bribes they had betrayed their own army to the African king, Jugurtha. For bribes a number of the senators had even conspired to bring mountain chiefs down through the Alpine passes to pillage Rome.

The Roman law-makers stand out as fat and greasy profiteers, waddling around in togas, who over-ate and over-drank, who, worn out with debauchery, spent much of their free time pawing over the bodies of their Greek boys and fine young Barbarian gladiators—of which every wealthy Roman kept a stable—, afterward to gloat sadistically over the butchery of the latter in the Forum or circus, who, in the senate-house, shrieked and wrangled in high-pitched voices, and not infrequently, having just lurched out from one of the combination tavern-brothels with which the city abounded, to take their seats in the Senate, vomited during their speeches.

The plebeians, whose votes elected the two annual consuls, were a venal rabble, composed largely of the farmers whom the gradual monopoly of all the good land in the vicinity of Rome had forced into the metropolis. The immense cattle-farms, and vineyards, of the millionaires, which used only slave labor, by making it impossible for the free Italians in the rural districts to earn a living, compelled them to seek their subsistence in the city, where they soon caught the easy-money spirit, selling their votes instead of working, and howling for free corn and public banquets; and where, likewise, urged on by the demagogues, they insisted on being entertained with great wild-beast shows and gladiatorial combats, and applauded, as the idol of the hour, whichever general brought back the biggest spoils.

In this republican city of millionaires and beggars, which created itself "guardian" of every foreign country where rich booty was to be expected, there existed the keenest competition for the higher political positions. The enormous sums it was necessary for aspirants to the consulship to expend in bribes and entertainment—often, in modern money, the equivalent of, or more than, a million dollars,—were amply compensated for by the rewards which fell into the lap of the successful candidate. Every consul, when his term of office expired, was appointed to the governorship of a province, and it was customary for these "proconsuls," as the governors were called, to leave for their governments heavily in debt, but to return in a few years fabulously wealthy with what they had extorted through every monstrous form of cruelty and crime from the wretched foreigners placed under their jurisdiction. If the proconsul, during his absence, developed a greed complex, which made him reluctant to divide his plunder honorably with the senators back home, he was impeached for misgovernment immediately on his return to Rome; otherwise he was welcomed back to civil life again as an exemplary citizen.

The Roman proconsul, when not leading his legions on pillaging expeditions, and thus, at the expense of the Republic, from whose state-chest his troops were paid, busy at his official task of building up his private fortune, led a life calculated not to overtax his energies; a writer of the period has handed down a description of how the tired executive of Sicily, one of the most exploited of the Roman provinces, used to travel when he made the circuit of his dominions attending to public business——

When the governor travelled, which of course he did not in winter, but only at the beginning of spring—not the spring of the calendar, but the beginning of the season of roses—he had himself conveyed, as was the custom with the kings of Bithynia, in a litter with eight bearers, sitting on a cushion of Maltese gauze stuffed with rose-leaves, with one garland on his head and a second twined about his neck, applying to his nose a little smelling-bag of fine linen, with minute meshes, filled with roses; and thus he had himself carried even to his bedchamber.

Rome's greed for gold had been given immense stimulus by the destruction of Carthage, which for the crime of being a commercial rival, had been hounded to extinction by the Republic on the north shore of the Mediterranean. A century before Cæsar's birth, the great Carthaginian general, Hannibal, in a last desperate attempt to throw off the Roman oppression, had landed in Spain and crossed the Alps with his elephants, to carry the war into Italy, where for ten years he defeated every Roman army sent against him. After his death, Rome made elaborate plans not merely to humble the hated Phœnician city but utterly to destroy it. At the first opportunity, the existing treaty was set aside, while the terms of the ultimatum presented to Carthage were made so monstrous that the city in desperation was driven to armed defense, with the result that the Roman *tormenta*,—the huge battering rams, operated by more than a hundred soldiers, and the great catapults throwing jagged rocks twice the weight of a man— finally, after a prolonged siege, broke through the walls, and allowed the legionaries entrance.

For days and nights now the city was given over to organized massacre, until, with the exception of a few thousand inhabitants reserved for the triumph, the entire population of half a million people had been exterminated. By order of the Roman Senate the depopulated Carthage was then burnt, the ruins being levelled and ploughed to eliminate as completely as possible all traces that might mark the site of this once flourishing metropolis; and, as final display of the malignant ferocity characterizing this atrocious crime, a curse was solemnly invoked upon whomsoever should rebuild the city.

The same year that saw the destruction of Carthage witnessed the similar extinction of the thriving Grecian manufacturing town of Corinth, doomed likewise for being in the eyes of the Romans too prosperous. The large indemnities collected from Carthage before the final siege, and the loot brought back from its ruins and those of Corinth, made Rome money-mad. From now on gold, and gold alone, interested patricians and plebeians alike. The generals became simply business men in uniform. With their armies went the contractors of the city capitalists, and to these the Roman commanders sold whole nations into slavery, dividing the proceeds with the politicians who had secured their appointments for them. The wholesale bribery at the elections began to assume such gigantic proportions that because of the heavy borrowing by rival candidates for the consulship, for the purpose of winning over the various voting divisions, it was not unusual for the rate of interest on money in Rome to double during the election periods.

Religion, the Romans had brought, for political purposes, to a high degree of refinement. By consulting the heavens, and declaring these unfavorable to legislation, either one of the consuls, when the people showed signs of voting in a manner unfavorable to the interests of the oligarchy, could have the elections postponed. The College of Augurs, whose members examined the livers of sacrificed animals and noticed the manner in which birds were flying, in order to determine whether the auspices were good or bad, was composed exclusively of the millionaire politicians; and the popular assembly could thus always be brought to terms, since either it voted as directed by the oligarchy, or its decrees, if it did not disperse, were pronounced illegal, and the Forum was cleared by the gladiators of the senators. When the oligarchy itself split seriously on some issue, the minority faction of senators usually led an armed insurrection against the party in power; inducing the lawless element of the city to join their ranks by proclaiming a general cancellation of all debts, and seeking to win the support of the slaves by declaring them emancipated.

This slave population, which had increased so enormously as Rome widened its protectorates, until at last it was twice that of the free population in the peninsula, was catered to with much unction at such moments, but at other times held down with ruthless severity. Already the Republic stood in such dread of a widespread revolt that once when the Senate was debating the passage of a law compelling the slaves to wear a uniform costume, different from that of the free Italians, to indicate their servile condition, the law was judged inadvisable on the grounds that it would show the slaves too markedly their numerical superiority. To keep them from gaining the upper hand, a system of terrorization was resorted to, runaway and rebellious slaves being crucified on posts put up by the roadside, and impaled upon wooden stakes, sharpened and hardened by fire, driven through the back below the shoulders and coming out through the mouth. On the occasion of one uprising in Sicily twenty thousand slaves were thus suspended from crosses, erected for miles, like modern telegraph poles, along the principal highways.

The misery into which foreign peoples were plunged when rounded up in the Roman man-hunts and sold into slavery remains to this day, perhaps, the darkest and most dreadful in the annals of history. Slaves were brought back from the wars in such huge quantities—there were times when ten thousand would be shipped to Italy from Asia and Africa in a single day—that it was far cheaper to kill them off quickly and buy new ones than to breed them. They were made to butcher one another in the gladiatorial combats, and to fight with lions, tigers and panthers, in the circus, for the amusement of the Roman mob. They were worked to death in chains in the Spanish mines, and on the great plantations and farms of millionaires, where they cultivated the fields, gathered the grape and olive harvest, and tended the cattle. And enormous numbers perished on every public project, such as the construction of a new road or aqueduct.

While the subjugated peoples forming this huge Roman slave-reservoir were all regarded by the Romans as primitive races, little above the level of animals in their morals and manners, the term Barbarian, in its strictest application, was referred to the European tribes north of the Alps. These, because the Roman burgess lived in constant dread of a raid from the north that might result in the destruction of Rome, lay utterly beyond the pale of civilization. The Romans hated the Barbarians—the Gauls and the Germans—not as commercial rivals, but as enemies of the entire human race.[1] They spat on the captive chiefs brought to Rome to be dragged in the triumphs, and roared applause when their corpses came tumbling down the long flight of stone steps leading to the Forum from the prison in the Capitol where they were strangled to death by the triumvirs.

But the truth about the Barbarians may be a different matter. They had tremendous problems to solve which the Romans, safe and sheltered in their sunny southern city, were never troubled by. The Barbarian "armies" which the Roman legionaries hacked to pieces were not armies at all, but migrating tribes, driven by cold and starvation to seek an easier existence in a new homeland. Pressed upon by equally wretched tribes further to the north-east they had to move on or die.

The Barbarians were children in much the same way that the American Indians were children. Such greed and hate as the Republic had displayed against Carthage was unknown to them. They were fighting, not to monopolize the wealth of the world, but merely to live, and to Rome, with its superior military science, they would never have constituted a menace except for Rome's internal corruption which constantly imperilled the safety of its own legitimate boundaries. But wherever they made contact with the Romans they were betrayed and exploited; the legionaries hunted them through their forests like wild beasts, dragged men, women and children away into slavery, and cut off the hands of the patriots who persisted in disputing the Roman "right of conquest."

[1] In this respect the Barbarians bear a suspicious resemblance to the modern "Bolsheviks."

As they came under Roman influence the Barbarians adopted the Roman standard of morals, and became, possibly, equally corrupt and treacherous. They began even to cut off their long picturesque moustaches so that they would look like Romans. But types of the true Barbarian, so scorned and hated by the Roman, were handed down to posterity by the Romans themselves in their sculpture—suddenly, from among the throng of rapacious faces in the Roman room of any large present-day museum there will leap at last into the vision of the visitor one that lacks the greedy vicious eyes, the heavy jowls, the bald head of the Roman—this piece of statuary will have written upon its name-plate, *"Head Of A Barbarian."*

And the head is a fine head, with frank and open features, framed in thick, long hair that tumbles down to the shoulders, and a mouth, that, half-hidden by the drooping moustache, is sad and wistful, as though this unknown Barbarian, staring with his stone eyes past the alien Roman faces surrounding him, were dreaming, as in Rome two thousand years ago, of the faraway rivers and forests of his native land.

He died, only too probably, as so many of the captive Gauls died; either torn to pieces in the arena by wild beasts, or goaded on with whips and hot irons to butcher, and be butchered by equally unhappy fellow-Barbarians—to make a Roman holiday.

2

Caius Julius Cæsar was born in Rome, on the 12th of July, in the Roman year 704 (Roman time dated from the founding of Rome), a hundred years before the birth of Christ in Bethlehem.

He is reported by some historians to have been delivered into the world under circumstances of unusual difficulty, surgery having to come to the aid of nature—hence the term, Cæsarean operation,—but others state he had a normal birth.

In an age of general corruption, the Cæsar family—Cæsar was the cognomen, being Moorish for elephant, which an ancestor, one of the *gens* Julia,[1] was said to have killed in Africa on a hunting expedition,—has been singled out as the honorable exception. The Cæsars, it is usually recorded, were moderately well-to-do Romans of the finer old-fashioned type, who for generations had remained uncontaminated by the prevailing viciousness of the times. The men held important political positions, but discharged their duties faithfully, some of them being consuls, but good consuls. The women were only concerned in making good wives and mothers. Of Cæsar's parents, his father was an upright praetor or judge, and his mother a simple home-loving gentlewoman, with a horror of wrong-doing, whose main interest in life was bringing up her son to follow the same straight and narrow path of rectitude in which the father had always walked.

This estimate of Cæsar's family antecedents is based unfortunately on purest conjecture. From the rapid manner in which he rose to power it is far more probable that the Cæsars, instead of being only moderately rich were extremely wealthy. They had unquestionably been in the foremost rank of the Roman nobility that profited in such a monstrous manner by the murder of Carthage, while their very considerable activity as politicians in an era of recognized corruption would seem strongly to indicate that there was little to choose between them and other Romans on this score. Certainly Cæsar himself, as his career showed, had been ably tutored in the science of distributing largesses where they could be relied upon to bring the greatest returns.

Perhaps, then, Aurelia, Cæsar's mother, was a simple old-fashioned lady who clung tenaciously to past ideals, but it is quite possible also that she was not greatly different from the wife of any modern war-time profiteer. Beyond a doubt she was exceedingly shrewd and worldly, with few illusions about Roman nature. Her sister, Julia, had married the dictator, Caius Marius; it was Aurelia, who, in later life, urged her son

[1] Only during the last days of the Republic did it become Roman custom to call the individual by the gens or middle-name. Thus, most of his lifetime, Cæsar was known as Caius Cæsar, and not as Julius Cæsar.

into the alliance he made with Marcus Crassus, the richest man in Rome.

As Caius grew into adolescence, she may have kept the strictest of watch over his morals, but certainly to little or no effect. Cæsar, from a delicate wayward child, developed into a slender handsome youth (looking more like a girl than a boy, however), whose main natural bent was towards having a good time. He has dark hair, and dark eyes, the former fine and silky, the kind that falls out early in life. He wears, not the short tunic of more masculine young Romans, but a long one that reaches almost to the ground, and has sleeves, with fringes at the wrist. The girdle, worn tight usually by men except when relaxing in the privacy of the home, he has loose at all times. With the exception of Cicero, his companions are all revellers, many of them bi-, some of them frankly homosexual. Cæsar, because he takes pride in tracing his ancestry back to the goddess of love, Venus, inclines mainly towards girls in his amours.

Cicero, several years older than Cæsar, but with a younger brother about his age, is a sickly intellectual.

He has a big head, a scrawny neck, and a long lanky body. A bitter envy consumes him as he watches Cæsar blossom out into one of the most popular young men about town. As a thinker, and conversationalist, he knows that he is immeasurably the superior of Cæsar, yet, at the same time, he grieves secretly because he fails to make an equal impression upon the world of fashion.

He too wants to be hailed as the best of good-fellows, but wherever he goes his uncontrollable urge to enhance his reputation as a wit by making highly personal remarks about his friends creates for him lifelong enemies.

He is jealous likewise of Cæsar's obvious sex-appeal. Cicero himself feels sex strongly, but while the girls admire his mind, and all of them predict for him a brilliant future, at the parties he always somehow has to give way to the rowdies.

So he grows up, a tragicomic figure in his period. His body

becomes leaner and longer, and his neck scrawnier, until it scarcely seems capable of supporting the large nervous head. Burning up with desire for fame, but realizing his physical unfitness for the army, he maps out for himself a splendid political career; for though he despises the common people he nevertheless yearns for the coming of that day, which he dreams so often about, when, slaves and all, they will be shouting his name from every housetop.

Cæsar cares nothing about book-learning. His tutor, Antonius Gnipho, a Gaul, spends weary hours trying to teach him Greek. His mind during the lessons is on the taverns, or the barber shops where he spends whole afternoons having his hair curled and scented in the latest foppish mode.

But from Gnipho he hears of the Barbarians who live on the far side of that great wall of mountain to the north, and his ambition is sometimes faintly stirred to imagine himself a victorious general dragging back to Rome with him for his triumph a long chain of captive kings. These thoughts, however, are vague and fleeting—the youth Cæsar is far too fond of Rome and its amusements to wish yet awhile to leave it for the northwestern wilderness. He has a certain admiration for his uncle Marius, the creator of the first Roman professional army, but military life in general, with its hardships and dangers, has little appeal for him. At the moment, good-fellowship,—wine, women and song,—sum up for him the whole of life. Some day, because his mother wishes it, he may stand for the consulship, but at present the office of ædile has the brightest glamour for him.

The ædiles, among other duties have charge of the public entertainment. They manage the gladiatorial combats and wild-beast spectacles. When these are less elaborate than the populace feels they ought to be, the ædile is hissed, while, on the contrary, if new numbers, more sensational than any previous ones, are offered the audience, it makes the Forum or the Circus ring with its applause.

Caius likes to be popular. He can think of nothing more

stirring than the sight of a sea of faces turned in his direction, every mouth shouting approval. So he means to be ædile some day, and when he is he will outdo all the efforts of former entertainers, by staging epic spectacles such as the city has never before seen.

Even the thrilling feature of the hundred lions matched against Numidian archers in the Circus by Lucius Sulla shall fade and vanish from Roman Memory when it looks on at the shows of Cæsar.

3

In his childhood he has more than one chance to become used to the sight of blood.

The Roman boys and girls gather in curious groups around corpses being torn to pieces by the dogs. . . . He is twelve when Lucius Cinna, placed in the consulship by Sulla before he leaves for Asia to war against Mithridates, conspires to bring about the downfall of the absent Dictator.

Cnaeus Octavius, Cinna's consular colleague, remains faithful to Sulla. He surrounds the Forum with his soldiers. They fall on the unarmed citizens collected here to listen to the harangue of the new demagogue; and when night falls after Octavius' day, ten thousand bodies lie outstretched upon the blood-soaked ground.

Cinna and the revolutionary tribunes have made good their escape. They collect an army in rural Italy, give the command to the exiled general Marius, and march on Rome, which succumbs after a desperate battle. Terrible reprisals for "Octavius' day" follow; the gates of Rome are closed, for five days and nights the city streets swim in blood; the heads and hands of the slain senators add a gargoyle cornice to the rostra; horses are driven full-gallop through the Forum dragging behind them the bodies of the wounded and dead patricians. What survivors there are, flee to the army of Sulla in Asia.

The triumphant Cinna, a lean shrewd man devoured by ambition, which he masks beneath a show of democratic feeling, now takes the place of Sulla as Dictator. He is four times consul.

That the youth Cæsar saw fit to join the party of Cinna can be judged no sure sign that he was especially interested in political reform, for then, as now, private motives frequently governed public actions. Cæsar was in love with Cinna's daughter, the beautiful Cornelia. His parents were trying to arrange a match between him and a rich heiress named Cossutia, but no sooner had his father died, leaving him free to plan his own future, than he broke off the engagement to marry Cornelia.

He was eighteen then. His uncle Marius had been dead two years. The old general had not been assassinated by the Senate, or stabbed in the back by mutinous soldiers, the usual fate of a Roman commander, but, at seventy years of age, crazed with jealousy of the younger commander, Lucius Sulla, who had once been his lieutenant, and whose exploits in the East were now eclipsing the fame of Marius, died a raving lunatic in his bed.

Marius was the son of an Italian farmer. Bred to the plough, he ran away from home to join the army. He seems to have possessed certain soldierly qualities for promotion was quick; in an age when senile old capitalists and degenerate boys were commanding the Roman armies, and when a Roman expeditionary force consisted of four times as many bakers, cooks, actors and harlots as soldiers, he built up for himself the reputation of being a military genius.

How great a soldier he really was is open to question. He was hailed as invincible when he brought Jugurtha in chains to Rome, but Jugurtha was nothing more than a petty African prince, whose success in warfare had always been dependent upon the bribes he paid the Senate. He was hailed again as the Saviour of his country when he slaughtered the Cimbri, but the Cimbri were only a vast unorganized collection of Gallic families grouped for migration like a herd of buffalo.

Marius *was* unquestionably one of the first Roman generals with enough common sense not to be scared by numbers. Instead of believing exaggerated rumors of the fighting strength of the enemy, he goes to see for himself. In the case of the Cimbrian army, he finds this, as he has expected, to consist mainly of women, children, old men and dogs. He watches it trekking wearily through the mountain passes of the Alps; choosing a favorable moment, when the covered wagons which have survived the hardships of the journey are no longer strung out for miles, but collected on the first open plain in encampment, he swoops down with his cavalry and swiftly sweeps the Barbarian peril out of existence.

His skepticism in the value of non-combatants as part of an efficient military machine he applies in turn to the Roman armies. He expels the audience of impotent octogenarians, and their simpering perfumed boys, who, no longer able to derive a thrill from the bloody mangling of bodies in the city combats and wild-beast shows, have hitherto been glad to wear armor in return for the privilege of peeping at battlefields from behind their gladiators. He throws out of camp all the harlots, male and female. He makes war, in short, strictly a business proposition.

His soldiers must be no amateurs, but experienced killers, willing to submit to rigid discipline. Their pay will be small,—480 sesterces, or twenty-five dollars, a year,—but let them only serve Marius loyally, and their welfare will be looked out for in the rapine and pillage they can indulge in after victories. Thus he creates the first Roman professional army.

It is he who makes the eagle its official emblem. Before his day the wolf, the minotaur, the horse and the bear were also carried as military standards. Marius discards the quadrupeds, keeping only the bird of prey.

As his reputation rises, the citizens of Rome begin to call upon him in every social crisis. He represents to their minds the clean-cut soldier, who can always be relied upon to restore law and order. He becomes military Dictator, and is seven times consul.

As a youth, Cæsar stands in no great awe of the old general, for he sees too much of him at his aunt's. Marius may have accomplished great things that will live forever in history (as he himself says they will), but in private life he is dull and boresome. Cæsar yawns at the mere thought of his interminable lectures on order and system.

The old man seems confident there has never been a general like him, and that there never will be, but Cæsar, though he may appear to concur in this opinion, feels that Sulla is much more of a real hero. For Sulla knows not only how to win wars, but how to have a good time also. He is twenty years younger than Marius and takes life far less seriously. His soldiers are as well-disciplined, but he makes no attempt to interfere with their pleasures, tolerating all forms of indulgence, and, himself licentious to an extreme, setting them an example for debauchery when there is no enemy to fight. In his camps he is always surrounded by dissolute young patricians, actors and dancers, and it is common knowledge that he has love affairs with both sexes.

Marius hates Sulla as partly responsible for the change in public sentiment which had put an end to his dictatorship and resulted in his banishment. It amuses Cæsar how his uncle endeavors to hide this hatred beneath contempt, speaking of Sulla as though the latter, instead of being a man of fifty, were a mere boy—he remembers well, he says, the time when Lucius first applied for an army position; it was during the war with Jugurtha—his grim, wrinkled face, scarred with wounds, breaks into an ugly smile as he says that to build up his first army he had deliberately enlisted Rome's most worthless citizens, and Lucius Sulla was one of them. All that he knows about war, he learnt, says the old general, from Caius Marius.

Marius dies, deliriously cursing the new hero of the Roman legionaries who, in Asia, is prosecuting a successful war against Mithridates. At Cinna's house, where Cæsar spends much of his time because of Cornelia, the sentiment is wholly anti-Sulla. But news of fresh victories won by Sulla over the eastern king keeps coming to Rome. The senators grow fearful. What will happen when he returns and finds that his town house has been razed to the ground, and his country estates laid waste?

Cinna, a persuasive talker, tells them not to worry. He knows how to protect the Republic in case of trouble. If Sulla tries to come back at the head of an army, he himself will raise troops and go out and defeat him. The senators, who usually find his speeches convincing, give one another furtive glances —what does Cinna know about fighting?

Cinna sends notes to Sulla ordering him to return to Rome —he is recalled for misconducting the war, and another general will be sent out to take his place. Sulla pays no attention to the notes, but continues his conquests. Cinna sends more notes.

At last, after a long silence, Sulla replies that he has still work to do in Asia which will keep him here for a few months longer, so cannot obey the wishes of the Senate immediately —he attaches a postscript saying that when he does return to Rome he means to bring his army with him.

The Senate goes into an uproar. The senators—the new ones approved by Cinna after Sulla's had been assassinated or had fled to Asia—meet in little groups on street-corners near the senate-house to whisper opinions upon the advisability of murdering Cinna to win back the good-will of Sulla. Cinna tries to make light of the letters. He tells the Senate that Sulla's conduct is only the commonplace one of another disobedient general. He thunders against the absent chief in the name of the Republic. The senators, their better judgment overpowered by his oratory, agree to stand firm.

But at home Lucius Cinna puts aside pretense somewhat, appearing less certain of the outcome. He has grown thinner, and very nervous. He sits with his head drooping into his hands, as though brooding upon what the future may hold in store for him. Cornelia is anxious about his health, and Cæsar begins to pity him.

At last he sends to Sulla the following ultimatum—either

Sulla disbands his army, and returns to Rome according to the instructions of the Roman people, or he will be decreed a public enemy and have a price set on his head. There follows another long interval of silence—then Sulla replies. This time his letter is little more than a brief memorandum to the effect that he has already drawn up proscription lists of those influential Romans who will be executed for treachery and abuse of office when he enters Rome with his army,—Lucius Cinna, and his entire Senate, are on these lists.

Rome, wild with terror, wails for dead Marius. The senators, frantic with despair because the old man is no more, yet blame him as being largely responsible for the present crisis—why did he accept the command of the army which brought Cinna back and massacred the Octavians, if only to die later, at this moment when he is most needed?

They feel equally vindictive towards Mithridates. That an Asiatic potentate should arrogantly title himself "Child of the Sun," and yet be unable to inflict a crushing defeat upon a Roman general that his own countrymen want out of the way, seems the most hollow of mockeries. For months there have been conscientious sacrifices to the gods in order that Sulla and his whole army in the East may be cut to pieces by the enemy, but instead of this happening it seems only too probable that in the last big battle Mithridates has been completely routed, leaving Sulla free, after four years' absence, to return for his revenge.

The Roman populace shakes its head when Marius the Younger, twenty years old, supports Cinna in his advice not to worry, declaring he will take the place of his father. He may have inherited some of his father's military ability, but who can tell?

So over the whole town hangs the dread of Sulla's return. And the very confidence of young Marius makes Cæsar think more of his dead uncle. True, the old man was not ornamental around the house, but on the battlefield he must have been competent. Certainly, today, were he alive, Romans would have something to cling to.

It was Marius, he remembers, who first ridiculed the Roman militia, and asked for real soldiers. It was Marius who made war a profession, and gave the legionary dignity.

Cornelia, a dark passionate girl, hates Sulla bitterly. She knows that if he wins his way into Rome her father dies.

Gradually Cæsar is influenced by her to the point of allowing himself to appear in sympathy with the party of Cinna. But he regrets lost opportunities. Cnaeus Pompey, whose father, nicknamed Strabo, the squint-eyed, had been one of the first patricians murdered by Cinna after he took over the government, has gone to Greece to join Sulla. Until Cæsar fell in love with Cornelia, he had been very friendly with Pompey. Then, because of her devotion to the avowed principles of her father, and the factional strife which put the Pompeys on one side and the Cinnas on the other, he was forced to see less of him. Now, while he cannot bring himself to do anything that would wound Cornelia, he is immensely envious of Pompey's opportunity to make a triumphal entry into Rome with the world's greatest living general. But it is quite impossible for him to go likewise to Asia, since this would mean fighting against Cornelia's father.

Much as he loves Cornelia, he doubts whether it would be advisable for him to take up arms against Sulla. He knows both Cinna and Marius the Younger too well personally to place much confidence in the generalship of either. Also he is very friendly with Marcus Cicero's brother, Quintus, and he notices that Quintus, though quite as wild as himself, is saying nothing about volunteering for service in the army with which Cinna expects to defeat Sulla. He feels reasonably confident that the shrewder Marcus has advised his brother not to risk his neck in a hopeless cause, and he is the more sure of this when the older Cicero, who he knows really dislikes him under a display of great affection, pretends to him he has heard rumors that Cinna has already given his son-in-law a commission, and warmly congratulates Cæsar on the splendid spirit which is taking him to the front in defense of the liberties of the Republic.

Public sentiment being against allowing Sulla to bring the war into Italy, Cinna is compelled to take an expeditionary force to meet him. He prepares to leave for Brundisium. Sulla, meanwhile, is giving Rome plenty of time to arm against him. He seems to understand perfectly that the longer the suspense lasts the more likelihood there will be of the defense forces becoming divided among themselves. He is returning from Asia Minor in a very leisurely fashion, occasionally sending the senators ironic notes to let them know that he still has them in mind. In Athens he lingers to collect paintings and statuary with which to decorate his Roman palace.

Cæsar has not left Italy with Cinna's expeditionary force, but has stayed in Rome to take care of Cornelia. All around him there is plotting and intriguing. Many of the patricians have slipped quietly out of the city to join Sulla, while others hurriedly depart for their provincial estates. Very few of them, though careful not openly to display antagonism to the party which still holds the city, are inclined to take an active hand in resisting the entry into Rome of the veteran legions commanded by the returning Dictator. Marius the Younger is drilling troops for defense of the city in the event that Cinna may be defeated, but Cæsar does not enroll.

The city mob, divining rightly that it will, as usual, on general principles, be massacred wholesale if Sulla takes Rome, has allowed itself to be worked up into a frenzy of patriotism, but Aurelia pleads with her son not to compromise his whole future career by a single rash act. Cæsar's own common-sense advises him to refrain from taking any step that may put him on the much discussed proscription lists.

He hopes, for Cornelia's sake, that Cinna will triumph over Sulla, but he decides to wait until one side or the other has obtained a decisive victory before he does anything. Meanwhile, very conveniently, he has his priesthood to fall back on.

For since the age of fourteen, he has been a priest of Jupiter;

his aunt Julia having talked her husband, old Marius, during his seventh consulship, into making her nephew a member of the Sacred College. Except for the handsome salary attached to it, Cæsar has always thought his priesthood a first-rate joke. In the wineshops, his fellow-revellers have often made merry over the fact that he is a *flamens dialis*. But during the present crisis he becomes more serious about religion. He looks up the duties of a priest of Jupiter, and finds it would be highly improper for a member of the Sacred College to take up arms, no matter how admirable the cause.

One day a courier, his horse lathered with foam, gallops up to the gates of Rome with the news that Lucius Cinna has been killed in a mutiny of his own soldiers.

4

The death of Cinna, ominous and terrible as it seemed to the citizens in the streets, did not come as unexpected news to most of the senators. Many of them had been in correspondence with the officers who executed the murder. Now that it seemed only a matter of time until Sulla would be in Rome, there was frantic competition among all to take the credit.

In Athens, Sulla, an indolent middle-aged man with red hair, blue eyes, and a face so blotched and disfigured by drinking and disease that his complexion has been likened by Cicero to a mulberry sprinkled with flour, reads their letters and smiles. Despite their fervent protestations of friendship and loyalty, he means, as soon as he is back in Rome, to turn over to his assassins all these now so penitent politicians who aided Cinna in usurping the dictatorship.

He lands in the south of Italy, and begins fighting his way northwards to the capital. The provincial Italians, especially the Samnites, sure that he will take the franchise away from them if he is successful in overthrowing the Cinna government, put up a fierce resistance. To strike terror into Rome, he destroys all the towns along his line of march, killing combatants and non-combatants alike. At last, in the late fall, after advancing slowly along the peninsula for nearly a year, and defeating the two armies sent against him by the city, he is camped outside the walls of Rome.

Plot and counterplot, treachery and reprisal, seethe in Rome. Patricians suspected of being in communication with Sulla to betray the city into his hands, are stabbed on the streets by the furious plebeians. Cæsar sees the head of the Roman church, the Pontifex Maximus, a venerable old man named Scaevola, dragged bleeding from his house by a frenzied mob, and his corpse thrown into the Forum, where there is already a large pile of the dead. Through the alleys, and over the rooftops, continues, night and day, the hunt for traitors; while, in the very heart of the city, the really dangerous sympathizers with the Sullan restoration, and Sulla's own spies, go quietly about their work of corrupting the defense army, undetected.

Desperately, Marius the Younger endeavors to create confidence in his troops before giving battle to Sulla, but without success—in the decisive engagement fought between the two armies, under the walls of Rome, the city companies are put to rout by the veteran legionaries, and, on the morning of the second of November, Sulla makes his triumphal entry.

With the exception of alley fighting continued here and there by survivors from the popular army, who know they will be given no quarter if they lay down their arms—the third day after the battle Sulla had marched his four thousand prisoners into the Campus Martius, and there put them to the sword—all resistance is now at an end, and Sulla once again Dictator.

Cæsar now fears for his life, for he knows that Sulla will direct his revenge, not so much at the rabble which supported Cinna's rebellion as against those members of the nobility who have displayed, whether in good faith or as a matter of policy, democratic tendencies. These Sulla views as class traitors; and has announced his intention of showing them no mercy. Be-

cause of his marriage to Cornelia Cinna, Cæsar passes sleepless nights, dreading the clank of armor and swords announcing the arrival of the assassins.

But Sulla has determined on a policy, which, ruthless towards the older Romans who have opposed him, will show
leniency to the younger generation. He might even, influenced
by a certain feeling he has always had for the old disciplin-
arian under whom he first soldiered, but whom, were he still
alive, he would, for state reasons, have no compunction about
executing, have spared Marius the Younger, had not this unhappy youth died on his own sword the morning after the fall
of Rome.

He calls Cæsar to him, and says that if he is willing to
divorce Cornelia, and to re-marry as directed by Sulla, the
past shall be forgotten. Cæsar talks to Cnaeus Pompey, who
has entered Rome with the victorious eastern army, and Pompey confides to him that because Sulla has asked him to do so,
he intends to put aside his own wife, Antistia, to marry Sulla's
step-daughter, Aemilia. His advice to Cæsar is, for his own
good, to sever all relations with the Cinna family by divorcing
Cornelia as Sulla requests.

Later in life, when he never allows sentiment to stand in
the way of ambition, Cæsar would not hesitate to obey what
is, he knows, less a request than a command, and failure to
comply with which may result in his death. But because he is
still scarcely twenty, and will never again love any woman as
he now loves Cornelia, he is tormented by indecision.

Weeks slip by . . . he continues to evade giving a definite
answer. When he sees the Dictator's litter being carried through
the streets he quickly slips up a side-alley to avoid a meeting.
But one day, while waiting in the public baths for the water
to be heated, as he is wandering about looking at the theatre
advertisements and announcements of gladiatorial combats
posted in the court, he hears the familiar voice, soft and drawl-
ing in tone, at his elbow, and turning, finds himself face to
face with Sulla.

They enter the hot-air chambers together, and sit talking

about topics of the moment—the re-building of the Capitol,
burnt down during the recent fighting, and the reconstruction
of which Sulla has assigned to Quintus Catulas—the new
senatorial bodyguard of ten thousand enfranchised slaves, who
had belonged to the proscribed nobility, that the Dictator has
created—until the ringing of a bell announces that the water
is ready. Not until Sulla picks up the little silver box in which
he carries his favorite perfumes, and they are ready to leave
the baths, does he mention the subject of the divorce. Then
he speaks about it, and beneath the amiable manner in which
he suggests that Caius seems to be taking rather a long time
to make up his mind, Cæsar this time detects a threatening
note. Before they part, the Dictator has spoken of Pompey's
willingness to marry Aemilia, he has reminded Cæsar of the
fact that his own father had never wished him to take Cornelia Cinna as his bride, and he has added that the Cæsar
family has quite a number of enemies in Rome who are im-
portuning him to put Caius on his proscription lists.

Cæsar goes home feeling more wretched than ever. He feels
deeply the truth of Sulla's remark about enemies of his family
being glad to seize the opportunity afforded by the proscription lists to have him murdered. Every day is adding to the
number of the prominent Romans being assassinated for their
property or to satisfy private animosities. Oppianicus of La-
rino, one of Sulla's agents, is openly killing every person he has
a grudge against, and then putting the names of his victims
on the lists as condemned aristocrats, to escape prosecution.
Sulla's reprisals, the worst in Roman history, are holding the
city under a reign of terror. Not an hour passes that more
patricians are not dragged out of their homes by the soldiers
and stabbed to death before the eyes of their wives and daugh-
ters, while confiscated properties worth 6,000,000 sesterces, or
three hundred thousand dollars, are being purchased by the
boon-companions and freedmen of Sulla, for sums as low as
a hundred dollars.

But despite the savage passions which are loose in Rome,
and that, he knows, need only a nod from the *tyrannis* to turn

to him as a further victim, Cæsar cannot bring himself to give
up Cornelia. He continues to avoid Sulla, hoping that some
member of one of the families the Dictator has brought misery
upon may waylay and kill him as he is being borne through the
streets in his litter.

Once again Sulla sends for him.

This time he begins by saying that he bears Cornelia not the
slightest ill-will. He himself has often admired her beauty,
so can well understand why Caius is opposed to the divorce.
She is simply the daughter of her father, and for this reason
he cannot have any youth, in whom he takes such keen interest as he does in Caius, living on as her husband. If Cæsar
keeps her for his wife, she will sooner or later poison his mind,
perhaps to the extent of persuading him to attempt the life
of the man who was the cause of her father's death.

Cæsar, with a nervous laugh, answers that Sulla need never
fear he will be dangerous in *that* way. He has always admired
Sulla greatly, both as a man and as a general. It is only chance
that had placed him with the opposition party. But for Cornelia, he would certainly have gone to meet Sulla in Greece as
Pompey and so many other young nobles did. This he says in a
sudden outburst of sincerity. Sulla replies that he quite believes
it—it is just because he does feel that Caius really likes him
that he wants to put opportunities his way. But surely Caius
must understand that as the husband of Cornelia Cinna there
cannot be any future at all for him. Suddenly raising himself
up a little on the divan where he is lying, and fixing his pale
blue eyes intently upon the dark ones of the younger man,
Sulla inquires if Cornelia may not already have put into
Cæsar's head the idea of becoming a second Cinna.

The suddenness of the question, when the Dictator had
seemed so completely to sympathize with his position, takes
Cæsar aback. Paling under Sulla's steady glance, he again protests that he has never subscribed to the political opinions of
Cinna—besides, while Cornelia may not have doubted her
father's sincerity as a reformer, he himself has always been

more inclined to see Cinna as a demagogue pure and simple, using the people, through agitation against Sulla's doctrine that the Senate, and the Senate alone, shall manage the affairs of the Republic, to advance himself to the supreme power.

Sulla watches the youth's face as he speaks and for a moment afterwards, then, getting up, asks Caius if it might not be pleasant to walk awhile in the garden. Moved by a genuine liking for young Cæsar, who reminds him somewhat of himself as he was at the same age, he rests a jewelled hand affectionately on his shoulder as they stroll in the shade of large plane trees and along little alleys formed by hedges of box and cypress, oddly clipped and twisted, at regular intervals, —where a statue or fountain stands in the center of a flowerbed in which crocuses and narcissi are blooming,—to form the shapes of animals and ships. He suggests with a smile that Cinna's daughter is not the only beautiful woman in the world —there are others, yes, many others. Why then will not Caius come to his senses and divorce her? Sulla guarantees to arrange a far better match for him—if Cæsar is hesitating because no one of the girls mentioned to him in their previous conversation is to his taste, it will not be difficult to find others to choose from.

And as far as Caius being so deeply in love with his wife is concerned, well is he not taking the idea of the divorce altogether too seriously—for what is to prevent him keeping Cornelia as his mistress after their separation? Once the marriage bond is broken, Sulla certainly has no intention of prying into their relationship. He is only concerned, as he has said before, for purely political reasons, that Cinna's daughter be no longer the legal wife of Cæsar.

Sulla's new palace—the confiscated property of one of the richest Romans marked for death on his lists—is on a hill-top which commands a magnificent view of the city.

The two men reach a terrace; here they linger, the younger silent and worried, plucking with nerveless fingers at his loose girdle, the elder, with occasional side-glances at his companion, talking on in his slow drawl.

Cæsar listens; but his eyes are on Rome. And the picture he sees is not one of dirt and squalor, but of vast splendor—never has the city with its great array of houses, its public buildings, its glittering Tiber, seemed to him grander than it does at this moment when he feels his life is in the balance.

He hears Sulla's voice telling him how Cnaeus Pompey is being sent as general to Spain to help put down the insurrection headed by Quintus Sertorius, one of Cinna's officers who had fled there after the defeat at Rome—he knows that the Dictator is intimating that Cnaeus, through his willingness to marry into the Sulla family, has assured himself a brilliant future, and that Cæsar, if he will be as obedient, can count on one equally so. Next Sulla mentions the Ciceros—both Marcus and Quintus, because they have shown themselves amiable, and anxious to help Sulla put order into his government, are to receive lucrative appointments, Marcus as a pleader in the courts of the Senate, and Quintus in the army. Jealousy and despair torment Cæsar as he contemplates this thought of Sulla making the fortunes of every young Roman but himself—why did his aunt marry Marius, why did Marius make Cinna Dictator, why, worst of all, did he, Caius Cæsar, fall in love with, and marry, Cornelia Cinna?

He stares hungrily at the outspread panorama of the city. What use, he asks himself, will he be to Cornelia dead? If Fate has decreed that he and she must be separated, why try to resist it? On the point of consenting to divorce her, he turns to Sulla.

The slanting afternoon light shines full upon the face of the Dictator. Every wrinkle, every ugly blotch made by intemperance and the grim blood disease which is slowly eating away his body, is revealed in pitiless clearness. The pale blue eyes have a bleached lifeless look, and when Sulla opens his mouth in a smile, as their glances meet, he exposes discolored and decaying teeth.

From this face of an old man, momentarily revealed in all

its ugliness and age, Cæsar recoils, the face of Cornelia, in all
its purity and beauty, rising suddenly between him and the
Dictator. He sees her dark and radiant eyes, her full richly-
red lips, all the smooth exquisite curves of her cheeks, and
throat, and neck; and a feeling of horror for those words, so
nearly spoken, grips him—though they have remained unsaid,
he seems already to have lost his wife. In a passionate and
rebellious outburst, he tells Sulla that no amount of persuasion or threatening can ever induce him to divorce Cornelia.

The Dictator looks from him to the town. He likes Caius
the more for defying him, and smiles indulgently. But to remind the youth that life is not all love he directs his gaze towards a nearby street where the proscription officers and their
soldiers are entering the house of a patrician on the lists.

A clamor breaks out . . . shouts of men . . . shrill de-
spairing screams of women. Swords flash in the sunlight. The
wounded men who have staggered from the house can be seen
falling under the blows of the soldiers, who begin dragging
out the furniture. The house bursts into flames.

From numerous other points of the city rise the smoke and
flames of similar fires. In the Forum, where the household
belongings of the murdered families are daily auctioned off,
a large crowd can be seen milling around.

To Cæsar, following Sulla's glance, Rome looks different
now. No longer does it lie outspread before him stirring his
imagination with ambitious thoughts. It rather crouches as a
misshapen monster, with blood-red eyes, and fierce smoking
breath, which only awaits a signal from the jewelled hand almost touching his own to rend him to pieces.

Sulla, watching his face keenly, puts friendly fingers upon
his arm, and invites him into the palace to have another bowl
of Chian wine.

5

When Cæsar would not divorce Cornelia, Sulla did not immediately hand him over to the assassins. First he took away

his priesthood, and confiscated Cornelia's dowry; a few weeks later, as a further disciplinary measure which might break down Cæsar's resistance, he confiscated his estate.

Except on the hypothesis that the Dictator was really certain that young Caius Cæsar was not a liberal aristocrat, it is difficult to explain such leniency. Already more than four thousand Romans of noble birth had been made away with for suspected sympathies with the people in their struggle against exploitation by the Senate. Had Cæsar been the youthful idealist and reformer so many historians have painted him, is it credible that Sulla, whose reprisals were directed mainly against the Romans judged by him guilty of attempting to undermine the power of the Senate, would have kept him, in a time of such wholesale slaughter, off his proscription lists as long as he is known to have done?

He undoubtedly saw Cæsar as just one of those wealthy young Romans, far more concerned with pleasure than politics, whom he wished to attach strongly to himself. Cæsar's marriage to Cornelia Cinna was simply an unfortunate love-match, which, when remedied by divorce, would have no lasting consequences. Once Cæsar was free, he would quickly drift back to the party in which he naturally belonged.

Cæsar's father had been thoroughly conservative. His mother had never liked Lucius Cinna. She feared, like Sulla, that though insincere in the reforms he had advocated, he had nevertheless set highly dangerous forces into motion when he increased the privileges of the people. Since the Dictator's return, Aurelia Cæsar had had several interviews with him, frankly confessing that she was worried for her son's safety. How did Sulla intend to interpret his marriage with Cornelia Cinna? Was there perhaps a likelihood of the whole Cæsar family being made to suffer because of the rash step taken by Caius? Sulla had reassured her with the statement that he bore the Cæsars not the slightest ill-will; all he expects from Aurelia is her assistance in persuading Caius to divorce Cornelia. Through her co-operation, this may be made no very difficult matter; her influence as a mother should bring Caius around quicker than any urging he can do. He proceeds to a casual outline of the glorious futures of Cnaeus Pompey and the Ciceros. Aurelia, a large thin-lipped woman, with evasive eyes, and a sharp profile, tries, by frequent smiles, to cover up her jealousy, but she leaves the presence of the Dictator vowing to herself that the girl Cornelia shall never be an obstacle in the way of her son becoming an equal success.

But neither his mother's entreaties, nor Sulla's veiled threats, have the desired effect upon Cæsar.

And each day his position in Rome is becoming more perilous. With all Romans against whom there is the slightest evidence of having been compromised in Cinna's insurrection being murdered right and left around him, there seems to exist no legitimate excuse for sparing the husband of the dead Dictator's daughter. Eventually, though still with reluctance, Sulla yields to the pressure exerted on him, and allows his favorite freedman, Chrysogonus, to add Cæsar's name to the lists.

But when the soldiers go in search of Cæsar, he has fled. The usual reward of 12,000 denarii ($2400) is now offered for his head, but the young outlaw manages to escape the assassins—whom he bribes once, with double the reward, to let him go free—until the Sullan reprisals begin to draw to their natural conclusion.

The toll of murders is nearing the five thousand mark. The confiscation of property has been so enormous that, in spite of the immense depreciation in value, Sulla has realized not less than 350,000,000 sesterces, or seventeen million dollars, from this source. The patience of Rome under the outrages committed has reached the breaking point. Sulla is too shrewd not to realize that even his most loyal followers are becoming weary of the slaughter.

Two very influential Romans, Aurelius Cotta and Mamercus Aemilius, close friends of the Cæsar family, have asked him to spare Caius, and the College of Vestal Virgins has also petitioned for his pardon. So Sulla lets it be known that Cæsar need no longer fear anything—he can come out of his hiding, he is pardoned. Never having wished the youth's death, he is genuinely pleased he escaped the assassins. But Cæsar, into whom his adventures while an outlaw have put a thorough scare, decides to place no trust in the Dictator's promise. He will show himself for a few days to give the appearance of being unafraid, and then avoid future risks by leaving Rome, which is still in too unstable a condition for him to be willing to try for any public office under Sulla—for should he be given a good appointment what is to hinder some resentful disappointed candidate for the same position from burying a knife in his heart, under pretense of believing that by doing away with Cinna's son-in-law he is rendering the Republic an important service?

Sulla seems to think the idea of leaving Rome a good one. He mentions the praetor, Minucius Thermus, who is taking a punitive expedition against the Mediterranean pirates, and suggests that Caius go along. In his usual amiable manner he adds that while Caius cannot expect any such considerable command as has been given to Cnaeus Pompey, who exhibited greater complaisance, still if he wants to go as an officer on Thermus' staff, there will doubtless occur opportunities for advancement.

Cæsar thinks it over, and decides that the army is unquestionably the safest place for him nowadays. For Cornelia will be in no danger if left alone in Rome, since with her dowry and Cæsar's estate confiscated, there remains no motive for doing her an injury; Sulla, now that all the sentiment is against continuing the bloodshed, would only injure his own cause by allowing harm to come to her. On these considerations, he resolves to accept the commission offered him by the Dictator.

He makes hasty preparations for the journey, says goodbye to his mother and Cornelia, is urged by both not to run any needless risks, or to venture into places infested by the pirates unless he has plenty of soldiers with him, and one fine July morning, accompanied by a modest retinue of slaves, sets out

to join the expedition of the praetor, which has already left
the city.

6

Rome falls behind, its seven hills melting into the horizon
haze.

The tombs and mausoleums lining both sides of the Appian
Way, along which Cæsar is riding, are no longer crowded together as closely as on the outskirts of the city; finally they
disappear altogether.

From the Great South Road there now stretch away the
lordly demesnes of the millionaires, made up of rich undulat-
ing meadows where the cattle wander, of wide sweeps of
vineyard and olive orchard, of exquisite ribbons of woodland
following the windings of little streams. The great villas can
be seen, with their summer houses and fish ponds. Here and
there on the road the prosperous beauty of the rural scenery is
marred by the miserable neglected farm of some small farmer
squeezed in between the boundary lines of two of the spacious
senatorial estates.

The road enters the region devastated by Sulla in his march
upon the capital. It passes burnt villages whose black ruins dot
the countryside between green trees, deserted camps where
tall weeds half hide the earthen walls, fields that are littered
with the putrefying bodies of the dead. Rusty spears and
shields lie where dropped in battle, overlooked by the victorious legionaries who stripped the corpses of their armor. Remnants of leather tunics, broken pieces of the forked sticks,
known as "Marian mules," on which the Roman soldiers carry
their packs, tufts of horsehair from the helmets of the centurions, can be seen scattered among the corpses from which
the hot moist wind brings over a noisome stench.

Bitterly indeed has the Campagna paid for its resistance to
Lucius Sulla. All this land laid waste by his army is now the
property of the capitalists, who will repopulate it with slaves.
In the north, where the farmers are still resisting the Dictator,

his cavalry generals have orders to treat the provincial Italians in arms as though they were not free men but slaves. For miles, as in the slave uprising of Sicily, the roads here are lined with crucified bodies. Rather than fall into the hands of the Dictator, all the inhabitants of Norba, one little country town up in revolt, set fire to their houses and kill each other a few minutes before the pillaging horsemen, waving their bloody swords, break through the pitiful barricade of trees and earth thrown hastily across the road, and come thundering down the streets.

The little cavalcade trots briskly along the magnificent highway, smooth as a broad pavement, which leads south to the port from which the punitive expedition is embarking.

Cæsar's worries in Rome have made him thin. The white delicate skin of his face is stretched tightly over the cheekbones, and the hand that holds the reins has a lean, almost emaciated, appearance. He has just passed his twentieth birthday, but looks older; his premature baldness—the hair has already receded a generous distance from his sloping forehead—partly producing this impression.

But now that he is safely out of Rome, with the neat milestones marking off the distance from the city slipping steadily by, his fears also pass away from him. Sulla, he thinks, will not live for ever. The disease he is suffering from, which the best Greek physicians have been unable to cure, may cause his early death,—if he is not assassinated. Looking back over the events of the past year, he feels they might have turned out a great deal worse than has been the case. His estate and Cornelia's dowry have been confiscated, but he has still large sums invested in the provinces. He is confident that the Cæsar family has always played too influential a part in the affairs of the Republic to suffer permanently through Sulla's return. When the Dictator dies there will follow one of the usual reorganizations—more reprisals—more confiscations—the present senators having to flee for their lives, and a new party, composed doubtless with refugees such as Quintus Sertorius for a nucleus, managing the affairs of the State; in which case, through

Cornelia, he will be in a position to regain all he has lost.

As he rides, he reflects that his own personality is perhaps a very fortunate one, which should help him greatly in the future to realize any ambitions he may have then. Because he is good-humored by temperament, and seems bent only on enjoying himself, there is no one who fears him as a rival. His fellow-nobles like him. He has never by any unnecessary display of arrogance aroused the antagonism of the people. Cicero, though he may have more brains, and the undoubted gift of oratory, has also his sharp tongue which everywhere creates enemies for him. Pompey is too much the aristocrat to please those capitalists of humble birth like Marcus Crassus who are becoming so important a factor in the government. Both may win their way to fame, but it will be at the expense of popularity—and of what use is the most glorious of careers if suddenly cut short by the dagger of an assassin, or a cup of poisoned wine?

On this expedition against the pirates, though beside him rides his armor-bearer carrying his greaves, cuirass, helmet, shield and sword, the youth Cæsar has no intention of putting his life in danger by engaging in any hand-to-hand fighting. He is not in the army to be killed, but to be safe. He will stay with Thermus until he can return to Rome without danger. And once well established in the life of the city again, he intends to work his way up to that ædileship which has always so appealed to his imagination.

His thoughts go again to Cicero and Pompey. To make even a single enemy through cutting words, as the former does, or with sneers, like the latter, seems foolish to him. Yet Cicero is perpetually insulting those who lack the wit to retaliate, and Pompey cannot repress the aversion he feels for a man with a dirty face. There is young Marcus Cato also, who, though he has scarcely discarded the praetexta of a child to don the toga virilis, yet, because he is the great-grandson of the famous censor, already feels himself obliged to deliver homilies against vice. Such behavior impresses Caius Cæsar as a needless and wilful stirring up of trouble. He himself is quick to sense the feelings of the majority when with a group of friends or acquaintances, and he always governs his conduct accordingly.

This, he knows, gives him a certain capacity for leadership, as any suggestion he makes is sure to be popular. In sex matters, for instance, he is not as abnormal as many of the young Romans he is friendly with, but this does not prevent him when the occasion arises, from enthusiastically joining them in their orgies. At other times, on the contrary, he can conduct himself in a very seemly manner. The result is that his weaknesses have come to be looked upon as the work of bad companionship, people saying that Caius himself is not really bad, only easily led.

And Cæsar wants to have plenty of friends, even if many of them have to be bought. If he ever makes a name for himself in Rome, he reflects, it will certainly not be through denouncing society as young Cato does, or by fighting the legal battles of the senators, which seems to be Cicero's ambition, but by spending money lavishly.

From himself, his thoughts turn to Cornelia, whom he has left pregnant. Will the child be a boy or a girl?

Only a boy, it is certain, can win his mother around to liking Cornelia. Should the child be a girl, she will have more of a grudge against his wife than she now has. For in the judgment of his mother the birth of a girl will be a convincing proof that the gods disapprove of the marriage.

He smiles faintly as he anticipates in fancy the triumphant expression of her voice as she exclaims that had the girl been a boy there might have been reason for believing that at least Venus felt kindly towards the love-match, but, as it is, even his own ancestress looks upon the marriage with disfavor. For Aurelia Cæsar, with all her worldliness, allows herself to have at certain moments a superstitious regard for religion.

He himself has no illusions in this direction. As he rides on towards the blue water beyond the hills he reflects that the same mysterious fate which brought him into life as Caius

Julius Cæsar instead of as Cnaeus Pompey or Marcus Tullius Cicero has already undoubtedly determined the sex of the child.

7

The Mediterranean pirates against whom the praetor Minucius Thermus, a short rotund Roman, whose principal interest lay rather in supper-parties and banquets than in war, was taking his punitive expedition, were composed, for the most part, of the survivors of those foreign peoples whose homelands had for years been a carnival ground of rapine and extortion for the Republic.

Their ships were manned by Illyrians, Greeks, Syrians, Carthaginians, Egyptians, Africans, Spaniards and Gauls. In these motley crews were also to be found many Italians from the rural sections, whose hatred of the great robber city by the Tiber was as great as that which united the foreigners. The cosmopolitan fleet had been augmented during the past few months by vessels from the defeated forces of Mithridates.

Rome, preoccupied with its civil war, had been indifferent towards the raids made by the pirate fleet on merchant shipping and the coast towns until it began to be rumored that the pirates had commenced to organize their resources not only for the plundering of provincial Italy but to launch a campaign against the capital. Then the city went into one of its usual panics.

The cry was raised that the pirates had entered into alliance with the Barbarians, that Rome was in imminent danger of being attacked simultaneously from the north and from the south, that from the dark heart of Asia mighty armies of warlike Parthians were already moving westward to effect a juncture with the Gauls and Germans, and that these combined hordes would then invade Rome, capture the city by storm, put all the able-bodied burgesses to the sword, and drag the children away into slavery—when they took their departure there would remain where Rome in all its glory now stood only a heap of smoking ashes.

Roman civilization—the Roman burgess in the most extravagant of his dreams could imagine none other—being thus menaced, Thermus had been hastily despatched to crush the pirate peril. But no sooner was the praetor in the theatre of conflict than he found that he needed ships. He was faithful to the traditional Roman policy in war of never sacrificing legionaries if there were auxiliaries who could be pushed into the bad places, when he decided to seek out an ally whose fleet could be used to bear the brunt of the fighting while the few Roman galleys stood by and took the credit.

He thinks of the old profligate king of Bithynia—Nicomedes. Nicomedes is a potentate who has never been popular with his subjects. They have made numerous attempts to expel him from the country, but on each occasion—as in the case of Ptolemy, nicknamed the Flute-Player, the half-witted tyrant of Egypt—Rome, for large sums of money, has put him back on his throne. Nicomedes owns a fleet, but he may not be willing to lend it, for though he has repeatedly vowed eternal friendship to the Republic, he is heavily in debt to the senators for their good offices. Like other allies of Rome, the civil war, with its heavy drain on the fighting forces of the Republic, has made him restless. Because of his debts, which victory on the part of the pirates will cancel, he is known to secretly favor their cause.

But the tyrant's weak point is his vanity. In Rome, which he has frequently visited, the senators have made many jokes about his absurd conceit in thinking because he has cut off his beard, and dresses like a Roman, that he is civilized. Thermus knows this—he knows also that Nicomedes excels in all the fashionable Roman vices. He believes that the right sort of ambassador, one who is young and good-looking, and who perhaps will not mind being the royal favorite for awhile, may be able to flatter the old king into lending his fleet.

So the praetor revolves in his mind the various officers of his staff, with a view to selecting his ambassador. He finds, to his disappointment, that the person he is looking for seems to be missing. The gruff old veterans he has to reject im-

THE YOUTH

mediately—any one of these, at the first advances made by the king, might in the red-blooded Marian manner draw his sword and run it through Nicomedes. The perfumed young degenerates, on the other hand, of whom there are many in his entourage—senators' sons mostly, sent with him by their fathers to acquire military experience—lack the necessary diplomatic ability. They will be amiable, but it is doubtful if they will bring back the fleet. More probably the aged tyrant, who is not wanting in shrewdness, will simply twist them to his own designs.

Thermus is still searching for the right ambassador to send to the court of Bithynia when Caius Cæsar arrives.

The praetor has known Cæsar in Rome, and he thinks he understands his character. Certainly Caius has a great talent for making friends. And though, from the rumors about him, he seems to have few moral prejudices, he does not by any means fit into the class of the young effeminates who wear veils to protect their complexions from the sun and spend the greater part of the day having their slaves anoint them with passionate perfumes. Cæsar may have a homosexual streak in his nature, but the praetor does not believe he will abandon himself so completely to the orgies at the court of Bithynia as to forget the purpose of his mission—bringing back the fleet.

So the stout praetor talks with Cæsar and explains the situation. He enters into no details of the manner in which the ambassador ought to conduct himself in order to win the king's favor, but simply stresses the value of the service Cæsar will be doing the Republic if he brings back the fleet. Socially, he does say, with a certain emphasis, he is sure Cæsar will please the king. In this case it should not be a difficult matter for him to persuade Nicomedes to lend his ships.

When Cæsar, glad to be given the mission, has departed, Thermus feels his worries are over. He wants, above all, to win popularity with his soldiers by defeating the pirates with small losses. The expedition will be a success if he can destroy the pirate strongholds in the Ægean Sea, and hardly lose a legionary. And he thinks he can do this with the aid of the king's fleet. For it will be manned by sailors who are far superior to the legionaries—the latter, excellent on dry land as infantrymen, where they can dig themselves a camp every night, lose their confidence on the water.

But the weeks pass, and the ambassador does not return. A month slips away—still no Cæsar. The praetor grows anxious.

He begins to wonder if, after all, Caius Cæsar was the right man to send. Can he be sure that he understood him aright about Nicomedes? Perhaps, for all the accounts told of him, Cæsar is more prejudiced against certain indulgences than Thermus imagined. Perhaps it is only his effeminate appearance which has led to the rumors.

With time, the praetor's doubts increase. His plump face begins to wear a harassed look. He tries to forget his anxiety in banquets with the gentry living in the neighborhood, but to no avail. The oyster and mussel pasties, the delectable purple shell-fish and spondyli, the fattened fowls and fieldfares, the hares and ducks, which he partakes of in such abundance at the palatial villas along the seashore, have lost their savor. Though he now takes the precaution of vomiting not only after, but also before, his meals, a health measure he has never had to resort to previously, he is troubled more and more with nervous indigestion.

The weeks have stretched into nearly two months when one day the praetor, having feasted more greedily than usual, is returning in a carriage to the port. His fat chin lies drooped upon his breast, and his expression is frowningly morose. Unless his ambassador makes an appearance within a few days he will have to send off another, as the pirates are fortifying Mitylene and other captured towns, with a view to using these as a base from which to conduct an offensive against the Roman expedition. His uneasy fancy is picturing a scene between Cæsar and the tyrant which may be responsible for the mission having failed.

He sees the depraved monarch, at first all cordiality towards the good-looking young Roman ambasador, finally

becoming impatient with the reserve shown by Cæsar. There
is a dramatic climax, when Cæsar, after a banquet, at which
much wine has been drunk, is induced by the old king, on
pretense of being shown some rare objects of art, to follow him
into a private chamber. Here the king, closing the door, tries to
force Cæsar to accept his embraces.

Cæsar, in his anger forgetting diplomacy and the fleet he
has been sent to bring back, slaps the tyrant's face. The king
screams hysterically. Armed guards rush into the room. At a
sign from the enraged monarch, they cut Cæsar down with
their swords, and the Roman ambassador, his mission unaccom-
plished, falls.

Thermus groans. There is no longer a doubt in his mind
but that he chose the wrong ambassador to send to the court of
Bithynia. For days and nights now his imagination has made
him wretched with this palace scene so disastrous to the success of his expedition. In an effort to rid himself of the vision
he passes a perspiring hand across his eyes. Appearances and
report, he thinks bitterly, have been his undoing.

But suddenly, as he drops his hand from his face, and looks
down at the sea which has come into view at a bend of the road,
his whole expression becomes radiant with hope. For the harbor is full of ships, and as he enters the port he sees Caius
Cæsar step on shore from one of them and come towards him
smiling.

8

With the aid of Nicomedes's fleet, the praetor captured the
town of Mitylene, and sank a number of the pirate vessels ply-
ing out of Lesbos. He immediately sent despatches to the Senate announcing an overwhelming triumph over the enemy
navy, and returned to Rome, where he was well received because of the booty he brought with him.

The Roman mob, with characteristic fickleness, had long ago
recovered from its pirate scare. It had, indeed, lost interest in
the punitive expedition almost the moment that this left the

town; and that the praetor had so successfully cleared the seas of the peril of invasion seemed only further proof of the invincibility of Roman arms.

Home affairs were now claiming the whole attention of the Roman burgesses. Sulla was known to be seriously ill. One morning it was rumored he was dead. But a few days later these rumors were publicly disproved when he appeared at one of the combats. It was said that when all the Greek physicians had failed to cure him of the sickness ravaging his body, an Egyptian magician had at last been found who by the simple utterance of a few occult words had restored him to complete health. Seemingly well again, Sulla, having instituted all the reforms which he considered necessary to tie the hands of the people and to make Rome safe for the nobility, now resigned the dictatorship and retired to civil life.

The Egyptian magician, it was reported, had effected in him so marvellous a rejuvenation that he was no longer compelled to abstain either from wine or from sexual indulgence as the Greek physicians had advised him to do during his last serious illness; he was not only living riotously, but actually growing younger each day. Then, of a sudden, there were again the rumors that he was desperately ill, that he was dead. And this time they were true.

His death, and the events immediately leading up to it, were, a century and a half later, in his *Lives of Illustrious Men*, described as follows by the historian, Plutarch——

Some few months after the death of his wife, Metella, at a show of gladiators, when men and women sat promiscuously in the theatre, no distinct places being as yet appointed, there sat down by Sulla a beautiful woman of high birth, by name Valeria, daughter of Messala, and sister of Hortensius the orator. Now it happened that she had been lately divorced from her husband. Passing along behind Sulla she leaned on him with her hand, and plucking a bit of wool from his garment, so proceeded to her seat. And on Sulla looking up and wondering what it meant, "What harm, mighty sir," said she, "if I also was desirous to partake a little in your felicity?" It appeared at once that Sulla was not displeased, but even tickled in his fancy, for he sent out to inquire her name, her birth, and past life. From this time there passed between them many side glances, each continually turning round to look at the other, and frequently interchanging smiles. In the end, overtures were made, and a marriage concluded on. . . . Notwithstanding this marriage, Sulla kept company with actresses, musicians, and dancers, drinking with them on couches night and day. His chief favorites were Roscius the comedian, Sorex the arch mime, and Metrobius the player, for whom, though past his prime, he still professed a passionate fondness. By these courses he encouraged a disease which had begun from unimportant cause; and for a long time he failed to observe that his bowels were ulcerated, till at length the corrupted flesh broke out into lice. Many were employed night and day in destroying them, but the work so multiplied under their hands, that not only his clothes, baths, basins, but his very meat was polluted with that flux and contagion, they came swarming out in such numbers. He went frequently by day into the bath to scour and cleanse his body, but all in vain; the evil generated too rapidly and too abundantly for any ablutions to overcome it. There died of this disease, amongst those of the most ancient times, Acastus, the son of Pelias; of later date, Alcman the poet, Pherecydes the theologian, Callisthenes the Olynthian, in the time of his imprisonment, as also Mucius the lawyer; and if we may mention ignoble, but notorious names, Eunus the fugitive, who stirred up the slaves of Sicily to rebel against their masters, after he was brought captive to Rome, died of this creeping sickness.

The mysterious and dreadful complaint beginning from unimportant cause which carried away the dissipated dictator, has doubtless, in the gruesomeness of its details, received exaggeration from the fertile imagination of Plutarch, who was not, as already mentioned, a contemporary of Sulla, and therefore no eye-witness to the loathsome dissolution he describes so vividly; but Sulla's reputation as a voluptuary and profligate in an age of unparalleled licentiousness, to which prophylactic and salvarsan were unknown, is sufficiently suggestive of the true nature of the "creeping sickness" which caused his death.

His death was an immediate signal for a change in public sentiment. Mass-meetings were held in Rome in an attempt to have his body thrown into the Tiber instead of receiving an honorable burial. But he seems to have died, as he had lived, popular with women.

It is said that the Roman ladies contributed such vast heaps of spices to his funeral, that besides what was carried on two hundred and ten litters, there was sufficient to form a large figure of Sulla himself, and another, representing a lictor, out of the costly frankincense and cinnamon. The day being cloudy in the morning, they deferred carrying forth the corpse till about three in the afternoon, expecting it would rain. But a strong wind blowing full upon the funeral pile, and setting it all in a bright flame, the body was consumed so exactly in good time that the pyre began to smoulder, and the fire was upon the point of expiring, when a violent rain came down, which continued till night. So that his good fortune was firm even to the last, and did as it were officiate at his funeral. His monument stands in the Campus Martius, with an epitaph of his own writing; the subject of it being, that he had not been outdone by any of his friends in doing good turns, nor by any of his foes in doing bad.

9

Cæsar was in Cilicia when he heard of Sulla's death. For the services rendered by him to Thermus, he had been decorated with the oak wreath. When the praetor returned to the capital, Cæsar had joined the expedition of another general, Servilius Isauricus, on its way to put down piracy in the creeks and river-mouths of Cilicia.

On the arrival of the news of Sulla's death, the pirates were immediately forgotten, and the sea-coast left to protect itself. The officers of the expedition hurried back to Rome to secure favors from the new administration. Once again, as had happened on so many previous occasions, the unhappy Mediterranean provinces, compelled to pay heavy taxes to Rome for military protection, were abandoned to the mercy of the enemy.

Sulla had already been gorgeously buried in the Campus Martius, among the ancient kings of Rome, when Cæsar arrived in the city. Without difficulty now,—for no sooner were the ashes of the Dictator safely deposited in their burial urn than the reaction began to gather impetus,—he recovered his estate and his wife's dowry. He was welcomed back to Rome as one of the refugees who should certainly be willing, nay eager, to help overthrow the party put in power by Sulla.

His brother-in-law, Cinna the Younger, who had escaped the hands of Sulla, came to him with a scheme for raising an army in Etruria and occupying Rome, when revenge could be taken for the reprisals of Sulla, and Cinna's government restored. With Cinna the Younger, in the conspiracy, is associated one of the consuls, Marcus Aemilius Lepidus, once an officer in Sulla's army, and by him made consul, but who aspires to greater power than is possible under the strong Senate created by Sulla.

Cæsar, approached by both conspirators, seems partial to the conspiracy, but has actually decided that he has a great deal to lose and not much to gain by joining it; from his knowledge of the leaders, he senses that they are going to fail.

Eventually he says no to them. But he says it in as friendly a way as possible, so that should the conspiracy be successful the leaders will remember that at heart, though he may have lacked the courage to join them, he favored their cause. The insurrection, as he had expected, comes to nothing, the Etrurian army, an unorganized rabble led by a few incompetent officers, being defeated in the Campus Martius by Pompey, at the head of a legion of Sulla's veterans; Cinna the Younger fleeing to the protection of Sertorius in Spain, and the consul Lepidus running away to Sardinia, where, a few months later, he dies from consumption.

Now that the conspiracy has failed, Cæsar makes no secret of the fact that he was asked to join it. His confession increases his popularity with both the Senate and the people. The former praise the stand he took in not allowing himself to be won over by the ambitious rebels. He receives as a present large tracts of land taken away from the Etrurians, and has his priesthood restored to him. The people, on the other hand, consider he acted discreetly in not giving his support to so carelessly planned a revolution. They realize that it is just such rash uprisings as this one of Cinna the Younger and Lepidus which do most harm to the popular party, since they furnish the Senate with an excuse for policing the streets with soldiers and cutting harmless gatherings of citizens to pieces—a way of telling the world that while the Roman rulers may have their little political differences they still know how to keep law and order.

He means to let Roman events shape themselves, while making the most of every opportunity. In his private life he is equally willing to bow to the inevitable. Cornelia has given birth to a daughter. He accepts the disappointment as what might be expected of fate, and grows fond of the child.

Nor does his mother's propaganda against Cornelia disturb his peace of mind. He allows her to gossip about his wife as much as she pleases, smiles, and seems to agree with her that he might have made a better marriage. He is not in the least discontented. Pompey may be making rapid headway in the army, but he has surely gained nothing by divorcing Antistia. During Cinna's administration Antistia's father had been killed by a furious mob for staying loyal to Sulla; her mother, a witness to the bloody spectacle of the mangled body being dragged through the streets, had gone mad and poisoned herself. Will Antistia ever forget the dead Dictator's ingratitude in forcing Cnaeus to divorce her in order to marry his step-daughter, or Pompey's cruelty when, for the sake of ambition, he agreed to the divorce? And Aemilia, a married woman and pregnant at the time she was compelled to become the bride of Pompey, had lived only a few weeks after entering his house. Cæsar feels he lost nothing . . . no, nothing . . . when that afternoon on the palace terrace he defied Sulla by refusing to separate from Cornelia.

His mother keeps urging him to show more ambition. But

he thinks his future is best cared for if he does not follow her advice too closely, but plans it in his own way.

Aurelia Cæsar tells her son he lacks energy. She tries to get him to show a keener interest in public affairs by exciting his jealousy of the other Romans of his age who seem to her to be really doing things. She talks continually about Pompey and Cicero.

The former is already known as "the Great," for his military exploits in Sicily and Africa which he was sent to colonize with the eastern veterans, and for which he was allowed the honor of a triumph by Sulla. The latter is springing into fame as an orator by his prosecution of Verres, a corrupt governor who failed to whitewash his misdeeds by distributing sufficient bribes among the senators. Both of these companions of his childhood, she tells Caius, will have covered their names with glory while his own sinks into obscurity, if he does not bestir himself. There is Marcus Crassus also, who, penniless a few years ago, has made an immense fortune by investing in the property of the nobles proscribed by Sulla, and is now one of the richest men in Rome.

Cæsar, who knows from experience how futile it is to attempt to curb his mother's tongue when she starts giving advice, lets her scold. He wishes he did have the will-power to carefully outline a career, and then never to swerve from a single detail, but by nature he seems far more inclined to allow circumstances to decide his actions.

To humor her he does finally, however, agree to go to Rhodes, there to study public speaking under the celebrated Greek rhetorician, Apollonius Molo. Aurelia Cæsar believes that Marcus Cicero, because he is at the senate-house so much, must be on the inside of all important developments. She wants Caius to have the same advantages. She tries to show him what a fatal business policy it is to have only idlers and spendthrifts for friends. If he wants to get ahead he must cultivate the friendship of the senators and politicians as Cicero is doing. Is it not only natural that a young Roman who has the interests of the Republic truly at heart should be anxious to have the older

men give him the benefit of their experience? Caius is too old
to be spending so much of his time in the wineshops. That may
have been all right when he was a carefree youth with no one
to think of but himself, but now that he is married and has a
wife and child dependent on him he ought to develop a greater
sense of responsibility.

Cæsar seems to reflect. He answers that perhaps she is right.
But with the seas in as unsettled a condition as they are at present, he suggests that the trip be postponed until the pirates are
less active.

Might it not be a good idea for him to take a preparatory
course in rhetoric here at home before going to Rhodes and
enrolling under Molo? Then the famous teacher's time need
not be wasted instructing him in the elementals.

His mother shakes her head doubtfully. Will he really
study? Caius promises he will, saying that his old tutor, Antonius Gnipho, will be glad to help, and that Cicero's vanity
has only to be flattered a little for him to become an enthusiastic instructor.

So for several months he studies public speaking quietly at
home. The old Gaul, Gnipho, schools him once again, as in
childhood, in the first principles of gesture and expression, but
it is Cicero as he had expected who is the greatest practical help.

The orator is vain enough of his own growing reputation to
be delighted to teach. The pleasure he takes in the frank manner in which Cæsar seems to look up to him as a master, admiring his command of language and the dramatic inflections he
gives his voice, is only too apparent. Soon Caius does not have
to go in search of him. Cicero comes to the Cæsar house of his
own accord. He even overcomes prejudice to the extent of
visiting the taverns in search of his pupil. The willing manner
in which Cæsar, when he enters, rises and follows him away
from his companions in revelry, seems to give him an immense
satisfaction.

It is a time of their lives when a more genuine friendship
exists between the two young men than ever before or after.

Cicero, whose bitterness against frivolity is mainly the result of the carefree Roman youths whose affection he secretly most covets not caring for his company, is proud to have the handsome young Caius Cæsar, everywhere so popular, for his companion. At his suggestion, to improve the carrying power of Cæsar's voice they often go off together to lonely spots in the hills, where Caius declaims while Marcus, his lanky body sprawled on the grass, criticises his delivery, and gives him advice on how to pitch his voice to throw it the furthest distance with the least straining of his throat. Cæsar, timid at first about speaking above a conversational tone, overcomes his embarrassment gradually as he grows interested, until he is shouting and gesturing as though haranguing a mob in the Forum.

But though his voice improves with practice it never acquires either the volume or the flexibility of his instructor's. Cicero likes him the more for this. Obviously, in the field of oratory, there can never be any rivalry between them. After listening awhile, the master rises from his lounging position to instruct by example. He clears his throat in an impressive manner, shifts his position as though to make sure that the ground is firm under his feet, frowns once or twice, glances to right and left with smirks of vanity as if, instead of being here on the hillside with Caius Cæsar as his only audience, he were in the senate-house, noticing how all the seats are filling up to hear him continue his pleading for the conviction of Verres. Striking an attitude, he begins a thundering denunciation of the manner in which the Roman governor in his greed had plundered not only private individuals, but even temples, of their statues and other works of art.

The sun sinks in the sky. From the Capitol, which Lucullus is rebuilding, and the gilding of which alone is to cost 12,000 talents, or, fourteen million dollars, half the war-indemnity exacted by Sulla from Mithridates, a long shadow reaches out to the two men on the hillside.

Both are seated now. Cicero has laid aside the wax tablets on which are the notes for his second pleading against Verres, to be delivered in the senate-house before the end of the week, and is talking about himself. He hints at his loneliness. His brother Quintus has plenty of friends, but with the exception of Atticus he himself seems to have none. And Atticus is not the kind of friend he means, their friendship being in the main intellectual. He would like to have one based more on sentiment.

Cæsar, always a good listener, leans towards him, his face sympathetic. Cicero overcomes his repressions and becomes jovial. He feels warm with a spirit of comradeship. The guarded expression goes out of his eyes. His lean features seem to fill out and lose their sallow unhealthy complexion. Each time he makes a witty sally, he touches Cæsar with his hand; slapping him on the shoulder, poking his thumb into his side, or thumping his knee.

And now, just when the orator feels most affectionate towards Cæsar in his own heart, the latter begins to tire a little of his company. Cicero, the great orator who can hold his audience spellbound with his golden voice, is no more—in his efforts to be genial, this man who has taken his place, with his repeated emphasis of his remarks by prods, and digs, and slaps, is only awkward and annoying; his overflowing cordiality, with its smirking gossipy overtones relating to mutual acquaintances, and its colossal conceit, obliterating completely the power and charm of the speaker.

Dusk falls, and they return to Rome. Sometimes Cicero, as though suspecting that his companion may have been secretly amused by his attempts at friendliness, becomes suddenly cynically aloof as they go down the hill together, but more often the day ends with a very affectionate parting.

10

Besides instructing Cæsar in public speaking and pleading, Cicero gives him advice.

He harangues him at home on the emptiness of a life not devoted to the public welfare, and, like his mother, urges him to break definitely with dissolute companions. Cæsar admits the truth of everything he says, particularly agreeing with Cicero that he ought to have more strength of character.

Cicero talks on . . . his voice to Cæsar is only a murmur like that made by running water, for he is able to apparently listen attentively when he is really hearing nothing, and his mind is a blank. He watches his daughter, Julia, crawling towards him across the court. She is not quite three years old—he picks her up, and swings her gently in his arms to keep her quiet while Cicero talks.

The child's large and beautiful eyes, inherited from her mother, stare up into Cicero's face, their expression profoundly meditative as they watch his mouth opening and closing—suddenly, struggling to free herself, and reaching up one of her small fat hands, she tries to seize the great orator by the nose.

Cæsar's fingers close over those of his daughter; keeping his eyes on Cicero's face, he quiets Julia. But Cicero is so preoccupied with what he is saying that he hardly notices the child. He is no longer talking about Cæsar, but about himself. An intolerable expression of pride shines in his face, and the large head seems to swell on its lean neck, as he announces that he believes he has the necessary qualifications to become the greatest Roman of all time. A note of querulous complaint enters his voice as he adds that a less short-sighted Republic would supply such a coming leader as he knows himself to be with opportunities for more rapid advancement. He is well aware, as others must be also, with the fact that there is not a single senator who can compare with him for intelligence, yet so far he has no voice in the government—petulantly he exclaims that by not allowing his genius sufficient room in which to expand, it is Rome, and not himself, which is the greatest loser.

These talks Cæsar accepts as a necessary concomitant of his instruction. Meanwhile, at Cicero's advice, he makes his first appearance in public as a speaker by prosecuting Dolabella in behalf of the Macedonians, who have grievances of misgovernment against him similar to those preferred by Sicily against Verres, but whom Cicero, for a large fee, is this time defending instead of prosecuting. Dolabella has bribed the Senate generously enough for his acquittal to be certain, and the orator, before all an opportunist, with a shrewd sense of when it is timely to uncover corruption and when it is not, intends to add to his glory by proving Dolabella innocent in the same way that he increased it by proving Verres guilty.

Since one of the other pleaders for the defense will be Aurelius Cotta, a kinsman of Cæsar, Cicero has little difficulty in persuading his pupil that the part he takes in the prosecution —which might otherwise offend the Senate—will not be viewed seriously; the senators will understand that he is merely seizing the opportunity to try out his eloquence. At the same time, Cæsar reflects, the people will look up to him as their champion, which may be of value to him in the future. There is also the consideration that Cornelia hates Dolabella bitterly, as having once belonged to her father's party and then deserted to Sulla.

So he is willing to appear at the trial as one of the pleaders for the prosecution. His speech is short, but Cicero tells him afterwards (when Dolabella has been acquitted), that it was much to the point—he says this pressing Cæsar's arm and beaming with delight, for his own pleading in defense of the governor of Macedonia has brought as much applause from the senators as had his previous exposure of the iniquities perpetrated by the governor of Sicily.

As he tucks up his toga, and they leave the senate-house together, Cicero bowing and smiling to the senators who come forward to praise and congratulate, the master feels in a very amiable mood towards the pupil before whom he rehearsed the one oration, and whose puny opposition he has so easily battered down with the other.

After his unsuccessful prosecution of Dolabella, Aurelia

Cæsar was more determined than ever that her son should go to Rhodes, there to study oratory under Apollonius Molo as Marcus Cicero had done. It vexed her greatly that the pleading of Cicero had been so much more rhetorical and effective than that of Caius, who had plainly shown that he could express his ideas only in a very brief and bare manner.

Preparations were made for the journey, and Cæsar took his departure. This time he travelled, not as when on the way to Thermus, with only a very modest retinue of slaves, but in all the state of a wealthy young Roman. A ship was waiting for him at the sea-coast. It had not been on the water for more than a night and a day when, as he had feared, it fell into the hands of pirates.

The captured vessel was taken to the island of Pharmacusa, Cæsar being allowed to keep three of his attendants, while the rest were put off on the mainland near the first Roman camp to raise the fifty thousand dollar ransom demanded.

Cæsar, when no longer fearful of being put to death, accepts the situation as not altogether an unpleasant one. The hatred which the pirates bear Rome cannot prevent them from holding in a certain awe any native of the great city who, like their prisoner, is obviously of high rank. They are flattered by the way he seems frankly to enjoy their society. One of them, a young Syrian, who speaks many languages, and whose secret ambition it is to some day go to Rome, the center of all opportunity, shows himself especially anxious to please.

Pharmacusa seems to the captive a perfect spot in which to forget all cares. He strolls along the beach, enjoying the blue sky, and the calm water of the Ægean stretching away with not a ripple upon its surface to the distant ring of the horizon. He plays games of chance with his guards, and questions them about their experiences. He joins them in their drinking parties.

The wine puts his body into a warm glow—the pirates have never known a companion more genial. They listen eagerly to the tales he tells them of great Romans they have heard about. They feel certain that if they are ever captured by one of the

Roman governors they have only to call for Cæsar to bring to
their rescue a friend who will surely do all he can to have their
punishments softened. Their prisoner, in a joking tone, tells
them that if they fall into his hands after he has been ransomed
he will have them crucified.

The ransom arrives, and he is released, the pirates, as they
promised, putting him ashore on the mainland near Miletus.
The while he has been their prisoner, Cæsar has known that a
fleet of Roman pirate chasers is shortly due in this port. Underneath his amiability has lain the comfortable assurance that
he will in all probability be able to recover his ransom money.
Now, as soon as the ships arrive, he takes them to Pharmacusa
and makes the pirates, in turn, his prisoners.

They are thrown into prison at Pergamus, while Cæsar com-
municates with Junius, the governor of Asia, to determine their
punishment. The governor, having heard there is a large sum
of money involved—besides the ransom, Cæsar has made all
the booty stored by the pirates at Pharmacusa his prize—replies that he will shortly arrive in person to mete out justice;
in the meanwhile, Cæsar can forward to him the captured
spoils so that these will be in safe keeping. He ends his letter
with warm praise for the efficient manner in which Cæsar has
made the capture, and with wishes that all travellers would
co-operate with the law to the same extent.

Upon reading this answer, Cæsar's mind is quickly made up.
The governor's flattery, and his zeal for the public welfare,
do not deceive him in the least. Had Junius agreed to an equitable division of the spoils, instead of being so avaricious
as to want all, he should, as governor, have been awarded
his share, but now the whole of it shall remain the prize of
Cæsar.

He has the pirates brought out of prison, and himself pronounces judgment on them, condemning them to crucifixion.
Crosses are constructed. With the same deadly amiability that
he had displayed when playing and drinking with them on the
beach at Pharmacusa, Cæsar walks around watching his

Between the crosses, which the setting sun will silhouette in dreadful starkness against the evening sky, walks Caesar.

wretched victims as the nails are driven through their hands and feet. Even now, in their agony, they cannot believe that this smiling young Roman, with his sympathetic glance, is the true author of their torture.

The young Syrian, dragged forward, throws himself at Cæsar's feet, imploring mercy. The Roman smiles at him, while with a little movement of the hand, unseen by the Syrian, motioning to the executioners to take him to his cross. He continues to smile in the same kindly manner as the spikes tear through the shrinking flesh of the Syrian, and his shrieks are added to those which already fill the air. His soft friendly glance seems to say that he bears none of the pirates any ill-will, and the young Syrian least of all—the law is simply taking its course as he had warned them it would.

The crosses, with their suffering victims, are raised from the ground to an upright position. The faces of the pirates, so child-like in their expressions of wonder when at Pharmacusa beside the blue water where their ships lay at anchor Cæsar had entertained them with tales of the exploits of his uncle, the great general Caius Marius, and with descriptions of Rome, and its grandeur, now stare down at him contorted with agony. . . . Blood drips from the maimed hands and feet. . . . Muscles stand out like cords on the necks straining to break loose from the torture. . . . The lips of the young Syrian, struck in the mouth by one of the executioners to quiet his frenzied writhings as he was being nailed to his cross, bubble a scarlet foam. . . .

Between the crosses, which the setting sun will silhouette in dreadful starkness against the evening sky, walks Cæsar. He promenades here as though in the shade of beautiful plane trees. He is still smiling his friendly genial smile.

He touches a cross occasionally to be sure it is in the ground firmly. As he leaves the scene of the crucifixions he lifts a dainty white finger to his forehead to brush back into place the thin lock with which he tries to conceal his baldness.

It is the same delicate gesture and the same lock of which Cicero will one day exclaim——

But when I see his hair so carefully arranged, and observe him adjusting it with one finger, I cannot imagine it should enter into such a man's thoughts to subvert the Roman state!

PART 2

The Demagogue

I

AFTER crucifying the pirates, Cæsar continued his journey to Rhodes, where he spent nearly two years studying the art of public speaking. He left Rhodes to take part in a campaign against Mithridates, once again threatening the Republic from the east. Then he returned to Rome, and began spending money lavishly to have himself elected military tribune.

He is now approaching his thirtieth year. He has become almost entirely bald. What hair he still has he allows to grow long so that it can be brought around to form the lock across his forehead. He is very sensitive about his baldness, and bears a grudge against Cicero for the latter's witticisms on the subject of his vanity in trying to hide it.

During the past few years his disposition has undergone a marked change. Subject since childhood to slight attacks of epilepsy, this nervous affliction, which the physicians had diagnosed as a mild distemper that he would outgrow as he approached manhood, has steadily grown worse. At Rhodes he several times fell to the ground foaming at the mouth, and his body convulsed with spasms, on one occasion nearly strangling himself by swallowing his tongue. It was because he had been told that an outdoor life might cure him of the disease that he had left the lecture rooms of Apollonius to take part in the campaign against Mithridates.

Both his mother and Cornelia tell him that his illness is the result of dissipation. Aurelia Cæsar in particular refuses to recognize any connection between his present serious attacks and the milder ones he was subject to as a child. She insists he was born healthy. She loses all patience with him when he mentions a sickness his father suffered from, remarkably similar to his own in its symptoms. The faintest suggestion that he may have inherited his disease, or a tendency towards it, from either one of his parents, brings an angry flush to her face.

Cæsar, for his part, would far rather believe that his distemper, as the physicians still call it, is a constitutional weakness, than an ailment contracted through riotous living, as the women say it is. At the same time he is willing to admit that rich food and heavy drinking may well aggravate the disease, so, fearful that one of the attacks may otherwise prove fatal, he reluctantly puts himself on a frugal diet.

But if his altered mode of living is good for his health, it does not increase his amiability. As he goes to banquets less and less, and ceases to frequent the wine-shops with his former regularity, he declines in geniality. In the days when he spent so many hours reclining on dining couches eating eels garnished with prawns, capon livers steeped in milk, boars' heads and peacocks, and washing his meals down with copious draughts of Greek and Falernian wine, his cordiality was genuine. Now his good-humor and affability are only a disguise.

He is no longer sincerely indifferent to what the future may have in store for him, but has grown shrewd and calculating. Indulging less in pleasure, he thinks more. Even his amours, for all their apparent recklessness, are now carefully planned to achieve their ends.

In appearance he has changed also. His nose looks longer and thinner. The bald sloping forehead, when not covered by its lock of hair, catches the eye more. His mouth, though it can still flash the same kindly smile, is often compressed grimly when he knows himself to be alone. And he has become introspective to the extent of realizing this change in himself, and taking pains to conceal it—to the end of his life he will stand in no fear of fat gross men like Marcus Crassus, or of robust voluptuaries like Mark Antony, but will mistrust just those lean and hungry-looking men in whose class, behind his disguise of affability, he feels himself really to belong.

He has grown definitely ambitious. He no longer covets the

ædileship for the glamour of its combats and wild-beast shows, but as a step towards the consulship. Once when gorged with rich food and languid with wine, his mother had had to urge him to go actively into politics, but no more. Now he himself is jealous of the success of others.

He keeps close track of the progress being made by Cicero, Pompey and Crassus, and, though retaining his outward composure, is easily worked up into moods of resentment and envy. When his mother exclaims that no one of the three,— though all are climbing to fame faster than he is,—have his ability, he feels she is right.

He agrees with her that Pompey is not a great general, but simply knows how to keep his name before the public, and to insist upon being given good commands.

Aurelia Cæsar points to the way her son distinguished himself when sent on the mission to the court of Bithynia. If he wanted to, she says, he could easily outshine Pompey as a military man. And Cæsar, listening, feels that that little affair he had had with Nicomedes,—which the old king, kissing him as he left, had called the grand romantic passion of his life (and by means of which the fleet had been brought to Thermus),—was not just the amusing adventure he had thought it at the time but an achievement which should have been rewarded with more than an oak wreath.

Nor is Marcus Cicero, in Aurelia Cæsar's opinion, really a greater orator than her son. There are many people, she insists, who dread to listen to him, he takes so long to say so little; Caius, now that he has been to Rhodes, would, if he practised more, make quite as good a pleader, as he is by nature more concise, wasting fewer words. And Crassus, she knows, as does everyone else, has only built up his immense fortune by keeping informed of every profitable business opportunity that comes along.

He sits brooding. Is not everything that his mother says true? He recalls Pompey's first efforts as a soldier. Was not Sulla only amusing himself when he allowed Cnaeus to call

himself "Magnus" and to have the honor of a triumph? For
Pompey had done nothing of note either in Sicily or Africa except to capture and crucify a few bands of robbers; and Sulla
himself, though he had humored Cnaeus when the latter had
refused to disband his troops as ordered by the Senate until
these honors had been guaranteed him, must have really been
disgusted with his arrogance and conceit, since, generous to
every other friend and relative in his will, he had left Pompey
nothing. Nor had there been much to boast of in the defeat of
the disorganized rabble of Cinna the Younger and Lepidus
with Sulla's eastern veterans. And in Spain, though at first
there were rumors that he had routed the forces of Sertorius,
Pompey had in reality been able to make no headway in his
campaign; by urging the Spaniards to throw off for once and
all time the crushing yoke of Rome, and the exploitation of the
country by one rapacious governor after another, Sertorius had
created a volunteer army that ignominiously put to flight every
Roman expedition sent against him; the Roman mob may believe that Pompey the Great won the war by out-generalling
the commander of the Spanish army, but the Senate knows, and
Cæsar knows, that he never defeated Sertorius in battle, but
finally, when the situation had become desperate, had managed
to bribe some of the Roman officers of Sertorius to assassinate
their general, after which, having scattered the leaderless
Spaniards, he was hailed as a warrior whose fame would eventually eclipse that of Marius and Sulla, and granted a second
triumph.

To Cæsar, on a level with Pompey's pretensions to greatness as a soldier, are those of Cicero as a champion of justice. A
contemptuous smile curls his lips as he asks himself whether in
the whole of the Republic there exists a man more governed in
his actions by self-interest than Marcus Tullius Cicero, who
now besides orator and idealist, styles himself philosopher.

He thinks of Cicero's defense of Sextus Roscius, whose father, during the period of Sulla's proscription lists, had been
lured to Rome by relatives and murdered for his estate. The
freedman Chrysogonus, who had put his own name on the lists,

had for a share of the estate proscribed the dead man, but the township of Ameria, in which Roscius had been one of the most honored citizens, protested so indignantly against this outrage that to cover their own guilt the Roman cousins had accused the son. Because of Cicero's magnificent oration in defense of young Roscius he had been acquitted. But Cæsar remembers how careful Cicero had been to fix no blame for the injustice upon Sulla, who, aware of the manner in which his favorite was selling pardons, had yet never seen fit to restrain, and still less to punish, Chrysogonus.

In his oration Cicero had artfully compared Sulla with Jupiter Optimus Maximus, the ruler of the universe, with too much to do to be able to look into the details of every wrong. And when the orator, after the acquittal of Roscius, had posed as the one citizen in Rome who could always be relied upon to come to the rescue of the weak and oppressed, he had neglected to give equal publicity to the fact that it was not until the tide of public sentiment had turned strongly against further outrages being committed under cover of the proscription lists that he himself had come forward to plead in defense of any of its victims. His prosecution of Verres, with shortly afterwards his defense of Dolabella, had been other instances of the shrewd way in which he only denounced infamy when he knew he could do so with complete safety; and a still further example that Cæsar thinks of is his present thundering against Lucius Lucullus, the general left by Sulla in charge of the East, and whom Cicero—knowing the feeling against Lucullus in the Senate, which resents the manner in which he is plundering Asia and sending his friends nothing—is agitating to have recalled as another embodiment of that rapacity of Roman governors and generals which is making the name of the Republic detested throughout the world.

Lastly Cæsar thinks of Marcus Crassus, who wishes to be looked up to as a genius of finance. But except for Sulla's proscription lists, would not Crassus still be poor and unknown? Is it not chance, rather than ability, that has brought him his fortune?

In his new mood, Cæsar is unwilling to admit that either
Pompey, Cicero or Crassus have more ability than himself.
Where once he accepted in good humor the knowledge that
no one of the three considers him a serious rival in any of their
fields, viewing him as an idle pleasure-seeker, with no particular talent for anything, he now resents as much as his
mother this estimate of himself.

So he sits brooding, a prey, despite his efforts at self-
persuasion, to the sense of inferiority that gnaws away inside
of him. Beneath the smooth temples, under the carefully arranged lock of hair, swirl veiled animosities. Has he nothing,
he wonders, which is peculiarly his? . . . He remembers his
smile. . . .

His face at the first sound of footsteps quickly loses its sharp
and furtive look, and he is safely behind his disguise of affability.

2

During his term as military tribune he makes use of every
opportunity to become popular with the Roman mob.

The fact that Cicero will certainly receive the strong backing
of the Senate when he becomes a candidate for the consulship,
determines him the more to ingratiate himself with the people.
He is bitterly jealous of Cicero's rising reputation. The tribuneship he buys as a first step towards the consulship. As the
Roman army is now organized, the *tribuni militum*, of whom
there are six attached to each legion, are merely political and
social favorites who go into the army for a year or two in order
thus to begin their public career. But under the new laws created by Sulla to strengthen the power of the Senate, only Romans who have first held the minor senatorial offices of praetor
or quaestor are eligible to the consulship. Cæsar therefore resolves, while he is tribune, to next buy himself a quaestorship,[1]
the money for his election expenses to be borrowed from Crassus.

Marcus Crassus, the richest man in Rome, is huge in

---

[1] The quaestors have charge of the treasury.

body, with small cunning eyes. Apparently he aspires to be nothing more than what he is—a fat and successful business man.

He frequently denounces war, stating that peace-time prosperity is what the government should really aim for. He pretends to have no sympathy with the politicians who are continually trying to drag the country into more wars for their own private profit. He explains away the fact that he has made all his own millions by buying up confiscated properties and dealing in the slaves which the Roman generals sell by the tens of thousands to his contractors who follow every Roman army, with the statement that this is not his fault but the fault of the times—if he did not take advantage of such situations, others would.

He has great influence not only with the spendthrift young aristocrats who count on him for loans, but also among the provincial Italians, to whom he is always willing to lend money at a high rate of interest. These smaller loans he considers good investments as they have less of a gambling element connected with them; the large political loans he feels he must make as a matter of policy, but he has a great deal of money outstanding among dissolute and extravagant patricians which he fears he will never get back. While always busy, therefore, acquiring public lands and contracts through graft, he is at the same time building up a reputation among the farmers and artisans as a politician who champions the rights of the poor man against those of the Senate.

Though himself the owner of immense areas of cattle land and vineyard in provincial Italy he does what he can to keep the senators from bringing the farmers to a state of utter ruin, knowing that if everything is taken away from them his loans will suffer. He sells the big Roman landlords their slaves, thus aggravating the misfortunes of the free Italians, but he attempts to restrain the other Roman capitalists from making an equal profit in the Campagna. His problem is thus largely one of finding the right balance between exploitation in two conflicting directions—he buys all the land he can to add to his own immense estates, but for the benefit of his country debtors puts every obstacle he can in the way of rival capitalists doing likewise.

Crassus dreads nothing more than force. As a boy he was timid, abhorring rough games, and sickening at the sight of blood. This horror of physical violence he has never outgrown. His blood runs cold at the thought of being transfixed by one of the seven-foot pilums of the legionaries, or of receiving a thrust from one of their short double-edged swords.

Yet he realizes that nowadays in the Republic, money, powerful though it may be, is not as powerful as the sword; that quicker even than to bribe is simply to take.

He watches the triumphs of the victorious generals, and sight of the plunder heaped high on the wagons preceding the generals' chariots in the processions to the Capitol, of the quantities of gold and silver plate, the jewelled ornaments, and the chests of money, fills him with greed and envy. In his heart he yearns to win military laurels. Though terrified by pain and death, he covets the Roman generals the booty they seem to make theirs so easily, and the honor and glory attendant upon a successful campaign. To ride through the streets of Rome as a conquering hero, to be known everywhere as a man of action, a great soldier, this, in reality, is what Marcus Crassus aspires to.

He intends to become a soldier as soon as he feels he can do so with perfect safety. He will wait a few years until there is no longer the slightest room for doubt upon the invincibility of the Roman legions, then insist upon being given a command in the East. For Asia, in the mind of Crassus, can always conjure up thoughts of limitless wealth. The Roman legions have marched through Asia Minor and crossed the Euphrates, but it is his intention to go much further than this. He will take an expedition beyond the country of the Parthians, journeying towards the rising sun until he reaches at last those great cities in India and China, where the walls of every house (according to the stories told by travellers) are gilded and bejewelled more richly than the Capitol. He knows that Alexander the

Great failed to conquer the Far East, but he believes that the Roman legions, superior as a war machine to the troops commanded by the Macedonian chief, will have no difficulty in doing so; once the warlike Parthians have been defeated, will it not be an easy matter to subdue the peace-loving and industrious inhabitants of the great wealthy countries beyond?

The greed of Crassus is particularly excited by the empire of China, which report says lies at the very eastern edge of the world, and is surrounded in its entire extent by a wall. The fat millionaire has thought much about this wall. He has come to the conclusion that because the natives of China doubtless rely upon it to keep out invaders, they have only a small defense army, the main body of the people being engaged in those useful occupations, such as mining and manufacturing, which have made the empire so immensely wealthy.

The little eyes of Marcus Crassus glitter greedily as he pictures the huge Roman siege engines battering down that impregnable wall surrounding the empire of China, and he sees himself, at the head of his army, riding through the breach.

Such is Marcus Licinius Crassus, the richest man in Rome, who longs to put aside the toga of a peaceful business man in order to don the purple military cloak of a general.

To him Cæsar goes when he needs money to insure his election to one of the quaestorships. He relies on a promise made him by Crassus when he was elected military tribune, to give him financial backing should he wish to try for higher political positions.

Will Crassus, he asks, lend him the money as he has promised? Crassus, an amiable expression replacing the look of cunning usually in his eyes, answers that he will. Of humble birth, he has always liked Caius Cæsar, who never plays the haughty aristocrat in his presence as Pompey, when he would humble Crassus, by making him feel his social inferiority, has a habit of doing. He is willing to assist Cæsar forward politically, since he believes the latter will always be under his control. Like Pompey he sees nothing of the rival in Caius Cæsar, but looks upon him as raw material for an ideal henchman, one who can be relied on to stay loyal under all conditions to the friends who have done him favors.

His little eyes beam cordially, then, as he tells Cæsar that the latter shall certainly have his most vigorous support as a candidate for the quaestorship. They beam with the same good-will when, after Cæsar has been elected, he becomes the pupil of Crassus in finance in the same way that he used to be the pupil of Cicero in public speaking; Crassus, as he talks over taxation and foreign revenues with the young quaestor, is more than glad to occupy the position of instructor, and to have Cæsar bring to him the various problems which arise in con-nection with his work, since, as long as Cæsar is quaestor, he is sure of a good friend in the Treasury.

Meanwhile Cæsar is in a similar manner cultivating the friendship of Pompey, who, capable or incapable, has been steadily growing more famous as a general.

At the present time Pompey is conducting a naval war against the pirates, who, because of the connivance of the cor-rupt governors of the Mediterranean provinces, and the half-hearted manner in which Rome has attempted to solve the pirate problem by sending out small expeditions that return to the city as soon as a single victory can be claimed, have grown so powerful that the Senate has given him supreme con-trol of all the Roman forces on the Mediterranean, with juris-diction over the entire coast to a point thirty miles inland. And besides this authority along the Mediterranean there is strong agitation to have Pompey made commander of the army in the East which is fighting Mithridates. Cæsar is especially anx-ious to stand in well with Pompey as he knows that Cicero is courting the latter's favor. Whenever he goes to the Pompey palace—where he is making himself as amiable as possible to Pompey's cousin, Pompeia—he finds Cicero there; and one day, passing by the Forum, he finds an immense crowd gath-ered here listening to an oration by Cicero in defense of the proposed Manilian law which will make Pompey generalissimo of the Roman armies. Rage gnaws at his heart as he listens to the golden voice of the orator extolling the absent general to the skies.

He knows from Cicero's confidences in the past that the orator in reality holds Pompey in great contempt. It is another instance of Cicero making what he feels is a timely speech. He is helping Pompey because he has an intuition that Pompey will be given the supreme command whether he does or not.

Cæsar leaves the Forum more than ever determined to win the love of Pompeia. She may not be beautiful, like Cornelia, but she is known to have considerable influence with her cousin. Through her, he thinks, he should surely be able to rise higher in Pompey's favor than does the arch-hypocrite, Marcus Tullius Cicero.

3

While he is quaestor his aunt Julia dies, and he delivers an oration at her funeral.

His aunt having been seriously ill for several weeks, he has had plenty of time in which to prepare his speech. He uses the occasion to revive popular feeling for his dead uncle, first haranguing the mob assembled at the bier on the manifold virtues of his aunt, then going on to recall to the crowd such illustrious achievements of Marius as the bringing of Jugurtha in chains to Rome, and the defeat of the Cimbrian migration. As he enumerates the exploits of the general who, because of the loot brought back by him from his various campaigns, had once been the idol of the Roman mob, but whose name during the days of Sulla's power had become discredited, a number of Marius's old veterans, whom he has carefully placed in the crowd, come forward and burst into tears.

After the funeral, followed by an enthusiastic mob shouting the praises of his dead uncle, he restores to their former places those images of Marius which were thrown down from their positions in the Forum by the victorious Sullan army when it entered Rome. For some time he has sensed a strong reaction of feeling against the Senate put back in power by Sulla, and he means to make all the capital he can out of his aunt's death. In subsequent street-talks he not only again dwells upon his relationship with the dead general, in order to make himself stand out as the living representative of the Marian ideals, but also weaves into his speeches the fact that he is descended on one side from the Goddess Venus, and on the other from the ancient kings of Rome.

Having played up his illustrious ancestry in order to lay stress on the idea that he is not to be viewed as any low-born popular leader animated only by personal ambition, he has himself, with the aid of Crassus, appointed chairman of an investigation committee authorized to examine into the wrongs committed under cover of Sulla's proscription lists; and also, at the urgent wish of Cornelia, obtains pardons for many of the refugees whom the Senate is keeping in exile, among these being his brother-in-law, Cinna the Younger.

There are two women who still play an important part in his life—the first is his mother, the second is Cornelia. Though both are glad he has changed his mode of living, and instead of remaining the wastrel of earlier days is now showing ambition, each judges him by a different standard of greatness.

His mother is too worldly to want more than material success for her son. She knows he is falling more and more in debt to Crassus and other Roman capitalists as a result of his aspirations to a political career, but takes it for granted that if he succeeds in becoming consul the province which will then fall to him as proconsul will lift him out of debt, and make the Cæsar family richer than it has ever been.

Cornelia's interest in her husband's political activities has other motives. Where Aurelia Cæsar thinks it merely a good stroke of practical politics for Cæsar to revive enthusiasm for Marius, Cornelia is tremendously in earnest when she encourages her husband to become leader of the people's party. She dreams of him carrying on the splendid reform movements for which she believes her father sacrificed himself. What Lucius

Cinna commenced, that must Caius Cæsar finish—namely, the freeing of Rome from the tyrannies of a corrupt Senate, the restoring to the city of its ancient republican glory. The civil wars that have convulsed Rome since her childhood convince her that a patriot is needed who will drive the oligarchy out of Rome in the same way that four centuries ago the Tarquin kings were expelled. And, more dearly than anything else, she wants her husband, Caius Cæsar, to be this patriot.

And the Senate is not inclined to belittle her influence over Cæsar. It traces back to the machinations of this proud dark-eyed daughter of Lucius Cinna,—who even during Sulla's life-time was fearless in her denunciation of the bloody revenge taken by the Dictator upon her father's supporters,—Cæsar's present activities; his laudation of Marius at the funeral of his aunt, and the exciting of the populace to the point of raising up in the Forum again the overthrown images of the dead general; his agitation for investigation of the crimes committed during the Sullan reign of terror, his securing of pardons for Cornelia's brother and the other exiles. They feel that day by day the march of events is approaching nearer to a position where their own security will be dangerously threatened. Is not the Roman mob already tired of being ruled by the five hundred elderly millionaires composing the oligarchy, and eagerly awaiting the appearance of another Dictator like Sulla, who though his faults may be many will at least stand out conspicuously as a personality instead of being only systematic misgovernment shapelessly disguised as democracy? Is not the real power already drifting into the hands of Pompey with his army, and Crassus with his money? Once again the ideal republic of the senators, in which Italy and the provinces are the property of the corporation, of which each senator receives his proper share, and where the lawmakers live in perfect harmony with one another, seems in danger of having its privileges usurped by a few.

For the senators there is hope in the thought that Pompey may be killed in the East. Cicero, though largely influential in obtaining the passage of the Manilian law, in order to win

Pompey's friendship for himself, has been careful to preserve the good-will of the Senate by privately stating this to be his belief. He has also promised to increase the power of the Senate all he can during his term of office if the senators will support him in his candidacy for the consulship.

The Senate stands in no fear of Cæsar himself; but Cornelia seems a real menace. At the present time there are many of the senators who are in enjoyment of estates confiscated from the murdered friends of her father; these meet privately and talk over the investigation being conducted by Cæsar, also the return of the exiles. How far will Caius Cæsar go, urged on by Cornelia? May not the present agitation be only the forerunner of far more serious trouble? Perhaps banishment, even death, has already been decided on as the fate of all Sulla's friends.

Cinna's daughter is not an old woman like the widow of Marius, whose grievances were not considered to hold any grave potential threat, because she might die a natural death at any moment. She is young and healthy. Is there any limit to the mischief she may be able to do unless perhaps—the senators glance at one another meaningly—accident or illness should suddenly send her to a premature grave?

Cornelia begins to sicken. The physicians—as she expects to be a mother again in a few months—advise her to be more careful of her diet in the future. She lies in bed, pale, everything swimming before her eyes in a strange dizziness.

One bright June morning when every window of the house shows a patch of blue sky and the country breeze brings over the fragrance of wild flowers Cæsar stands looking down at his dead wife. She died at dawn. As the sun was rising above the seven hills of Rome, bringing a new day to the Republic, here in this room, where he had watched in agony all night, he had stooped and caught with his mouth her last breath.

Is it only Cornelia who is dead? Has she perhaps taken with her a part of himself? The bald-headed man at the bedside lifts a hand to his forehead and twists nervously in his fingers the lock of dishevelled hair that has fallen down over his eyes. Very far away seem to him those days of his youth when he had risked life itself by opposing the wishes of Sulla. Will he, he wonders, ever again risk anything for love?

The house is very quiet. Softly, slaves move to and fro in the rooms beyond the one in which lies their dead mistress. Little Julia comes to the door, and cries as an attendant, with a frightened glance in the direction of the master, takes her hand and leads her away.

Cæsar sees only the face of his dead wife. He remembers the days when old Marius was still alive and her father's position as Dictator, with Sulla away in Asia fighting Mithridates, seemed so secure. How little he had cared then what were the political ambitions of Lucius Cinna! How much he had cared for Cornelia!

The hot summer nights when walking with her in the garden he had sworn he would never marry the heiress with whom his parents had arranged a match for him, come back in memory. He remembers the gondola rides at Baiae, moonlight strolls on her father's splendid estate in the Campagna. He sees again the full moon rising from behind one dark hill as they watch, shedding upon the night the magical radiance of a faraway world in which, to the lovers, love seems the only reality. He catches his breath at the white and mysterious loveliness of her face in the moonlight.

But the light in this room is that of pitiless day, which reveals harsher realities than love—in which love becomes only a dream. Though a voice, speaking it seems through the mist of tears blurring his eyes, tells him he has loved Cornelia too much to be able ever to live with another woman, to hear another woman laughing and talking in this house where she now lies dead, another louder voice is already repeating in his ear the name of Pompeia.

Yet if, from now on, ambition, and ambition alone, will govern all his actions, the world shall at least know that his love for Cornelia was a great, pure, and disinterested love.

A surprised mob fills the Forum, and all eyes are on Caius Cæsar.

It is true, then, as has been rumored, that he intends to deliver a funeral oration for his dead wife, the daughter of Lucius Cinna?

No oration has ever been made for so young a woman—Cæsar when he rises to talk is violating the Roman precedent that only elderly matrons, usually widows of great men, shall be thus honored after death. But as he extolls the virtues of Cornelia he becomes for the first time in his life really eloquent.

The crowd presses closer. There are whispers, however, that his ardor is rather political than based on sentiment; that he is praising his dead wife, not because of any great love he bore her, but because she was Cinna's daughter.

Can it be otherwise when the licentiousness of his private life is common knowledge? When he is known to have had love affairs with Servilia, the sister of Cato, and almost numberless other Roman women, married and unmarried? When on his return to Rome after visiting King Nicomedes the town wits had jestingly called him Queen Bithynia? When at the very time Cornelia fell sick he was said to be intimate with Pompey's cousin, Pompeia?

Senators in the audience wonder if Cornelia's death has come too late. Has she planted in Cæsar's breast seeds of hate that will live after her to the peril of the oligarchy? Cicero, likewise one of the listeners, stares at the impassioned orator, conjecturing for the first time whether Caius Cæsar, beneath his careless exterior, may not be shrewder than is commonly thought.

Only Cæsar knows the truth. The fragments of talk that come to his ears on this day of the funeral fill him with bitter malice. Does no one believe his love for Cornelia was genuine? Is he to be judged only by those past acts of his which seem to prove the contrary?

That night as he sits in his lonely home, an ungovernable and womanish fury sets his nerves twitching when he reflects upon the manner in which his sincere tribute to his dead wife has been misinterpreted. He feels himself on the verge of one of his epileptic attacks. With an effort he brings himself under control.

His thoughts leave Cornelia, turning to his own future.

One day, a few weeks later, two men walk in the garden of a magnificent villa on the Bay of Naples. They are Cæsar and Pompey the Great. The child between them, holding a hand of each, is Cæsar's daughter Julia.

Because of the way his own ambition is being crowned with success, Pompey can the more readily sympathize with Cæsar in the loss of his wife. He is glad to have seen Cæsar before he leaves for the East to take command of the Roman army in the field against Mithridates. They talk about Cicero, who will doubtless strive to be elected consul while Pompey is away at the wars. Pompey knows that Cicero spoke in behalf of the Manilian law, and has expressed his gratitude to the orator for this support, but now he lets Cæsar know privately that with Crassus he intends to oppose the efforts of Cicero to become too powerful; unless Cicero will drop hypocrisy, and let them know frankly he is willing to join the party of Pompey and Crassus against that of the Senate, their plan is to try and defeat his election to the consulship by putting their money and influence behind Lucius Catiline as a rival candidate.

With Cæsar, says Pompey cordially, the case is different— he can depend on being backed for any political position he wants. In a more intimate tone, Pompey the Great, who talks with a slight lisp, adds he hopes that when time has softened somewhat the sorrow of his friend there may be made between their two families a marriage alliance which will cement the strong friendship already existing between them.

And while they talk of Pompeia, to obtain whose hand Cæsar has made the journey to visit Pompey, now one and now the other smile down at the little girl walking between them. Yet little does either guess that the day is to come when she will be the only link holding them together, or that her death will precipitate the Republic into that bloody civil war which will cost Pompey his life, and from which Julius Cæsar will emerge the first of the line of Roman emperors.

4

The next five years are years which move swiftly for Cæsar. In 65 B. c. he is ædile, in 63 Pontifex Maximus, in 62 praetor, in 61 propraetor in Spain, and in 59, at forty-two years of age, —consul. It is half a decade in which his life, political and private, is packed tightly with significant events: his marriage with Pompeia before Cornelia has been dead a year, and his separation from her scarcely two years later, the Catiline conspiracy during the consulship of Cicero, the alliance between Cæsar, Pompey and Crassus known as the First Triumvirate, the banishment of Cicero, Cæsar's marriage with Calpurnia Piso, his departure for Gaul . . . half a decade in which he becomes balder, shrewder, more ambitious, while his daughter Julia grows up into the beautiful girl, each year more resembling her dead mother, with whom Pompey falls in love on his return from Asia.

They are five years during which the last trace of the naïvely cruel and debauched young Caius Cæsar vanishes. . . . The new Cæsar suffers from indigestion. He has sleepless nights that he spends brooding on wrongs. Already the soldier-politician who will soak the ancient world in blood has been born.

The scene is the Circus Maximus, and the occasion a Roman holiday.

From all parts of the city the burgesses are hastening towards the Circus. For it has been rumored that the new ædile and demagogue, Caius Julius Cæsar, has prepared for their entertainment the most magnificent combined gladiatorial and wild-beast show yet seen in Rome.

The eyes of the mob, quick to notice improvements and innovations, dwell with approval on a canal, ten feet wide, that Cæsar has had dug around the field to protect the lower seats from invasion by the wild beasts. This is a distinct improvement, as in the past the pleasure of watching the hunting has been alloyed with fear that one of the lions may jump the wall of the arena, as has happened on several occasions, and begin tearing to pieces, not the Barbarians supplied them for this purpose, but the Roman spectators.

Many of the burgesses, before the performance starts, visit the dark vaults supporting the seats of the Circus, which are let out to women of the town. Others prefer to postpone the trip to the brothels until the show is over, when the bloodshed in the arena will have sharpened their appetite for pleasure.

The great sunlit arena is empty except for armed guards standing by the entrances through which the gladiators and animals will be driven into the Circus. But the seats of the Circus, which, though not any such magnificent stone structure as the later Colosseum, being built almost entirely of wood like a modern baseball grandstand, will hold more than a hundred thousand people, are rapidly filling up; the audience putting in the time until the show is due to start craning their necks to watch the arrival of celebrities.

The focus of attention is the senatorial section, where the seats, unlike those occupied by the plebeians, are shaded from the hot sun by gorgeous awnings. Here each new arrival bustles forward smiling and bowing in the hope of attracting to himself the applause of the mob.

Cicero enters. Casting frequent glances around him to be sure he is well under observation, he walks to and fro, throwing himself into dramatic poses, and gesticulating, as he talks now with one and now with another of the senators, in the studied manner of a professional orator. He beams delightedly when he hears his name howled by the mob, which thinks well of him for having supported Pompey for the supreme military command. Continually bowing and smiling, he throws out his arms towards the sea of faces, as though inflamed by an ardent desire to take the whole of Rome in his embrace.

Crassus waddles in. His face, likewise, is wreathed in smiles

until he notices Cicero. Then a sulky scowl darkens his heavy
features. It deepens as several of the senators surround Cicero,
and the group, glancing in his direction, begins to titter. For
the orator has made a bitter enemy of Crassus by indulging
in humor at his expense; not long ago he delivered an oration
in praise of the fat capitalist, then almost the next day got up
in the Forum when Crassus was again present and thundered
against him with such graphic allusions to his personal appearance that the mob was convulsed with mirth—on Crassus
demanding an explanation of his extraordinary conduct in one
day eulogising him and the next making him the butt of public
ridicule, Cicero with a smirk at the listeners, had replied that
no harm was meant—both speeches had been merely delivered
for oratorical exercise, in order to try the force of his eloquence
upon so bad a subject.

Now the two ædiles, Cæsar and Marcus Bibulus, are seen
taking their places. A slight hiss greets Bibulus, who is known
to be one of Pompey's strongest opponents, for which reason,
to counteract Cæsar's influence, he was put forward by the
Senate as Cæsar's colleague in the ædileship. Bibulus, short and
portly, with a bull neck, turns his back to the arena, and en-
gages in conversation with the senators. Cæsar, left standing
alone, receives tumultuous applause. He smiles his genial smile,
then surveys the Circus through half-closed eyes, turning to
glance in every direction, as though noting how thoroughly his
preparations for the comfort and entertainment of the crowd
have been carried out by subordinates.

Among a group of young patricians, lounging with their
courtesans and favorites, is a middle-aged man with sunken
cheeks and flashing black eyes—his name is Lucius Sergius Catiline.

Many in the mob are pointing him out, the drunkards and
gamblers eyeing him admiringly while coupling his name with
coarse jokes that bring shouts of laughter, the more respectable burgesses casting angry glances in his direction.

Catiline, a close friend of Sulla, had been with the Dictator
in Asia, and on his return to Rome was foremost among

those followers of Sulla who committed the worst crimes under cover of the proscription lists. Even in Rome his reputation as an expert in every form of crime is outstanding. As a boy he sold himself, like Mark Antony, as a male prostitute to whichever Roman millionaire would pay highest for his favors. His whole life since has been divided between carousal and the committal of crimes necessary to supply him with money for his pleasures.

To obtain their property, he had both his brother and his brother-in-law put on the proscription lists and murdered. To marry a female voluptuary, Aurelia Orestilla, he murdered his first wife, later poisoning his child by this marriage at the instigation of his new wife who hated her step-son. For extortion in Africa, where he was recently praetor, he is now being prosecuted, in order to prevent his becoming consul.

For Catiline, who left for Africa heavily in debt, had secured the praetorship of that province with the avowed intention of exploiting the inhabitants to an extent where he would be able to return to Rome with sufficient wealth to buy the consulship. His impeachment for misgovernment, however, having disqualified him as a candidate until the trial is decided, he used his money to secure the election of two friends, Autronius Paetus and Cornelius Sulla, both of whom have been unseated for bribery at the elections, the defeated candidates, Aurelius Cotta and Manlius Torquatus being raised in their places to the consular dignity. It is known throughout Rome that he recently plotted to murder Cotta and Torquatus, but so powerful is his influence with the disorderly element of the city, the bankrupts and adventurers who need only a leader to rise at any time in insurrection against the existing government, that the Senate dares neither to convict him of his crimes in Africa or of the one planned in Rome. Cneius Piso, another dissolute aristocrat belonging like Catiline to one of Rome's oldest families, and his partner in the murder plot, has fled to Spain but Catiline remains in Rome, openly contemptuous of arrest.

Because of his violent temper, and evil reputation, there is no one who dares lay hands on him. The senators hate and fear him, but he is the darling of the Roman underworld, to which his great personal courage, his skill with the assassin's dagger, and his derision of what the Senate pleases to call law and order in Rome, make him a highly romantic figure.

And at the moment he has Cicero's friendship—the orator, knowing through his elaborate system of spies that Pompey and Crassus are scheming to make Catiline his opponent for the consulship of the coming year, is at this very moment making advances to Catiline in the Circus—smiling and bowing he has approached the little group of patricians, and taken Catiline aside—from the direction of their glances and their gestures they are apparently discussing the new canal dug by Cæsar around the arena, but in an undertone Cicero is offering his golden voice for hire if Catiline will express his willingness to enter the consulship as his colleague.

Nor is this the first occasion on which he has broached the subject; in a honeyed voice he has already several times suggested to the impeached praetor that a burst of impassioned oratory—coming, as it would, from the mouth of an orator and philosopher renowned the world over for his honor and integrity—is the only thing needed to secure his speedy acquittal. But today for the first time Catiline agrees to the bargain.

With a jaunty step Cicero leaves Catiline and goes to converse with other senators. The moment he turns away, a quick smile crosses the wolfish face of Catiline, then the sunken cheeks are grim hollows again.

But the orator feels he has accomplished successfully another piece of masterly diplomacy, and before the Circus events—which he pretends to watch with interest, but at heart despises for their brutality—are half over, he is hurrying home to start an optimistic letter on the subject to his friend Atticus——

"At present I am thinking of defending my rival, Catiline, We have the judges whom we wish, and the prosecutor is most obliging. I hope, if he secures acquittal, that he will be more ready to join me in my candidature, but if otherwise, I shall bear it patiently. . . ."

A trumpet sounds. The hubbub of conversation in the Circus quiets down as two gladiators enter the arena.

Both are Gauls, and unknown. In their armor, of the same build and height, they look alike; but the moment they begin to fight, one of them, due to some wave of psychic feeling which sweeps through the vast audience, becomes the popular favorite. Every advantage he gains is applauded with frenzy, while equal skill shown by his opponent brings only growls of discontent or angry silence.

The unpopular gladiator, dripping blood from many wounds, fights on obstinately. The audience, finding this first number on the program beginning to drag a little, howls for a quick finish. Conversations recommence, women lean back and yawn. Cæsar fumbles nervously with his girdle.

But suddenly there comes a roar of delight as the favorite breaks down the guard of the other Gaul long enough to deliver a fatal thrust, and the stricken gladiator, vanquished as much by the malignity of those cries issuing from the multitude of throats, by the sight of that sea of faces cruelly anticipating his death, and the mysterious hate of the crowd which makes him seem to be fighting not a single man but a monster with a thousand faces and a thousand arms, as by the sword of his opponent, sinks slowly to the floor of the arena.

Circus attendants run forward with hooks to drag out his body through the porta libitinensis into the spoliarum or court where the corpses are stripped of their armor. The crowd returns to its gossiping.

Cæsar is thinking of Catiline. He is aware of Cicero's efforts to convert Catiline from a rival into a colleague. But will Catiline allow himself to be won over by Cicero? Let Cicero plead as magnificently as he will in his corrupt client's defense, is it not improbable that Catiline, once acquitted, will feel himself any longer bound to the cause of Cicero?

His thoughts are interrupted by the arrival in the arena of

an archer. Unlike the gladiators, the archer wears no armor or helmet, nor does he carry a shield; he is clad only in a light tunic, and for sole protection has a bow and arrows, and a knife in his girdle.

Tall and lean, he swaggers forward, greeted with a roar of welcome, for his expert archery in the arena, where he has already nearly a hundred wild beasts to his credit, and his audacious courage, have won him fame and popularity with the Roman mob. When a lion appears he disdains to notice it, but negligently traces a pattern on the ground with the tip of his bow.

The lion, driven out from one of the dens which share with the brothels the underneath section of the grandstand by attendants who prod at it with long spears and hot irons, has leaped into the arena with a roar—it stands quite still now facing the archer, a few paces away. When it seems bewildered by the huge audience, and stands quiet, refusing to attack, hisses and curses are hurled in its direction. The archer suddenly takes aim with his bow and wounds it in the side.

A deafening yell of applause rises from the Circus as the lion with a roar of pain tears at the arrow with his teeth and licks the wound with his great red tongue. Again the archer, going a step closer, takes aim. Now there are two arrows in the animal, one protruding from either side, but neither deeply imbedded.

The wounded beast, seeming of a sudden to connect its pain with the man opposite, lifts its head and stares at him. It begins to lash its tail. The archer at this moment sends a thrill through his audience by approaching still closer to the lion, while in a loud voice shouting insults. The great beast crouches. Stretching itself almost flat along the ground, it moves slowly towards him, its tail continuing the angry lashing. The archer stands squarely in its path with his bow raised until it gathers itself for the final spring when he releases a third arrow which driven from the bow not at the half-speed of the other two but with terrific velocity buries itself in the lion's throat.

Rising on its hindlegs like a rearing horse, the lion gives a

strangled roar, claws the air an instant convulsively, then col-
lapses into a quivering heap. When its death agonies have
ceased, the archer approaches, prods the carcass contemptuously
with his toe, and cutting off one of the paws with his knife,
throws it over the canal to be scrambled for as a souvenir by
the admiring populace. He next despatches a tigress and a
panther as expeditiously as he has the lion, then amid immense
applause leaves the arena.

These two preliminaries being over, and the seats of the Circus having filled until there are few vacant places, the show
now proceeds to more rapid butchery. In quick succession, gladiators, single and in teams, on foot and mounted, oppose one
another. There are *hoplomachi* wearing complete suits of armor, *mirmillones* having the images of fishes on their helmets,
retiarii whose weapons are a three-pointed lance and a net,
laqueatores who use a noose, *dimacheri* who fight with a sword
in each hand, *thraces* armed like the Thracians with round
bucklers and daggers, and, most popular of all, the *andabatae*,
who wear helmets that have no eye openings, and whose chance
thrusts at one another as they stagger blindfolded around the
arena, now stabbing only the air and then again burying their
swords in the bodies of unseen opponents, convulse the audience with laughter.

Besides these special classes of gladiators performing in
the arena, the Circus ground is covered with the *ordinarii*, or
regular gladiators fighting in pairs in the ordinary way, some
of them prisoners of war, others condemned criminals whose
death sentences have been revised to allow them to be made use
of for the combats but who must be killed within a year, and
still others free men who have sold themselves to the Circus
for board and wages as gladiatorial slaves whose contracts require them to be willing to let themselves be "chained,
scourged, burnt, or killed without opposition, if the laws of the
institution should so require."

Now panthers, lions and tigers, starved for days until they
are crazed with hunger, are driven by scores into the arena and
goaded by the attendants with their hot irons, spears and whips,

to tear each other to pieces. . . . There are combats of young patricians who have voluntarily entered the arena as a new excitement; these, however, do not fight to the death as the other gladiators must do, but as soon as they receive a wound are conducted respectfully to their servants who place them carefully on litters and bear them home. . . . Famous Capuan swordsmen step out onto the blood-soaked ground and thrust at one another. A miniature war is staged. . . . There is a battle between Arabians on camels and Parthians in scythed chariots. . . . Once again a menagerie of wild beasts is turned loose in the arena, but this time mixed with the snarls and roars of the animals are the shrieks of the unfortunate slaves left to fight them. . . . Two novel features that win much applause from the crowd are a fight between naked Ethiopians and some crocodiles imported by Cæsar from the Nile, and the slaughter of a number of giraffes—when these strange long-necked creatures, seen by a majority of the audience for the first time, fall under the arrows of their pursuers, making no sound of terror or of pain, a piece of natural history information which greatly interests the audience runs from burgess to burgess; these foreign animals, it seems, are silent because nature has furnished them with no organs for making a noise of any sort,—no matter how much they suffer they must remain mute.

But the most spectacular event of the day, and the one which Cæsar has counted on to win him most popularity is an elephant hunt. Now and again a single elephant has been sacrificed in the arena before, but such a spectacle as the Roman mob now gazes on has never been presented by any previous ædile. The huge crowd rises as one man, delirious with excitement, to watch an elephant herd numbering close on to a hundred specimens thunder back and forth across the arena in pursuit of archers and javelin hurlers who attack them with their darts. And Cæsar, smiling genially throughout the uproar, feels, as he watches the mob go wild over the men caught up by the great trunks and hurled through the air, or trampled under the massive feet, and the elephants crashing wounded to their knees, that if the show made a poor start it has certainly in the opinions of all wound up in a manner that will reflect honor upon him for many a day.

The show is over. The audience is filing out, a large proportion of the men, with tingling nerves, hastening to direct their steps toward the brothels in the vaults.

The hum of pleased voices fills the air. Here and there in the arena where men and animals lie in heaps which attendants with teams of horses are dragging out as fast as they can, agonized faces smeared with blood lift themselves with an effort from the floor of the arena an instant, then drop to the ground again and lie still.

Cæsar, as he leaves the Circus, passes by a spot where a number of the animal cages, all made of solid silver, are on display. He catches the sound of his own name frequently repeated by the admiring crowd. The moment seems a fortunate one in which to enhance that reputation for liberality which he so much relies on to aid him in achieving his ambition.

Pushing his way through the crowd he singles out a citizen who with trembling and covetous fingers is touching one of the shining cages, and in a voice loud enough to be heard by all tells the man it is his.

5

When Cæsar's term as ædile expired he was in debt to the extent of 25,000,000 sesterces, or a million and a quarter dollars. It was one of the inevitable consequences of the costly games and shows which the ædiles had to exhibit in order to have their later candidacies for the consulship received with favor, being given not at the public expense but at that of the ædiles, that corruption in the higher offices of consul and proconsul followed. And no ædile had ever spent more out of his own purse to win the favor of the Roman mob than had Cæsar. Besides the enormous sums he lavished on the combats and wild-beast shows he spent money freely decorating the city with new buildings and ornamental architecture, most impor-

tant among these being a large temple erected to the Dioscuri
and a row of columns placed in front of the Capitol. He also
borrowed heavily to improve the roads leading into Rome;
another form of philanthropy expected of the Roman who as-
pired to become a successful demagogue.

His future political career was now a matter of necessity.
Having invested a fortune in it, he now had to proceed through
the consulship to the proconsulship of a province the exploitation of which would recompense him for the immense outlay
in the minor senatorial offices. In 63, the same year that Cicero
became consul, he was made praetor. It was during this year
also, made notorious by the Catiline conspiracy, that he paid
out enormous sums of money to have himself elected Pontifex Maximus, a position of immense importance, the Pontifex
Maximus bearing the same relation to Roman religion that
the Pope later did to the Christian. The Senate, now keenly
aware of the perilous situation in which the oligarchy was
placed by the alliance between Pompey and Crassus, and knowing Cæsar's friendship with both, opposed him for election
with two candidates of their own, Quintus Catulus and Servilius Isauricus, but with the millions of Crassus behind him
Cæsar captured the election.

His mother's joy when she hears the result of the election
exceeds all bounds. Besides the prestige attached to the office
of Pontifex Maximus, it is an extremely lucrative one, being
accompanied also by a magnificent official residence into which
she immediately makes preparations to move. She sees her son
at last well on the road to Success. The fact that he is so heavily
in debt does not alarm her—what ambitious Roman has not
been at the outset of his career?

His extravagance as ædile had worried her a little, mainly
because she doubted whether the party of Crassus and Pompey
was strong enough to wrest power from the Senate and guarantee her son the further political advancement he required. She
saw money going out all the time, and none coming in. Each
lion and elephant she watched killed in the Circus made her
grieve for the great expense her son had been put to to import

the now useless beast. She felt the same way about the gladiators, killed off so rapidly that Cæsar's stables in Rome and Capua could scarcely supply the demand.

Conservative to the extent that she did not favor the ruling class being divided among itself, it had been a time when she was not certain that Caius was doing a sensible thing allying himself with the general and the multi-millionaire at the expense of making enemies in the Senate. It seemed to Aurèlia Cæsar there was plenty for all the rulers if the government was run rightly. She dreaded the armed disorders that raged in Rome when two parties came into active conflict. She saw no reason why Caius, whose family connections were far more powerful than those of Cicero, should not be able to attain the consulship without bloodshed. The Cæsars had so many relatives in the Senate, many of whom were constantly complaining to her that her son was making a serious mistake in joining Pompey and Crassus, that for a while she had allowed herself to be persuaded over to their viewpoint; seeing Cæsar not so much as a partner of Pompey and Crassus as their innocent accomplice, won over by flattery and gifts.

But gradually she had ceased to doubt. Pompey's successes against the pirates, and the equal success with which he seemed to be conducting the war against Mithridates, made her suspect he would return from Asia more powerful even than Sulla had been. So she strongly favored Cæsar's marriage with Pompeia. And now that Cæsar, with the aid of Crassus, had been elected Pontifex Maximus against the united opposition of the Senate, she had nothing but good to say of Crassus. That her son had had sufficient foresight to attach himself to their party seemed to her entirely of her own doing. In her talks to him nowadays she expresses her frank opinion that there is in the Senate a great deal of dead wood which needs cutting away.

She even comes out boldly with the statement that a very excellent thing for the country might be the centralization of authority—not in a Dictator of course, as this is something which the Roman constitution distinctly forbids—but in a little group of two or three men who, unhampered by the

advice of a large body like the Senate, and by short term of
office, as are the two annual consuls, would be in a position to
act with much greater vigor. And for this reason, she tells
Cæsar, she has always wanted him to make staunch friends of
Pompey and Crassus, each the most prominent figure in his
field; Pompey as general, Crassus as financier.

But Cæsar, unknown to his mother, has for some time been
less easy about the future. Though Pontifex Maximus, a position he will hold for life, and praetor, his enormous debts
weigh more heavily on him than she thinks. The determination
of the Senate to break Pompey's power, or to have him assassinated, and their equal determination to do the same thing to
Crassus, have made him uneasy about the consulship and
province on which he is staking all. The present consul, Cicero,
is known to be a strong partisan of the Senate; he had pleaded
in favor of the Manilian law and defended Catiline only out
of political expediency; since occupying the consulship his
whole policy has been a reactionary one calculated to preserve
the rule of the oligarchy. And not only has he throughout his
term of office, now drawing to a close, instituted no single reform in favor of the people, but he has likewise played up to
the senators by fostering legislation that will diminish the
power of the generals. Pompey's eastern victories have made
him a hero with the people, but like all victories of Roman
generals have only earned him the jealousy and mistrust of
the Senate; and it is already rumored that Cicero's last act
before he vacates the consulship will be the recalling of Pompey, and his replacement by a less competent general of whom
the Senate feels more sure. To safeguard their interests during
the coming year, Cæsar and Crassus therefore intend to support Catiline, who opposed Cicero for the present term of office, but lost the election, as Cicero's successor. And should the
Senate carry the election for its candidates, they have planned
to take the desperate step of seizing control of the government
by force.

In this conspiracy Lucius Sergius Catiline has been chosen

by Cæsar and Crassus as their tool because of the desperate condition of his finances. His African fortune has already been used up in election bribery, and he is deep in debt.

To Catiline have flocked all his friends among the nobility who are equally on the verge of ruin, and to whom the inducement to join the conspiracy is the general cancellation of debts which the new party will proclaim if it comes into power.

Crassus, though foremost among Roman money-lenders, is willing to be a secret leader in the conspiracy since he is gambling for a share in the kingship of Rome. But while he and Cæsar are the real heads of the conspiracy both mean to hide behind Catiline until its success or failure is decided. In the former case they will reveal themselves as the leaders, in the latter they will repudiate all connection with Catiline.

The period of elections, held at the close of every year, draws near. For several months, Catiline, acting under the advice of Cæsar and Crassus, and with the approval of absent Pompey, has been assuming the rôle of an aristocratic demagogue, similar to that adopted by Cæsar; he harangues meetings of the people in the Forum, pleading for their suffrages as a champion of the poor against the rich, and stirring them up to fury against the Senate by citing the numerous instances of its corruption and incompetence.

Cæsar, while remaining in the background, makes use of his growing popularity with the tribunes of the people to indirectly secure votes for Catiline. Crassus, still further out of sight, supplies the campaign funds and also money with which to equip an army for the purpose of seizing Rome in case Catiline is not elected. But both of them, as election time approaches, are worried for the success of their desperate enterprise by one element they had not taken into consideration at the beginning —the audacity of their henchmen.

Catiline's reckless courage, which at the outset had seemed ideal for their purpose, begins to alarm his more discreet employers. He goes about Rome openly announcing that if the Senate prevents his legal election, he means to cut his way to the consulship with the sword. When accused in the Senate by

Cicero of planning to carry the election by force, he defiantly
answers that he intends to be consul whether Cicero and every
senator listening to him wants him to be or not, and that if any
agitation is kindled against him he will put it out "not with
water but with revolution." Each day that sets the election
date nearer his language towards the consuls and the Senate
becomes more threatening and insulting. Though he does not
mention the names of Crassus and Cæsar, he admits the truth
of all the rumors circulated about himself; justifying his intended violation of the law with the remark that the Republic as he sees it is composed at the present time of two
bodies; one weak—the senators—with a weak leader—Cicero
—and the other the great mass of the citizens, strong in themselves but without a head—he himself intends to be the missing
head.

The election day arrives. Cicero and the Senate, afraid at
the last moment that Catiline may be constitutionally elected,
have decided to carry the election themselves by violence if
necessary. Though the law prohibits the presence of armed
men on the voting grounds at election time, Cicero places a
large guard here, and himself, as though he feared for his
life, appears wearing a breastplate. The guard, he explains to
the people, is made necessary by the lawlessness of Catiline,
who the government has been warned intends to fall on the
party of the senators with a gang of gladiators.

But Catiline, yielding to the persuasion of Crassus and
Cæsar, who see in the soldiers brought to the election by Cicero
an opportunity to place the Senate in the wrong, as having
taken the first illegal step, comes unattended. Cicero, taken
aback at first, and realizing his mistake, decides nevertheless to
make sure of the election now that he has gone this far—with
his soldiers he intimidates the voters until they elect as consuls
the Senate's candidates, Decimus Silanus and Lucius Murena.

Catiline, having lost the election, now works furiously at
the revolution. With continued cries of debt cancellation and
hints of emancipation to the slaves he gathers around him
fresh supporters. His plan is to so time the insurrection in the

capital that it will occur simultaneously with the march on Rome of the army raised by the conspirators, which, under command of a soldier of fortune named Caius Manlius, is now at Fiesole.

But it is at this point in the conspiracy that Crassus and Cæsar, alarmed by Cicero's precautions in posting guards throughout the city, by the suspicion that Cicero has bribed some of Catiline's accomplices so that these are betraying his plans to the consul, and by Catiline's negotiations, in order to make the success of the revolution a certainty, with an embassy of Allobroges which happens to be in the city, to the end that these Gauls may be persuaded to reinforce the revolutionary army with cavalry—that, losing courage at these developments in the plot, the real leaders resolve to go no further with it. When they discover that Catiline is planning the murder of Cicero they even send the latter warnings to be on his guard. But Catiline refuses to allow the conspiracy to drop. If Crassus and Cæsar have grown faint-hearted he will carry it on alone.

Cicero, when the unsigned messages warning him his life is in danger reach him, flutters nervously from the house of one senator to another to tell them the dreadful news.

At home—he has managed to marry a homely invalid named Terentia, and is now the father of a daughter, Tullia—he terrifies his wife with descriptions of the fate in store for him, and keeps her in constant dread of the assassins. He has the Senate offer a large public reward to the first discoverer of the plot to murder him.

At the senate-house, which Catiline attends regularly, he thunders against Catiline—the latter, with his wolfish smile, answers these accusations by broadly denying he has ever had any intention of killing Cicero. To prove his good faith he says he is willing to deliver himself to the custody of anyone whom the Senate chooses to name. Which of them asks Catiline, looking around, wants to have him as his guest?

The senators, whose whole efforts since the election have been concentrated on keeping Catiline and the concealed dagger he always carries, *out* of their homes, shrink back in their seats and make no reply. Catiline turns to the consul. Would Cicero perhaps like to have him—then at least he will be sure of his whereabouts, and not have to worry about this imaginary murder plot the details of which he thinks Catiline spends his nights arranging. But Cicero likewise refuses to take Catiline into his house.

So he remains at large, and on the evening of the sixth of November makes definite arrangements to have Cicero murdered the following morning.

The plan is to have two of the conspirators call at the consul's house shortly before daybreak, and to ask to see him on important business, the implication being that they have information to give him on the murder plot. When admitted they are to kill him in his bed.

But Quintus Curius, an informant of Cicero, happens to be at the meeting held by the conspirators this November night. When he leaves it he goes straight to his employer and reveals all. Cicero, frantic with fear at the thought of his narrow escape, hurriedly fills his house with guards. When the assassins, with their band of gladiators, call in the morning, they are told the consul is unwell. No matter how important their business he cannot see them. They must come again some other time when he is feeling better.

The assassins signal to their gladiators, waiting in the nearest alley. They try to force their way into the house. The guards rush out and drive them back. In the interior of the house, Cicero,—in his nightgown to give the impression of being unafraid, but with armor on underneath,—stands listening intently until the sound of angry voices and the clash of weapons has died away and he knows the assassins have been driven off, then he dresses in haste and despatches messengers to summon the senators to a special meeting in the temple of Jupiter in the Capitol, a place only used by the Senate on occasions of great danger.

Bursting with the news he has to impart, Cicero, at the hour appointed for the meeting,—it is the morning of the 8th, the

consul having allowed a day to elapse so that the senators will
have time to collect—strides into the temple. Gathering up his
purple-bordered toga majestically, he fixes the assembled
senators with a dramatic stare, and is about to disclose to them
the details of his narrow escape when he sees a familiar figure
entering the temple. It is Catiline, come to the meeting as an
uninvited guest.

The senators have seen him also. They shrink away from
him as from the plague. Silently, his black eyes flashing a fierce
humor, he takes his seat.

Cicero, appalled at his enemy's audacity, staggers back-
wards, then recovering himself, draws a deep breath, and
swinging around to face Catiline, now left alone on his bench,
launches into his famous first oration against Catiline. (Appendix, page 291.)

6

For all the eloquence he had put into his invective against
Catiline, it was plain to the whole of Rome that Cicero made
public acknowledgment of his own weakness when he dared
not arrest Catiline, but left him free to join the rebel army in
Etruria.

At the conclusion of the oration Catiline, far from showing
either shame or humility, had risen and requested the Senate
not to be too hasty in believing everything said to his prejudice by one who had always been his enemy.

He had mentioned his high birth and the stake which he
had in the prosperity of the commonwealth as arguments to
prove how improbable it was that he should seek to injure it.
He had called Cicero, descended from a family of provincial
Italians, a stranger and a new inhabitant of Rome. Then he
had quitted the temple, the same night leaving Rome to join
the army of Manlius; but telling his friends (in order to
excite odium against Cicero as having driven him out without
any trial or conclusive proof of his guilt) to spread the report
that he had gone into voluntary banishment at Marseilles.

This report caused Cicero no little anxiety. To counteract the sentiment being worked up against him he has notices posted summoning the people into the Forum, and there delivers himself of his second oration against Catiline.

The hoots he receives from friends of Catiline in his audience while he is making it, and the general restless condition of the city, fill him with uneasiness. In public he continues to put on a bold front, but in the privacy of his home he wrings his hands and wails. Tormented by uncertainty whenever he has to make an important decision, and always certain afterwards that any step he has taken has been the wrong one, he bitterly regrets having let Catiline leave the city alive. He walks up and down, not with the cool deliberate stride of a general and commander-in-chief who "thoroughly despises that army composed of desperate old men, clownish profligates, and uneducated spendthrifts," but nervous as an old woman. Why did he not have Catiline arrested and killed? Why, though he knows the names of all the minor conspirators still in the city—Crassus and Cæsar have been too discreet to attend any of the meetings, and with the little proof he has against them Cicero dare not mention their names—does he not have Catiline's accomplices, at this very moment urging the citizens to rise in arms against him, done away with?

He knows he is too little the man of action to dare to carry out any of his threats until he feels he has public opinion entirely on his side. Until the conspirators commit some monstrous outrage which will alienate from them the good-will of the whole of Rome, his hands are tied. He may talk his head off but he will do nothing.

Crassus and Cæsar, seeing how Catiline, by his very audacity, has become a popular favorite, now regret that they dropped out of the conspiracy. They talk the situation over, and decide that whether Catiline wishes it or not, they will step forward if he is successful and claim their rights as the organizers of the plot. They hurriedly try to make friends with him again. Their messengers leave Rome for Etruria to tell him they hope to see him in Rome soon with his army.

They quietly get into touch with his friends in the capital.

Then, suddenly, news of the conspirators' plan to have the Gauls raid Rome is brought to Cicero.

It is such news as he has longed for, prayed for. Faint with joy, he can scarcely believe his ears. For at last he sees his way clear to act, to visit summary punishment on the conspirators in the city, to conduct a popular war against Catiline's Etrurian army. What a panic he can throw the burgesses into when he reveals that Catiline has gone so far in his iniquity as to make arrangements to turn their beloved city over to the plunder and rapine of the BARBARIANS!

So far, for all his thundering against Catiline, he has been forced as an astute politician to realize that civil wars are much too commonplace in Rome for Catiline to seem to the people to be guilty of any enormous crime when he, in his turn, tries to gain control of the government. It may be possible to fool the Romans about strangers, but not about their own kind—Catiline, no matter how black Cicero may try to paint him, is no worse in the opinions of many than a hundred others who have gone before him, and who had only to be successful to be showered with honors by that very party of optimates or "good" citizens, to which Cicero is so proud to belong.

But tampering with the Allobroge ambassadors, conniving to bring the Gauls—those dreaded foes about which the average Roman citizen has his worst nightmares—to Rome, is a far different matter. If convincing proofs of this can be obtained, Catiline and his accomplices in the conspiracy, as Crassus and Cæsar had foreseen, will in the opinion of all Romans have put themselves definitely beyond the pale of the law.

Cicero's informant, Quintus Fabius Sanga, tells him that when the Allobroge embassy returns to Gaul, which it will do in a few days, it will carry with it letters to Catiline, whom the embassy expects to meet on the way—these letters ought to be sufficient proof. But Cicero, when Sanga adds that it is the Allobroges themselves—approached by Catiline as known to bear the present Roman government no good-will, but who, after first inclining favorably to his proposals, had later doubted the ability of Catiline to make the revolution a success, so, dreading the Roman reprisals to their country if it failed, and they were known to be implicated, had revealed the plot to Sanga, the patron of their largest city—who notified him of Catiline's attempts to make them his allies, sees immediately a chance to obtain much more complete evidence against Catiline than any casual letters might contain. He tells Sanga to persuade the Allobroges to continue to listen to the proposals of Catiline's friends until they are able to furnish him with full evidence against the conspirators. They can best do this, he thinks, by requiring the conspirators to individually, and each in his own handwriting, as tokens of good faith, give the embassy letters to take to their countrymen stating the concessions that will be made to the Allobroges if they will co-operate in the attack on Rome. Having made these arrangements, Cicero now, at the request of the embassy, to make it appear that they have not betrayed Catiline but that the vigilant consul through his spies has found out about the plot, sends a party of soldiers into the suburbs of Rome, who, when the Allobroges are leaving the city, make a feigned attack on them, place the ambassadors under arrest and get possession of the letters.

Cicero's eyes dance with triumph as the letters are put into his hands. Almost too great is the impulse to open them immediately. But no, it is better to wait. He has Catiline's chief friends, Publius Lentulus, Caius Cethegus, Publius Statilius, Gabinius, Annius and Bestia, arrested. He calls another special meeting of the Senate; goes to it taking the ambassadors, and the conspirators, with him, and the letters—breaks the seals open in the presence of all—most of the conspirators, confronted by their own writing and the testimony of the ambassadors, break down and confess.

When the Senate adjourns, he hurries to the Forum to tell the people in his third oration against Catiline how he, Marcus Tullius Cicero, the consul that sees all and hears all, has saved the city from destruction.

The discovery of the plot to make allies of the Gauls had seemed to Cicero to sound the death-knell of the Catiline conspiracy, but in this grotesque political charivari there is still a last act—and this the most sanguine one—which has yet to be played.

For Cicero's triumph had been premature. The city conspirators have been exposed and arrested, but their cause is by no means hopeless. Rumors reach Cicero's ears that their slaves, to whom the reward of emancipation is still held out if the conspiracy succeeds, are secretly worked up to a state of excitement where they may attempt the rescue of their masters. He also discovers that popular sympathy is by no means as completely on his side as he had hoped it would be. The city, because of the guards he has posted everywhere, may appear quiet on the surface, but underneath it is smouldering with revolution. If the trial of the conspirators is postponed, as there is every indication it will be due to the efforts of the many influential friends the accused men have in Rome, it is a question whether they will be convicted.

And if they are not, Cicero knows he has proceeded too far against them for his life to be safe in the future. For in a few weeks his term as consul will have expired, and he will be a private citizen invested with no authority of office to protect him. In his anxiety to crush the conspiracy while still consul he has committed the blunder of giving up the province of Macedonia, which had fallen to his lot—each year the two consuls draw lots for the provinces they will govern as proconsuls, so that there shall be no argument about which gets the best—to his colleague, Antonius, in order to tempt the latter to co-operate with him against Catiline, and for the same reason has given Cisalpine Gaul, which he had accepted in exchange for Macedonia, to another powerful Roman, Quintus Metellus.

What he fears most is a general uprising against him. And when he hears that the conspirators intend at their trial to implicate Cæsar, Crassus and Pompey in the conspiracy, his terror exceeds all bounds.

For the people, beyond a doubt, when three such influential names are added to the list of conspirators, will cease to view the conspiracy as a conspiracy at all but as a legitimate revolution. Panic-stricken, he decides that all the minor conspirators must be put to death immediately, before they can talk too much. But the authority for this illegal act must seem to come not from himself but from the gods. How shall he manage this?

Suddenly he remembers the Bona Dea festival, a celebration in honor of an important goddess held annually at the house of one or other of the principal magistrates, and at which the Vestal Virgins officiate. This year it is to take place in his own home, his wife, Terentia, being mistress of ceremonies.

Immediately he sees his opportunity. Having outlined his plan to Terentia, he so disposes of his time that on the night of the festival he is at a conference of the senators. They are discussing the sentence of the conspirators. Some of the senators, though all are fearful for the future of the oligarchy if the names of the three major conspirators come to light, are still timid about having Lentulus, Cethegus, and the others now under arrest put to death without trial. Cicero has just made a long speech urging this. Suddenly into the conference bursts Terentia. She implores the pardon of all present for interrupting the consul and his council in their deliberations, but says she must inform them of a prodigy which has just happened during the celebration of the mystic rites of the Bona Dea. It seems that after the sacrifice in which she, as presiding matron, had been engaged, was over, *the fire which had gone out suddenly revived spontaneously.*

Turning to face her husband, she tells him the Vestal Virgins have sent her to him, to acquaint him with this marvellous happening, and to bid him pursue what he is thinking of and intending for the good of his country, since the goddess has given this sign of her approval and that she is watching over his safety and glory.

To take care of the situation Cicero has doubled his publicity staff. They now hurry through the streets of Rome, cry-

ing the news of the miracle, and posting glaring notices of it
in the Forum, and on the walls of houses. That he may not
seem to be lacking in reverence for the Bona Dea, he calls
another special meeting of the Senate, to carry a motion for
putting the conspirators to death without further delay.

Glancing over the assembly, he notices that many of the
senators, unwilling to have any share in sentencing prisoners
of such high rank to death without allowing them the legal
appeal to the people, are absent. But he feels it is his neck
now, or those of the conspirators. Cato, he knows, will be for
immediate execution. He sees Cæsar among the senators. Will
he talk? And to what purpose? But now Silanus, the consul-
elect, and a protégé of Cicero, is on his feet. He gives his
opinion—that the conspirators in custody should all be put to
death. Next rise other senators who also see the conspiracy as
a dangerous menace to the oligarchy—they all agree with
Silanus. Then Cicero is suddenly tense—Cæsar is getting up
to speak.

Cæsar, while ready to repudiate any share in the conspiracy
should this be brought up against him, has agreed with Crassus
to do what he can to get the death sentences of the prisoners
commuted to life imprisonment. Both of them are aware that
as soon as the present agitation dies down, if Cicero does have
the conspirators killed it will be no difficult matter to make
trouble for him when he is no longer consul—also that by ad-
vocating leniency they will make themselves popular with the
people. So in his speech, though he is careful to show no sympathy for the conspirators, he expresses himself as strongly
against capital punishment, suggesting that Lentulus, Cethegus,
and the rest of Catiline's associates, shall instead have their
estates confiscated, and be themselves kept in perpetual con-
finement. Cato gets up, and vigorously opposes this.

But Cicero, closely observant of the senators' reactions to
Cæsar's proposition, can see that many of them have been
swayed by it as safer than voting for death. The moment is a
critical one. If the Senate votes for life imprisonment Cicero
knows that sooner or later the conspirators will be released or

escape. To insure his own safety they must die. Only a burst of eloquence can save the situation. Springing to his feet, he launches into his fourth and last oration against Catiline.

The oration has persuaded the senators—they vote for immediate death.

And Cicero is determined not to have the conspirators alive another day to plot mischief against him. This same evening of the 5th of December, after the Senate adjourns, he goes with an armed guard and collects the conspirators from the various houses where they are being held in custody, and marches them to the Capitol.

Will a rescue be attempted? The streets are packed with people. Cicero's eyes dart nervously to right and left. He is himself walking with Lentulus, the most important of the conspirators in Catiline's absence. All the conspirators believe they are being taken not to execution, but to a safer prison, and Cicero, as a matter of safety, has not undeceived them.

He conducts them to that subterranean vault at the foot of the Capitol—which had once served as a well-house—where the captured kings led in Roman triumphs are murdered. There he hands them over to the triumvirs who conduct the executions, and they are strangled to death in the vault by torchlight.

Nervous up to the last minute that his victims will be snatched away from him, he stands guard in front of the dungeon door until the executions are all completed, then striding to the edge of the Forum announces in a loud triumphant voice to the assembled mulitude that the conspirators are dead.

And thus ends the Catiline conspiracy, with Rome, "home of illustrious empire, most fortunate and beautiful of cities—light of the world, and citadel of all nations," as fitting setting for its climax.

For when the news of the executions reached the army of Catiline in Etruria his followers quickly began to desert in large numbers, and a few weeks later the consular army (led not by Cicero, however, but by Metellus, to whom he had given

Cisalpine Gaul, and by Antonius, who was so reluctant to actually attack his friend Catiline that on the eve of the battle he feigned a severe attack of gout, and turned over the command of his legions to his lieutenant Petreius) surrounded the remnant, cutting this to pieces, and killing Catiline.

7

Cæsar was not present in the senate-house when Cicero made his fourth oration. After his own speech, and Cato's sharp reply, a number of Cicero's supporters, the sons of senators loyal to the oligarchy, whom Cicero had brought with him to the meeting for just such an emergency as this, had rushed at him with drawn swords, shouting that they knew his real reasons for not wishing the conspirators to be put to death, and threatening to kill him—but for Cato throwing his toga around him and leading him, thus protected, out of the senate-house, he might have been killed here almost on the very spot where seventeen years later he will be assassinated.

This attempt on his life, and the execution of the conspirators later in the evening, determined him to revenge himself on Cicero. His mother and Pompeia are equally furious with the consul, Cæsar's wife suggesting to him that he write immediately to her cousin in an effort to induce him to bring his army to Rome. Cæsar listens to the excited exclamations of the women with his usual surface imperturbability. He is thinking of something else—that Cicero's consulship has only a few more days to run, and that, as it is customary for outgoing consuls on the last day of their year in office to make a speech in the Forum in which they review what they have accomplished and also take an oath that they have served the Republic as faithfully as they swore to do when inaugurated, Cicero, who, thinks his consulship has been the greatest in Roman history, will unquestionably try to seize the occasion to play up his suppression of the conspiracy.

But what of the provocatio—that right of appeal to the people which is the Roman burgess's most jealous privilege, and which Cicero denied to Lentulus, Cethegus, and the rest of Catiline's friends? Can Cicero swear he has served the Republic faithfully when he has violated its laws?

Cæsar talks with Quintus Metullus Nepos, one of Pompey's officers, sent to Rome by the general to agitate for a second consulship for Pompey. Nepos, Pompey's agent in the conspiracy, has bought himself a tribuneship in order to influence the people to re-elect his master. Together Cæsar and Nepos arrange a plan which should make a good beginning for that reaction of feeling against Cicero and the Senate which Crassus, Cæsar and Pompey hope to bring about.

First Nepos is to immediately call the people's attention forcibly to the crime Cicero has committed. This he does in an assembly of the people, when, referring to the consul's valedictory-address to be delivered a few days from now, he exclaims that "the man who has punished others without suffering them to be heard ought to be denied the privilege of being heard in his turn!" Then, if possible, he is to prevent Cicero from taking the oath.

So on the last day of the year as soon as Cicero rises to deliver his carefully prepared speech, he is greeted with angry shouts rather than applause, and no sooner does he come to the part where he is about to take the oath that he has "faithfully and zealously discharged his trust as consul" than Nepos jumps up and forbids him in the name of the people to swear to a lie, since all Rome knows his hands are still red with the blood of murdered citizens.

At this, the mob, largely bought up by Crassus, roars its approval. Fists are shaken at the retiring consul, sticks and stones fly through the air in his direction, the crowd, each time he opens his mouth, drowns his voice in an uproar. When he persists in his attempts to make the oath, several of the large vessels placed by the fullers at street corners for the collection of urine, which have been quietly dragged towards the speaker under cover of the confusion, are hurled at the rostrum, where they shatter, and scatter their contents over the renowned orator.

Thereupon Cicero, convinced at last of the futility of continuing to try to make the formal oath, raises his hand for quiet —he shrieks that at least he can swear truly to *this*—that he has preserved the Rome and the Republic from destruction!— that he is the Saviour of his country!!!

Stopping at the public baths on his way, he goes home to prepare an invective against Nepos, which he delivers in the Curia a few days later.

Nepos retaliates by the threat to impeach Cicero. Meanwhile Cæsar has decided to adopt Pompeia's suggestion of bringing Pompey back to Rome. He talks it over with Crassus and Nepos, and the three of them draw up a written resolution to the effect that on account of the disorder existing in the city Cnaeus Pompey, the conqueror of Mithridates, be recalled with his army to restore law and order. This resolution Nepos takes with him to the assembly, and amid great applause from Cæsar and Crassus, and their paid mob, is preparing to read it to the people when Cato snatches the scroll out of his hands. But Nepos, as a precaution, has memorized the resolution—in a loud clear voice he goes ahead reciting it. . . . The party of the senators suddenly rush armed men into the Forum and clear it with their swords. . . .

Both Nepos and Cæsar are too wise to resist when the Senate now goes into open war with them by taking away from Nepos his tribuneship, and from Cæsar his praetorship. The more they can make the Senate unpopular by leading it to the committal of acts of intolerance, the easier it is going to be to effect the recall of Pompey, whose presence in Rome now that the conspiracy has failed both Cæsar and Crassus feel is vital to the success of their struggle for power with the Senate. In less than a month the Senate has flagrantly violated Roman law twice—first when it strangled the conspirators without trial, secondly when it used force in the Forum. Nepos leaves Rome for Asia to tell Pompey what has happened, Cæsar accepts his dismissal as praetor and closes his court, apparently entirely acquiescent to the commands of the Senate, no matter how arbi-

trary and unjust these may be, but secretly through his large
following in the streets stirring up resentment against the Senate for the manner in which it has treated him, to a point where
the crowds gathered in front of his new home, the Pontifical
palace, shouting his name, and applauding him whenever he
appears, and the equally noisy threats made against the Senate,
coerce it into giving him back his praetorship.

But just at this time when Crassus and Cæsar, sure of Pompey's return, since he has recently written to Rome of great
victories he has gained over Mithridates, feel they are going
to have little difficulty breaking the power of the Senate—
just now, Cicero, no longer consul, is trying desperately to
destroy the alliance by securing Pompey's friendship for himself. He hopes to be able to justify the stand taken by him towards Catiline, also to stir up trouble by hinting that the
strongest partisans of Pompey in Rome nowadays had in the
past hoped he would be destroyed by Mithridates. He writes
the following letter to Pompey——

To Pompey the Great, Imperator.

Your letter to the Senate afforded inexpressible satisfaction,
not only to myself, but to the public in general; as the hopes
it brought us of peace are agreeable to those expectations,
which, in full confidence of your superior abilities, I had always encouraged the world to entertain. I must acquaint you,
however, that it entirely sunk the spirits of that party, who,
from being formerly your declared enemies, have lately become your pretended friends: as it utterly disappointed their
most sanguine hopes.

Notwithstanding the letter which you wrote to me by the
same express discovered but very slight marks of your affection,
yet I read it with pleasure. The truth is, I am always abundantly satisfied with the consciousness of having exerted my
best offices towards my friends; and if they do not think proper
to make me an equal return, I am well contented that the
superiority should remain on my side. But if my utmost zeal
for your interests has not been sufficient to unite you to mine,
I doubt not that our co-operating together upon the same

patriot principles, will be the means of cementing us more strongly hereafter. In the mean time, it would neither be agreeable to the openness of my temper, nor to the freedom of that mutual friendship we profess, to conceal what I thought wanting in your letter. I will acknowledge, then, that the public services I performed during my late consulship, gave me reason to expect, from your attachment both to myself and to the commonwealth, that you would have sent me your congratulations: and I am persuaded you would not have omitted them, but from a tenderness to certain persons. Let me assure you, however, that what I have performed for the preservation of my country, has received the concurrent applauses of the whole world. You will find when you return hither, I conducted that important scene with so much spirit and policy, that you, like another Scipio, though far superior, indeed, to that hero in glory, will not refuse to admit me, like a second Laelius, and not much behind him, I trust, in wisdom, as the friend and associate of your private and public transactions. Farewell.

The same courier who carries this letter to Pompey takes to the same destination another note from Cicero in which there is gossip of a more intimate nature that he prefers to keep separate from the main epistle.

This second note bears fruit. One day all Rome knows that Caius Cæsar is carrying on a love affair with Pompey's wife, Mucia. The rumors state that Pompey, having in some manner heard of his betrayal by the man he supposed his friend, intends to divorce his wife while he is still in the East.

Cæsar treats the rumors as mere propaganda on the part of his enemies, but when alone, frowns. For he knows they tell the truth. Though moderate in eating and drinking nowadays, he has remained the promiscuous lover he was in his youth. Not only has he had intrigues with Mucia, and the wives of many of the officers serving under Pompey in Asia, but he has also been receiving favors from Crassus's wife, Tertulla.

Just when the future looked bright, out of a clear sky has dropped this thunderbolt of ruin. Instead of friend, Pompey will now be enemy. And the same person—he guesses it to be

Cicero—who ferreted out his discreetly managed relationship with Mucia may discover that with Tertulla. Both Pompey and Crassus, instead of supporting him for the consulship, will now doubtless oppose him; and he already has alienated the Senate, so can expect no backing here. Has his weakness for promiscuous sexual indulgence destroyed his career?

The fact that his own wife is Pompey's cousin does not at first seem to help the situation. Pompeia has reproached him bitterly for his unfaithfulness. She vows she will never forgive him for having made her the butt of public ridicule. Cæsar listens to her outbursts with affected incredulity that she can believe every idle tale told about him. When she herself makes investigation of his alleged intrigue with Pompey's wife, uncovers the truth, and reproaches him with his hypocrisy, he treats her accusations in the same light manner, though shifting his ground of argument—he now pleads as the excuse for his indiscretions the fact of his descent from the Goddess of Love which necessarily, he says, though he struggles hard to conquer the weakness, makes him more amorous than an ordinary man.

Can he still persuade Pompey that the reports of his wife's infidelity represent merely the latest effort on the part of Cicero and the Senate to break the power of the popular party? He writes the general a long letter, phrasing it in a way that makes it have the appearance of frankly relating every detail of the town gossip while at the same time revealing this in its proper light. His courier leaves—Cæsar impatiently awaits an answer. . . . None comes. . . . Weeks pass. . . . Still no reply. . . . But one day Rome hums with the latest development in the scandal—Pompey, as he had threatened, has divorced Mucia.

Not only Cæsar is now genuinely worried, but Crassus also. The fat millionaire querulously inquires of his lieutenant why it is he cannot leave women alone when there is serious business demanding his undivided attention. Has Crassus any suspicions about Tertulla? Cæsar, apparently absorbed in thought, avoids his friend's eyes. But Crassus, as he grumbles on, soon reveals his main cause of worry—what he fears is that Pompey may believe he connived at the adultery, or at least knew of it, yet kept it a secret from him.

They must not forget, Crassus reminds him, that Pompey has the army. Suppose in a fit of passion he chooses to come back with it and put them both to the sword? What is Cæsar going to do about it, asks the fat man plaintively. Since it is his lechery which has brought all this trouble down on their heads, he is in honor bound to find a way of ridding them of the odious burden. And he must think fast, for any day now Pompey may start his return journey from the East.

Cæsar, too, realizes he must think quickly. At first his only course of action seems to be that of continuing his pretense of innocence after Pompey's return—but is not all the evidence against him? Then, suddenly a real loophole of escape presents itself; from a mere glimmer introduced into his train of thought by reflection on the unfortunate fact that his own wife should be Pompey's cousin, so that he has thus effected a double betrayal in the family of the general, it expands into an idea that dazzles him. Suppose he can compromise Pompeia? The Mucia scandal, because of Pompey's popularity, is daily losing him more of the people's good-will—is it not possible he can win all this back again, as well as conciliate Pompey, by creating an equal or greater scandal in which the Pompey family, through the actions of Pompeia, will be put in the wrong this time, while he, Cæsar, receives pity as the deceived husband?

But the occasion? Suddenly Cæsar thinks of Cicero, who has made all this trouble for him . . . of the miracle by which he gained authority to strangle the conspirators. . . . An ironic laugh peals and reverberates inside of him, though his lips show only a faint smile.

For in a few days it will be time for the Bona Dea festival again, and this year, with Pompeia as mistress of ceremonies, the festival is to be held in the palace of the Pontifex Maximus.

The scene is the Pontifical Palace on the day of the Bona Dea festival.

The festival is strictly a ladies' affair, no men being allowed admittance to the sacred rites under any circumstances whatsoever—their presence would be a sacrilege. Cæsar is away from home, and will not return until the festival is over. Pompeia and the Vestal Virgins are therefore supposedly alone in the house.

But suddenly, like wildfire, a rumor runs among the Virgins—there is a man in the house disguised as a woman—a maid saw him going into the bedroom of Cæsar's wife—the latter, taking advantage of her husband's absence, has an assignation with a lover . . .

The rumor seems to be correct, for suddenly the man, hotly pursued by several of the Virgins, comes into view. He has rosy cheeks and a mincing gait—his whole appearance is effeminate enough for him to be able to pass as a Virgin in his woman's attire—but in the tussle with his assailants enough of his clothing has been torn off him for his identity as a male to be established to the satisfaction of even the most sceptical of the Virgins.

There is a general shriek of Sacrilege! From all directions the Virgins rush at this infamous wretch who has dared invade the privacy of their festival to indulge his adulterous passion. As he flees through their midst, the nearest objects handy —wine-bowls, incense burners, Grecian urns—are flung at his head by the enraged women.

But the youth—his name is Clodius Pulcher, and he is a cousin of Metullus Nepos—is in too carefree a mood to notice the scratches he receives. Before setting out on the adventure he had warmed his courage well at the taverns. He runs about, dodging the missiles aimed at him, and deliberately shedding the few garments that still flutter in rags on his body.

He does not leave the house immediately. Seeming to lose his way, he rushes from room to room. A large crowd begins to gather in the street before the palace.

Clodius, for all his effeminate appearance, has the sinewy

strength of a gladiator. Shouting and yelling, he ploughs to and fro among the Virgins, tripping some up, and jostling one against the other, until, feeling he has created enough commotion, he at last makes his exit from the palace, running down the steps naked and being quickly swallowed up by the crowd.

In an hour all Rome has heard the news. How Clodius Pulcher,—whose name, coupled with his delicate woman's face and graceful figure, Cicero has played upon in the past, calling him Pulchellus Puer, "the pretty boy,"—has not only for some time been carrying on an adulterous relationship with the wife of Caius Cæsar but has actually this afternoon of the festival had the audacity to enter the Pontifical Palace disguised as a Vestal Virgin in order to be present at an assignation planned by him and Pompeia during Cæsar's absence.

The street rabble is hilarious over the escapade. The Sacred College of Priests views it however as a serious sacrilege which cannot be passed over as a joke. As Pontifex Maximus, and therefore president of the College, it becomes Cæsar's unpleasant duty to head an inquiry into the past conduct of his wife and Clodius. He announces that he does not intend to press the prosecution of Clodius.

The decision is popular as Clodius is a favorite of the people. In the East, where he soldiered under Lucullus, his brother-in-law, he had led a mutiny against Lucullus for not giving the soldiers a large enough share of the plunder. He has the reputation of being excessively wild and disorderly; though he took no prominent part in the conspiracy he was a friend of Catiline; he may be girlish in appearance, but he bubbles over with a rowdy humor that appeals greatly to the mob.

But both Cicero and Cato press for prosecution. They have no conclusive evidence, but they feel sure that the Pompeia scandal was planned by Cæsar to offset the harm done him by the exposure of his intrigue with Mucia. For while merciful towards Clodius, Cæsar, from the rumors that go round, is by no means inclined to be as lenient to Pompeia, whom the rumors state he considers the really guilty one of the two.

They try to induce Clodius to confess—he laughs in their faces. Then, at least, even though Cæsar gains his end by divorcing Pompeia as he is said to intend to do, this henchman in his vile plot shall suffer! But the great orator, the ex-consul and "Saviour of his Country," changes his mind temporarily when Clodia, the sister of Clodius, a beautiful woman of very loose character, whose fine figure he has long admired, and in connection with whom he has had many a suppressed desire, offers herself to him if he will plead in her brother's defense at the trial, instead of, as he now plans, being the chief orator for the prosecution. Cicero, whom Clodia avows she has long had a passion for, and whose beautiful voice she declares she often hears in her dreams, agrees to defend Clodius until he discovers that the sister, once he has secured her brother's acquittal, has no more intention of keeping her end of the bargain than did Catiline—once again he will be tricked, but this time, worse, by a woman. He again changes his mind, and presses for the prosecution of Clodius more vigorously than before. Of the two consuls, one of these, Piso, is a friend of Clodius, but the other, Messala, is for the oligarchy and Cicero. When a bill for the indictment of Clodius is submitted to the assembly, the people say they will pass it if recommended to them by both consuls.

By a large majority the Senate votes that the consuls must recommend the bill. Piso, acting under instructions of Crassus and Cæsar, gives way and joins his colleague in the recommendation—a court of fifty-six judges is appointed to try Clodius. But it disturbs the triumph of Cicero and Cato somewhat that these judges instead of being appointed in the usual way have been drawn by lot—Clodius has had the privilege of challenging as many as he pleases—the judges finally chosen are all of them bankrupts and debauchees who will be open to bribery.

But how can they acquit Clodius when he himself admits his crime—being present at the festival disguised as a Vestal Virgin? Cicero cannot believe that the judges, though corrupt, will dare to let him go unpunished.

He breathes more easily, however, when at the close of the first day of the trial, the judges, intimating that the verdict of guilty they intend to deliver in the morning may endanger their lives overnight, ask for a guard. But he anticipates the worst when that same night rumors reach his ears that, one by one, Crassus has sent for the judges. . . . In the morning thirty out of the fifty-six vote Clodius innocent—he has not committed sacrilege is their decision *as there is no positive proof he was present at the Bona Dea festival*—and he is acquitted.

Cicero, after the verdict is announced, hurries home to relieve his pent-up emotion in a letter to his friend Atticus, who though wealthy and influential has a horror of the noisy tawdriness of the capital and its incessant political intrigues so unfeigned and genuine—in this respect he is different from the orator, who only effects to disdain the hubbub of Rome; the noisier it is the more Cicero likes it, provided he himself remains always the most conspicuous figure—that he lives in the country most of the year. His hand trembles as he describes how Crassus, to make sure of winning over the judges, had bribed some of them not only with gold but also with more monstrous temptations——

"He summoned them to him; he made promises, gave security and gave them money. Moreover, oh ye immortal gods! even favors from certain ladies and young men of rank he offered to some judges to add to the amount of the inducement!"

In his vexation, he cries like a woman as he continues——

"We thought that the foundation of the Republic had been surely re-established in my consulship, all orders of good men being happily united. You gave the praise to me, and I to the gods; and now unless some god looks favorably on us, all is lost in this single judgment. Thirty Romans have been found to trample justice under foot for a bribe, and to declare an act not to have been committed, about which not only not a man, but not a beast of the field, can entertain the smallest doubt!"

Cæsar has taken no part in the Clodius trial. He is not even in Rome when the trial takes place. His term of office as praetor having elapsed shortly after the date of the Bona Dea festival, he had immediately arranged to go to Spain as propraetor. But before leaving Rome he had divorced Pompeia—he had done this sorrowfully, not because there was any evidence of her having committed adultery with Clodius, but because, as he said, "Cæsar's wife must be above suspicion."

In Spain he put in his time suppressing the banditry being carried on by survivors from the army of Sertorius, and it was here that he received the news of Pompey's return to Rome. Pompey's triumph, the accounts state, has eclipsed in magnificence all those of previous Roman generals. It moved through the streets of Rome for two days. Among the captives who preceded the chariot of the conqueror were the children of Asia's three mightiest kings; Tigranes, Phraates and Mithridates. The wagons carried gold and jewels worth 200,000,000 sesterces ($10,000,000), for the state-chest, and besides this amount 16,000 talents ($20,000,000) which after the triumph were distributed among his officers and soldiers. The honors paid to Pompey include a golden chaplet which he is to be allowed to wear for life, permission also to wear his triumphal robe, a gold-embroidered toga over a flowered tunic, in the Senate as long as he pleases, coins struck in his honor which show the world resting on the triple laurels brought home by him from Africa, Spain and Asia, and surmounted by the golden chaplet, and a magnificent column to be erected to him with inscriptions enumerating the twelve millions of people killed or subjugated and the 1538 cities and strongholds stormed by his army. Cæsar also hears that Pompey and Cicero are being seen a great deal together, that Pompey and Crassus have quarreled, that Pompey has been completely won over by the Senate. His own letters, Pompey answers with coolness, as though he by no means considered that the scandal involving

Pompeia had balanced that in which Cæsar and Mucia were the principals.

But time brings a change. Before Pompey has been in Rome many months he begins to have trouble with the Senate. Despite the urgings of Crassus and Cæsar, because he feared it would make him unpopular with the people he had disbanded his army before returning from Asia, only having it re-unite for his triumph, as custom allowed; soon, without his soldiers, he finds himself helpless.

The honors granted him by the Senate are all empty ones. He may wear fine clothes but he is refused what he most wants —a second consulship, and land for his soldiers. When he tries to insist on the former he is reminded that he was consul with Crassus eight years previously, and that therefore the ten years' interval, prescribed by Sulla, between the first and the second term, has not yet expired. He does not get the latter as there is too much opposition on the part of the senators to the passage of an agrarian law which will doubtless force them to give up a portion of their immense provincial estates to the soldiers.

Aurelia Cæsar is keeping her son informed of the situation in Rome. Her letters encourage him to hope for a renewal of his alliance with Pompey and Crassus in the near future. The temporary estrangement between Pompey and Crassus effected by the Senate—mainly through Cicero's unctuous handling of the general—is almost patched up. Cicero himself has largely contributed to this. Once again his uncontrollable desire to shine as a wit has defeated his carefully laid political plans. His recent attempts to win for himself the friendship of both Crassus and Pompey, while at the same time trying to stir up each against the other, and both against Cæsar, have come to naught because of his tongue. Crassus is furious with him because of a recent smart saying of the orator which has made the town laugh even more than the "bad subject" witicism; in casual conversation with Cicero Crassus had mentioned that no one of his family had ever lived beyond sixty years of age—afterwards he had denied it, asking what should put it into his head to say so? Whereupon Cicero, smirking at the friends who were with them, had answered, "It was to gain the people's favor—you knew how glad they would be to hear it."

And Pompey he has equally infuriated by coining a nickname for him which all the general's enemies are repeating, as it burlesques his exploits in Asia, his vanity in continuing to wear his triumphal robe, and his weakness for the homage and pomp which should go more appropriately with the person of an Oriental potentate than with that of a rugged Roman soldier—the name is taken from a petty Arab chief with whom Pompey had a skirmish while in the East—it is *Sampsiceramus*.

Cæsar's mother also tells him that Pompey is beginning to lose his resentment over the Mucia affair. The general has fallen deeply in love with Julia, and the latter's influence more than counteracts Pompeia's efforts to keep her uncle estranged from Cæsar. Since neither Pompey nor Crassus can become consul yet, there is no question but that both will support Cæsar for the consulship of the following year if he will pledge himself to help them into office when the legal ten-year interval has expired, and also get Pompey's agrarian law passed.

So in the fall of the year 60 Cæsar returns to Italy to submit himself as a candidate for the next year's consulship. But he also wants a triumph for his military exploits in Spain. In this second ambition the Senate sees an opportunity to keep him from becoming consul. For while there is one law which compels a Roman general who has petitioned a triumph to remain outside the gates of Rome until the day fixed for the celebration, when he and his army are officially welcomed by the Senate, and allowed to enter, there is another law which forces a candidate for office to be present in person on the day of the election. When Cæsar, as has been done previously by candidates in a similar position, applies for a dispensation enabling him to be a candidate in his absence, the Senate refuses to grant it. Will Cæsar, wonders Cicero, be vain and stupid enough to take the triumph instead of the consulship, as he cannot have both?

But Cæsar, though disappointed about not getting the triumph, withdraws his petition as soon as he realizes the Senate will set a date for this too late for him to appear at the elections, and that there is no chance of receiving the dispensation; he enters Rome as a private citizen, stands as a candidate for the consulship, and with the backing of Crassus and Pompey is elected.

8

"Sampsiceramus is causing trouble. There is every reason why he is to be feared. He is avowedly preparing a tyranny! For what is the meaning otherwise of that unexpected marriage connection, of the land in Campagna, of the lavish expenditure of money? If these were the last, they would be too much evil, but the affair is such that they cannot be the end. . . . *They* would never have come to this unless they were preparing for themselves the ways to other evil deeds!"

Thus writes Cicero to Atticus of the events which are taking place during the consulship of Cæsar; jealousy preventing him from seeing the latter as anything but a catspaw in the hands of Pompey the Great.

Cæsar's year in office is being spent making laws, most of these forced through by illegal methods, which will so undermine the influence of the Senate that from now on all real power will be centered in himself, Pompey and Crassus. But though consul, neither Pompey nor Crassus considers him their equal. He has no military reputation comparable with that of Pompey, the conqueror of Mithridates, and he lacks the great wealth of Crassus. He is the junior, and in their opinion, the far least important member in the triumvirate.

But Pompey and Cæsar are now on the best of terms. Pompey has married Cæsar's daughter, Julia, and all the past trouble involving Mucia is forgotten. Cæsar is to marry Calpurnia Piso, the daughter of one of the candidates for the consulship of the year following his own term of office. When Pompey helped him into the consulship Cæsar had promised to obtain grants of land for Pompey's veterans and he makes this one of the main issues of his consulship. Another equally important number on the program of the triumvirate—and one which as yet the orator knows nothing of—is the ridding Rome for good and all of Cicero.

The agrarian law to give land to the soldiers is bitterly opposed by the senators who hate to give up any part of the public lands they have annexed to their estates. They try to block legislation by having Marcus Bibulus—Cæsar's old colleague as ædile, and now consul with him; the Senate, while not able to prevent Cæsar's election, had been powerful enough to put Bibulus in office as a check on him—constantly postpone the voting for the law by declaring the heavens unfavorable to legislation. Finally Cæsar takes the law away from the Senate and goes with it straight to the people.

A huge crowd, one of the largest in Roman history, is collected in the Forum. Nearly the whole of it, because of Crassus's money, Pompey's fame as a general, and Cæsar's power as a demagogue, is composed of adherents of the triumvirate.

Yells of approval greet Cæsar when having mounted the rostrum he expands on the selfishness of the Senate. Drunken ex-soldiers in the crowd shriek out furious oaths as he suggests that the Senate seems not to care in the least what becomes of the men who fight the battles of the Republic, once the enemy has been vanquished, and there is no longer any danger of invasion.

Pompey and Crassus come forward and place themselves beside the consul. First Pompey speaks in favor of the law. "Will you support it if it is illegally opposed?" asks Cæsar. "I will bear the shield if others draw the sword!" answers Pompey the Great grandiloquently. Crassus then makes a speech, is asked the same question, and gives a similar answer.

Both receive roar after roar of applause. The mob cannot feast its eyes enough upon, or shout loud enough for, this trinity of disinterested champions of the people fighting to rescue the poor and oppressed from the clutches of the Senate.

But Bibulus has no such illusions. His face is scarlet, his pulse throbs furiously in his bull neck. When the time for voting arrives he rushes forward as usual, looks up at the sky, and shouts that the assembly is dissolved—the gods not only forbid all further action on the law that day, but also during the whole rest of the year.

This time however Cæsar is ready for his obstinate colleague. While Bibulus is still talking, the front rank of the mob, at a prearranged signal—the same slight movement of Cæsar's hand which sent the young Syrian to his crucifixion—rushes at the rostrum and knocks him off it. Along with Cato and the other senators most bitter against the law who have come forward to support him, he is dragged away by armed guards, and in their absence not only is the law passed but also a resolution compelling every senator who wishes to keep his seat in the Senate to take an oath to obey it.

After this demonstration, Bibulus, realizing the futility of further opposition, shuts himself up in his house, and refuses to have anything more to do with running the government. During the remainder of Cæsar's consulship the Senate virtually abdicates, letting it be known, however, that at the first opportunity after his term of office has expired all the Julian acts will be declared illegal.

The triumvirate now rules Rome firmly, and before Cæsar's year runs out it has been able to close a big deal with the Flute-player, Ptolemy, king of Egypt.

Ptolemy is one of two brothers—his brother is king of Cyprus—whom for some time past Rome has refused to recognize in order to compel them to pay heavily for this official recognition. Both have been outlawed as usurpers; if they want to be known as "allies of Rome" they must send in large sums to the Roman treasury. Ptolemy of Cyprus refuses to bribe his oppressors—Cyprus is accordingly declared to be annexed to the Roman dominions. But the Flute-player is willing to pay —he is officially recognized by a decree of the Roman people after the triumvirate has successfully extorted from him 6000 talents, or seven million dollars.

Cæsar's share in this bribe helps to lift him out of debt.

Having passed Pompey's agrarian law, his chief interest now, and it is one which is shared by Pompey and Crassus, is to safeguard the future. Pompey's veterans, whom, since his trouble with the Senate he has had no compunction about gathering around him, Crassus's millions, and his own authority as consul, have smoothed out all difficulties for the time being, but the triumvirate must insure against the danger of power slipping back into the hands of the Senate when Cæsar has gone to Gaul, and before Crassus and Pompey are consuls again.

Both of the consuls for the year 58 are henchmen of the triumvirate, Piso being Cæsar's father-in-law, and Aulus Gabinius the tribune who obtained the passing of the decree by which Pompey had been invested with his three years' supreme command over the Mediterranean in the naval war against the pirates, but Cæsar knows that as soon as he leaves for Gaul, Cicero, if he is allowed to remain in Rome, will start to make trouble. The triumvirate has made advances to the orator to induce him to join the party, so that it may have the use of his golden tongue for justifying its acts, but, jealous of Cæsar, he has remained true to the Senate. To get him out of Italy, Cæsar has offered him a command in Gaul, but this also he has declined. He is now sulking on one of his provincial estates.

The plan by means of which Cicero's political career is to be definitely cut short, is an ingenious but simple one.

Cæsar thought of it: namely, the passing of a law which will define as a criminal any Roman official who during his term of office has put citizens to death without a trial. To the burgesses, weary of the arbitrary handling they have received of late years from the senators, the law will seem designed expressly to protect the humble citizen. But the first official brought to trial for murder under it will be the ex-consul and Saviour of his country, Marcus Tullius Cicero.

And to make the law fit in even more neatly with the triumvirate's slogan of the people's welfare first and last, neither Cæsar, Crassus nor Pompey shall seem eager to have it passed. All three will stay in the background. A tribune of the people is to propose it and push it through.

Who shall be this tribune? Cæsar has his answer ready— Clodius.

Clodius, so useful to him in the past, will, Cæsar knows, be glad to do anything for the money Crassus is prepared to offer him. He is aching to revenge himself on Cicero for ridiculing him as "the pretty boy" and telling stories about his scandalous private life during the Bona Dea trial.

But Clodius is a patrician, and tribunes of the people must be plebeians. This difficulty quickly disappears when Clodius, interviewed by the triumvirate, says he has no objection to transferring himself from one class to the other if the compensation is made sufficiently inviting. The cause is such a good one, he says, he would almost do it for nothing. Crassus, his fat face beaming with smiles, assures him his future will be well taken care of if he will do this little favor for them.

The voluntary exchange of patrician rights for those of plebeian is not without precedent. The most important formality to be gone through is the obtaining of the consent of the Sacred College to the transfer. Cæsar being president of the College, Clodius's appeal is quickly granted. The "pretty boy," now a plebeian, and duly elected tribune, immediately proposes the triumvirate's law in the assembly, and the people pass it.

Meanwhile Cicero, back in town, is encouraged to live on in a fool's Paradise. Scenting trouble for himself when he sees Clodius making an active entry into politics, he has swallowed his pride and requested each member of the triumvirate separately not to permit that brainless pervert—Clodius is known to have been intimate with his own sisiter, Clodia, a circumstance of which Cicero had frequently reminded him and the public during the trial—to vent his spite on him in any way; and he has been assured that he is held in much too high regard by all three,—though there may have been little differences in the past,—for Clodius to be permitted to do him an injury.

In a letter to Atticus, Cicero writes——

"Pompey bids me have no fear about Clodius, and professes the greatest regard for me in all his speeches."

And in another he is equally optimistic——

"For myself, as far as I believe, and hope, and can ascertain, I am supported by everybody's good-will!"

But after Clodius gets his law passed, and rumors begin to spread that Cicero is to be brought to trial for illegally putting the conspirators to death during his consulship, the orator can no longer doubt that his life is in danger.

If convicted—and there is no question, the rumors state, but that he will be—his fate will be the same as that which he meted out to Lentulus, Cethegus, and the rest of Catiline's friends.

The thought of that cold damp dungeon at the foot of the Capitol, and of the noose tightening around his neck, makes Cicero break out in a perspiration of terror. He cannot believe that he, the Saviour of his Country, called also by Cato the "Father of his Fatherland," whose consulship was so glorious that he himself has written a long poem about it, is to die the ignoble death of a conspirator or a Barbarian. Surely the people must realize the sacrifices he has made for them!

He puts on his dirtiest toga, one which has not been sent to the fuller's for months, lets his hair and beard grow long—the Roman way of going into mourning—and in this attire of a suppliant wanders around Rome begging the intervention of all honest citizens. But instead of melting the hearts of the populace with pity, as he had expected, his unwashed appearance only brings down on himself ridicule and ignominy— for wherever he goes, Clodius, immaculately attired in a long tunic with frills on the sleeves, and with a chaplet of flowers on his head, follows him with his band of abusive fellows— just when, stopping to address the crowd, Cicero has reached the most touching point in his supplications, they shower him with dirt, stones and one or two of the fullers' pots.

In despair he tries to gain access to the triumvirate to remind them of their promise. But Crassus is out of town, Cæsar, whose consulship has expired, and who is waiting near the city with part of the army he will take with him to Gaul to watch developments and to back Clodius up with troops in case of necessity, will not see him, and Pompey, whose house he visits one day to implore mercy, sees him coming from a distance, slips out by a rear entrance while Cicero is announcing himself, and also goes to the country.

Cicero's friends urge him to leave Rome while there is still time. He swears that no matter how great the danger he will never run away. For once right shall triumph over might. The power of his eloquence as he says this is so great that his friends, particularly Cato, and Hortensius, a rival orator but also belonging to the senatorial party, embrace him passionately for his noble courage, saying that if he is strangled he will at least die a martyr to a splendid cause, and that his murder should fortify the souls of more timid enemies of the despots and fill them with the determination to avenge his death.

But bold as a lion in the presence of his friends the orator is timid as a hare as soon as they leave him, and he is alone, with night falling. He groans in his sleep; wakes up with a start, trembling like a leaf, from dreams of being pitched into the dungeon and strangled. As little a thing as the clatter of a saucepan dropped by the cook in the kitchen, which rings in his ears however as the clash of swords in the hands of armed men come to arrest him, puts him into a fury.

His wife, Terentia, is at a loss to understand what ails her husband. For he keeps assuring her in his sonorous phrases that he fears nothing—who dare molest Cicero, the consul who saved his country?

One day he goes to see Piso and Gabinius, the two present consuls, both of whom he has made targets for his wit in the past. Each tells him curtly he can do nothing—the law must take its course. Cicero hurries home. He tells Terentia he has important business in the provinces which demands his immediate attention, and that he must leave Rome as soon as night falls.

No sooner has he left the city than the law does take its
course. Officers go to his house to arrest him: his departure is
taken as an admission of his guilt. He is pronounced an exile.
He may no longer wear that honorable and unique garment of
the Roman citizen, the toga. If he comes within five hundred
miles of Rome he will be executed. For anyone to give him
shelter shall be a criminal offense punishable with death.

His property is confiscated. His houses both in Rome and in
the country are burned. On the ashes of his Roman palace is
built a temple dedicated to the Goddess of Liberty.

And Clodius, as a final act of sardonic revenge, takes his
riotous followers to the Capitol, publicly erases Cicero's name
from the bronze tablet on which he is commemorated as the
Saviour of his Country, and puts his own name there instead.

Cicero, fleeing from Italy, knows as yet nothing of these
later outrages. But he has heard of his banishment. Where
shall he go?

He thinks of Sicily, the present governor of which, Caius
Vergilius, he believes to be his friend. He writes to Vergilius,
telling him he is coming. Vergilius replies with a very affectionate letter, saying he is indeed glad to have heard from him,
but to go elsewhere.

Then it is that the great orator, struck suddenly by the full
meaning of his exile, breaks down completely. The wise counsels he has always been able to give so plentifully to others,
the philosophy of fortitude of which he is so proud, drop out
of him, leaving only a hollow shell of wretchedness.

After leaving Rome he had written to his wife confessing the
true reason for his abrupt departure, but now, from Brundisium, where he has found a friend who will give him temporary
shelter, he pours out his anguish in a letter to his family the
writing of which blinds him with weeping——

To Terentia, to my Dearest Tullia, and to my Son.

If you do not hear from me so frequently as you might, it
is because I can neither write to you, nor read your letters,

without falling into a greater passion of tears than I am able
to support; for though I am at all times, indeed, completely
miserable, yet I feel my misfortunes with a particular sensi-
bility upon these tender occasions.

Oh! that I had been more indifferent to life! Our days
would then have been, if not wholly unacquainted with sorrow,
yet by no means thus wretched. However, if any hopes are still
reserved to us of recovering some part at least of what we
have lost, I shall not think that I have made altogether so im-
prudent a choice. But if our present fate is unalterably fixed—
Ah! my dearest Terentia, if we are utterly and for ever abandoned by those gods whom you have so religiously adored,
and by those men whom I have so faithfully served, let me
see you as soon as possible, that I may have the satisfaction of
breathing out my last departing sigh in your arms!

I have spent about a fortnight at this place, with my friend
Marcus Flaccus. This worthy man did not scruple to exercise
the rites of friendship and hospitality towards me, notwithstanding the severe penalties of that iniquitous law against
those who should venture to give me reception. May I one
day have it in my power to make him a return for these generous services, which I shall ever gratefully remember.

I am just going to embark, and purpose to pass through
Macedonia in my way to Cyzicum. And now, my Terentia,
thus wretched and ruined as I am, can I entreat you, under all
that weight of pain and sorrow with which, I too well know,
you are oppressed, can I entreat you to be the partner and
companion of my exile? Or must I then live without you? I
know not how to reconcile myself to that hard condition; unless your presence in Rome may be a means of forwarding my
return, if any hopes of that kind should indeed subsist. But
should there, as I sadly suspect, be absolutely none, come to
me, I conjure you, if it be possible; for never can I think
myself completely ruined, whilst I shall enjoy my Terentia's
company. But how will my dearest daughter dispose of herself? A question which you yourselves must consider; for,
as to my own part, I am utterly at a loss what to advise. At
all events, however, that dear unhappy girl must not take any
measures that will injure her conjugal repose, or affect her
in the good opinion of the world. As for my son—let me not

at least be deprived of the consolation of folding him for ever in my arms. But I must lay down my pen a few moments: my tears flow too fast to suffer me to proceed.

I am under the utmost solicitude, as I know not whether you have been able to preserve any part of your estate, or (what I sadly fear) are cruelly robbed of your whole fortune. I hope Piso [1] will always continue, what you represent him to be, entirely ours. As to the manumission of the slaves, I think you have no occasion to be uneasy. For with regard to your own, you only promised them their liberty as they should deserve it; but, excepting Orpheus, there are none of them who have any great claim to this favor. As to mine, I told them, if my estate should be forfeited, I would give them their freedom, provided I could obtain the confirmation of that grant: but if I preserved my estate, that they should all of them, excepting only a few whom I particularly named, remain in their present condition. But this is a matter of little consequence.

With regard to the advice you give me of keeping up my spirits, in the belief that I shall again be restored to my country; I only wish that I may have reason to encourage so desirable an expectation. In the mean time, I am greatly miserable, in the uncertainty when I shall hear from you, or what hand you will find to convey your letters. I would have waited for them at this place; but the master of the ship on which I am going to embark, could not be prevailed upon to lose the present opportunity of sailing.

For the rest, let me conjure you in my turn to bear up under the pressure of our afflictions with as much resolution as possible. Remember that my days have all been honorable, and that I now suffer, not for my crimes, but my virtues. No, my Terentia, nothing can justly be imputed to me, but that I have survived the loss of my dignities. However, if it is more agreeable to our children that I should thus live, let that reflection teach us to submit to our misfortunes with cheerfulness; insupportable as upon all other considerations they would undoubtedly be. But alas, whilst I am endeavoring to keep up your spirits, I am utterly unable to preserve my own!

[1] Cicero's son-in-law.

I have sent back the faithful Philetaerus, as the weakness of his eyes made him incapable of rendering me any service. Nothing can equal the good offices I receive from Sallustrius. Piscennius likewise has given me strong marks of his affection, and I hope he will not fail in this respect also to you. Sicca promised to attend me in exile, but he changed his mind, and has left me at this place.

I entreat you to take all possible care of your health; and be assured, your misfortunes more sensibly effect me than my own. Adieu, my Terentia! thou most faithful and best of wives, adieu! And thou, my dearest daughter, together with that other consolation of my life, my dear son, I bid you both most tenderly farewell!

Brundisium
April the 30th.

At the date of the writing of this letter Cæsar has already left Italy for Gaul. As soon as he received word from Clodius that Cicero had fled he had set out for his province.

And before the forlorn orator, leaving a trail of tears behind him, has arrived in Greece, where he will remain during his exile, Cæsar is north of the Alps, engaging in the first of his Gallic wars, the campaign against the Helvetii.

PART 3

Gaul, The Lucca Conference
and
The Mysterious Island

I

CÆSAR is forty-three years old when he exchanges the purple-bordered toga of a consul for the paludamentum or military cloak of a general.

His command in Gaul is to last five years. The Senate, afraid to give him a province where he could raise an army, had planned to assign him the "department of woods and forests," where he should have no need of soldiers as he ought to be occupied only with roadbuilding and other public projects; but when the triumvirate came into power it quickly changed this—he was made proconsul not only of Hither Gaul but also of Transalpine Gaul, the Roman province lying north of the Alps.

He leaves Italy well satisfied with the way affairs have shaped themselves during his consulship. Piso and Gabinius are consuls. Not only Cicero, but Cato also,—who has accepted the governorship of Cyprus, and by so doing has made impossible a later attempt to declare all the Julian acts illegal (as he had intended doing on the grounds that the heavens had been declared unfavorable to legislation), since the annexation of Cyprus was one of these acts—is out of the way. And Clodius will be watchful over his interests in Rome.

He chose the two Gauls for his provinces as the war with Mithridates has squeezed Asia dry of treasure for the time being. Also Pompey and Crassus have both insisted upon being given eastern provinces after their second consulship expires.

The Mediterranean provinces—Sicily, Spain, the north coast of Africa—have had their revenues farmed out to Romans for so many years that their natural wealth is almost exhausted. The north-west, on the contrary, is a comparatively new region which should be able to support a great deal of exploitation. Hither Gaul may have been looted not infrequently by previous governors, but the province beyond the Alps rests on the edge of vast unexplored territory.

Cicero, at the mention of Transalpine Gaul, would scoff at it as a province hemmed in by the wilderness which was costing Rome more for military protection than it was worth, but Cæsar sees it differently. If the boundaries of Further Gaul are only hazily defined, may they not well be worth extending? Who can say what the great forests to the north and west conceal?

He remembers the stories told him in his childhood by Gnipho of the immense gold and silver mines from which the Arvernian kings drew their wealth. He has heard of the great river called the Rhine, beyond which there is no telling what rich cities may lie, and of a mysterious island far to westward where the inhabitants dye their bodies blue and pearls of an incredible size are to be found.

Gaul has stirred his imagination. And not only for its own mysteries, but also because his ambition has already soared higher than the triumvirate. He will use the army of the Republic for conquering new nations in Gaul, and then turn the Gallic spoils against the Republic, to make himself supreme. He is going to Transalpine Gaul with unlimited authority to do as he pleases with the peoples living across the frontier from the province; before he left Italy it had been understood between him and his two partners in the triumvirate that he should miss no opportunity for a profitable war with the Barbarians; in Rome, Pompey and Crassus will justify the expense of these wars by urging their necessity as a defensive military measure against the inroads of another such Barbarian horde as the Cimbri, they will also stop obstacles being put in the way of his recruiting fresh legions as he needs them and get him his appropriations from the state treasury for conducting the wars, in return for which he is to use the army for the sole purpose of building up the private fortunes of himself and his two colleagues.

Besides the spoils taken in war, and the tributes levied on the conquered tribes, the triumvirate expects to realize gigantic profits from the sale of slaves, as the Gauls are much in demand because of their large stature and strong healthy bodies, a handsome boy often bringing as high as 100,000 sesterces ($5000) from the wealthy debauchees, and the gladiatorial combats consuming each year larger and larger quantities. The contractors of Crassus will accompany Cæsar's army ready to buy up the Barbarians as fast as Cæsar captures them.

But while co-operating with Pompey and Crassus sufficiently not to arouse the suspicions of either, Cæsar intends, all the time he is in Gaul, to be mainly working for himself. In five years of warfare against the Barbarians should he not acquire enough military experience to be able, when he feels the right moment has arrived, to hazard a split with his colleagues? He means, from the first, to impress his soldiers favorably. If he can make his maiden battle in Gaul a great victory, the legionaries will immediately feel confidence in their new general. And if the victory is important enough for him to be hailed Imperator by his soldiers—to win this honor he must slaughter not less than five thousand of the enemy, while losing very few men himself—he can have Clodius magnify this success in Rome so that at the very beginning of his wars he will acquire the reputation of a military genius.

So, as he crosses the Alps, he makes his plans. He will be careful not to match his forces with any tribe capable of a strong resistance; such a blunder at the outset of his career as governor might be fatal. At the same time he will try to so arrange his first battle that it will appeal greatly to the imagination of the city mob. The ideal situation would be one which would allow his despatches home announcing the victory to describe how with scarcely a handful of legionaries he had completely annihilated a huge army of the enemy already on the march over the Alps to sack Rome.

And when he arrives in his northern province he finds this ideal situation awaiting him.

The Helvetii, who inhabit the north of Switzerland, have for years found it so hard to make a living here because of the barren soil and rigorous climate that they have decided to migrate westward across Europe to the Bay of Biscay, where the winters are milder and it will be easier to grow their crops; in their travels they have reached Lake Geneva and now, as the only practical route for them to follow on the next lap of their journey—there is one other way down the Pas de l'Ecluse, but the Pass is so narrow that two wagons cannot go abreast here —crosses the edge of Transalpine Gaul, they send ambassadors to the Roman governor begging his permission to go west by way of the Province.

Cæsar hurries to Geneva to see what the migrating tribes, said to aggregate a huge number of families, look like. From a hill-top he looks down on the Barbarians.

The smoke of the camp stretches for miles. A vague uproar, composed of the shouts of men, the higher voices of women and children, the barking of innumerable dogs, rises to his ears. . . . For a moment the thing he contemplates doing seems an impossibility. . . . Then he remembers the information brought in to him by his spies—in this vast multitude of human beings, numbering more than three hundred thousand people, with 8500 four-horse wagons, and which on the march is spread out over forty miles, *there are not as many as fifty thousand men capable of bearing arms*—the food supply, only sufficient for the three months in which the tribes hoped to make the hundred mile journey when they left their homes, *is already dwindling*.

He tells the ambassadors there is little doubt about their being allowed to cross the Rhone and pass through the Province if they will promise to pay for all damage done, but that as a matter of form he must consult the consuls. He needs fifteen days in which to send a courier to Rome. Let them return on the day before the Ides of April (April 12th) and he is sure he will then have the authority to grant their request.

He quickly destroys the only bridge across the Rhone, and for eighteen miles along the river, where it might be forded, has his soldiers throw up a sixteen-foot earthen wall. When the Helvetii, mistrusting these warlike preparations, want to know the meaning of them, he gives a banquet in their honor, assures them of his friendship, and smilingly explains the destruction of the bridge and the building of the wall as a precaution he has thought it necessary to take in case the Germans living to the north of Switzerland, seeing the Helvetii leave their villages, should try to pursue and plunder their rear.

The day before the Ides of April arrives. The ambassadors present themselves. To their surprise and indignation the new Roman governor, instead of giving them the favorable answer they had expected, tells them abruptly that the Helvetii cannot go through the Province—it is not the custom of the Roman people to allow foreigners to invade their territory. He gives them a lecture on the improprietry of their whole expedition, and tells them the best thing they can do is return to their homes.

The Swiss, understanding too late that Cæsar had raised their hopes only to gain time, decide to revenge themselves for this treachery by crossing the river by force. They build rafts, a bridge of boats. But the Roman legionaries are prepared for their coming; safe behind their fortifications they have little difficulty in repulsing every effort made by the Barbarians.

Their artillery—the large *catapultae* and *ballistae*, of which the former shoot great arrows in a horizontal direction, like a cannon, while the latter hurl heavy rocks through the air in a high curve, as a mortar throws bombs, both being operated by the elasticity of twisted rope and sinew, and the range varying between 1500 and 2000 feet—and the smaller scorpions or dart-throwing machines with a range of about 350 feet—play havoc with the Helvetii. The rafts are capsized, the bridge of boats destroyed as fast as it is built, wherever an attempt at fording is made the disorganized rabble is easily driven back. Wagons overturn, the river becomes choked with the bodies of dead and dying horses and human beings. What survivors there are among those who attempted the passage arrive at the Roman side of the river only to be impaled on the long pilums of the legionaries.

Cæsar, standing on the bank watching the slaughter, hopes that their rage at being tricked will make the Helvetii persevere in their efforts to cross the Rhone. It may be that he can annihilate the whole confederation of tribes without the loss of a single legionary, in which case he will certainly be hailed Imperator by his soldiers, and can justly claim a triumph for the victory when he returns to Rome.

But the Swiss, realizing the impossibility of entering the Province with the barrier of the river between them and the Roman army, and the latter holding its fortified positions, give up their attempts. Again they send ambassadors to Cæsar pleading for permission to pass through the Province. They detail the difficulties of such huge numbers taking the route of the Pass. They tell how already the delay has eaten into their food supply. They again promise to pay for all damage done. Will not the Roman governor allow them to go the easier way, since they will never be more than a few miles on the Roman side of the frontier? With all that passion of a primitive people which the Roman theatre audiences find so amusing when they look on at burlesques in which Barbarians with long moustaches are the comic characters, their eyes flashing as they talk, their arms flung out in appealing gestures, they try to make the governor understand how immensely their journey will be simplified if they can pass down the valley of the Rhone a short distance before turning west.

Cæsar, surrounded by his lictors, is cool and collected. Now and again he smiles indulgently as though listening to the unreasonable requests of headstrong children. His expression shows sympathy when he is told about the shortage of food and how disease and the hardships of the journey are killing off the old men, women and children. His answer is a point-blank refusal to let the Helvetii go through the Province.

That night, expecting that the Barbarians, driven desperate by necessity, will try more determinedly than before to effect

the passage of the river, he doubles the guards along the fortifications. His conjecture seems correct when the sentries report unusual activity in the enemy camp. He mounts one of
the earthworks and strains his eyes to see across the dark water.

He watches the black figures of the Barbarians passing in
confused masses across the red glare of their camp fires, and
listens to the distant clamor of voices. At his feet murmurs the
river, while against the sky, bright with glittering stars, but
without a moon, the forest stretching away on either side of
the Roman camp rises, stirred into motion by the night wind,
in two hills of rustling shadow. It is spring but the nights here
in Gaul are colder than in the sunny peninsula south of the
Alps—Cæsar wraps his cloak closer around him.

What is happening over there? Will the Barbarians make a
formidable night attack, or are they massing their fighting men
to cross at dawn? With the northern night all around him, there
comes a sudden sense of his distance from Italy, and he feels a
prick of uneasiness. He has only a single legion—four thousand men—with him. Has he perhaps over-estimated the
strength of his position?

He realizes the immense superiority of his army, small as it
is, as a well-disciplined fighting machine, unencumbered by
non-combatants, and where most of the troops are veterans of
previous wars, and each soldier knows his place in the machine,
to the unorganized host of the Barbarians; yet now, in the
night-time, against his calmer judgment, their numbers
frighten him. The sense of the nearness of this vast body of
humanity he has tricked fills him with doubts. Their stirrings
across the river come to him menacing as the shouts of the proscription officers that day when he stood on the terrace with
Sulla.

But as suddenly his fears leave him. For through the night
has come the blare of a Roman bucina announcing the change
in the night watch. He hears the tramp of the guard making
the rounds. His eyes, as the footsteps pass and fade into the
distance, no longer try to penetrate the mysteries of the om-

inous darkness but are fixed on the alert figure of a Roman sentry silhouetted against the stars.

And his gaze as he looks out over the water again is full of expectation and triumph. Let the Barbarians attempt another crossing; the river and his army will drive them back. Tomorrow may be the day when he will be hailed Imperator.

But the night and dawn pass without an attack, and in the full light of a clear morning the legionaries stand watching, on the opposite bank, the leather-topped wagons of the Helvetii streaming across the country in the direction of the Pas de l'Ecluse.

Cæsar's officers compliment him upon the scare he has put into the enemy, but he feels himself cheated. The victory has been won too easily. Why did not the Barbarians make that effort to storm his position he had hoped for?

He sees, in this column of retreating wagons, his big victory slipping away from him. The attempts at crossing made before the ambassadors came a second time to plead with him, while resulting in the loss of many lives to the Helvetii, had not involved the camp as a whole but only adventurous bands here and there whose destruction is insignificant compared with that wholesale annihilation he had planned, the news of which would bring him so much glory in Rome.

But they shall not escape. He gives quick orders. Mounted couriers cross the Rhone, overtake the Swiss, and tell them that in the name of the Sequani, whose territory they will have to travel through if they go by way of the Pass, the Roman governor orders them to go no further. The Swiss reply that they have the permission of the Sequani to pass through their country. Cæsar's answer is that the chief who gave them this permission had no authority to do so—he is a traitor to his country—the true patriots among the Sequani have asked Rome to aid them in repelling the invaders.

When the Helvetii keep on moving towards the Pass, Cæsar leaves Titus Labienus, one of his lieutenants—the tribune of the people who with the money put up by Crassus had carried

for him the election by which he became Pontifex Maximus—
in command of the Rhone forts, and hurriedly re-crosses the
Alps for more troops. He has three reserve legions stationed
at Aquileia in his southern province—he raises two more at
Turin—with these reinforcements he returns to Transalpine
Gaul.

Several weeks have passed. The Swiss are now out of the
Pass. With his new army of twenty-five thousand men Cæsar,
following in pursuit, crosses the Rhone near Lyons, catching
up with the emigrants at a point on the river Saone, a branch
of the Rhone, fifty miles from the Roman frontier. He camps
in the forest several miles from the Saone, which he hears the
Helvetii are crossing on rafts, and orders his scouts to let him
know when three-quarters are across. When he gets this news
he leaves camp at midnight with three legions.

And as dawn breaks the Roman army bursts out of the forest
and falls upon the unfortunate Barbarians who have not yet
crossed the Saone. A cold horror numbs the senses of those who
have gained the far bank as they watch the systematic massacre
by the legionaries of the families left behind . . . as they
see the legionaries, busy as ants, drop their swords and shields
to seize mattocks and shovels and begin burrowing industriously in the blood-soaked earth, while others make the forest
ring with the blows of axes. In less than three hours a Roman
camp, surrounded by a ditch nine feet wide and seven feet deep
and a ten-foot wall, and with four gates, has sprung magically
into existence . . . a bridge sturdily supported on piles, and
carrying a road, is almost across the river.

The chiefs go to Cæsar, and throw themselves at his feet.
Let him only stop his army from repeating on the west bank
of the river the dreadful massacre of the eastern one, and they
will go wherever he wants them to go. Cæsar says they must return to Switzerland. For invading the territories of the Sequani
and the Aedui they must pay a heavy indemnity to these tribes,
which he will take charge of. As a guarantee of good faith
they must give him as hostages the children of all their important chiefs.

The Helvetii, though they burnt their villages when they left so that there would be no turning back, agree to return and to pay the indemnity, but they refuse to give him the children. For they know that this seizing of children as hostages is the usual Roman method of bringing defeated tribes into a state of utter subjection. The children will be sent to Rome. The first act of the Helvetii which displeases the governor will draw from him the threat of having them put to death.

They refuse, and when Cæsar insists, decide to continue their journey to the Atlantic since whether they go on or turn back, as they will not give the children as hostages, they are in equal danger.

Their decision does not displease Cæsar, though he pretends to the chiefs that he can take their refusal to give hostages, and their intention of continuing their journey when he has expressly ordered them not to, as nothing but an open declaration of war.

He follows the immense horde at a distance of five miles behind the mounted warriors which now form the rear guard, waiting for his opportunity to fall on them, and repeat on a larger scale his massacre of the Saone. He bribes Divitiacus, the chief of the Aedui through whose country the Helvetii are now passing, to lend him cavalry and to keep him supplied with provisions. But in every engagement with the Swiss rear guard the Gallic horse suffers defeat, and at last he is forced to the realization that this is not because they are inferior fighters but because their sympathies are with the Swiss, so that despite the urgings of their Roman officers they only make a show of attacking. Nor have the corn carts promised by Divitiacus arrived.

He summons Divitiacus to him, and lodges a complaint. The Aeduan chief replies that it is his brother Dumnorix who is to blame—Divitiacus frankly confesses that his brother has a deadly hatred for the Romans, viewing them as the incarnation of all treachery, cruelty and viciousness—Dumnorix has said that Cæsar and his legionaries are infinitely more to be

feared than the Helvetii—it is he who influenced the Sequani
to allow the Helvetii to go through their country, taking guarantees from the latter that they would do no mischief and
from the former that they would not harass the Helvetii on
the march—Dumnorix, the leader of those Aeduan patriots
who have no patience with the manner in which Divitiacus is
allowing the Romans to cultivate his friendship for the purpose of strengthening their position in Gaul, is indignant at
Cæsar's presumption in ordering the Helvetii to keep out of
a part of Gaul which is not Roman territory, and at the manner
in which he has marched his army over the border in pursuit;
and is exerting every effort to stir up the inhabitants against
him. Cæsar has Divitiacus send for his brother; he delivers a
stern lecture to the Aeduan patriot, threatening to lay waste
the country if there is any more treachery. Dumnorix seems to
be impressed, makes promises, and goes away. But still the
corn carts do not come, and now the cavalry begins to desert.

Cæsar's confidence begins to fail him. He is fifteen days'
march from his province. Though he has worried the flanks
of the Helvetii, so that every mile of progress is marked by
dead bodies, and the charred remains of wagons captured and
burnt, the opportunity for the overwhelming blow has not yet
presented itself. His legionaries are grumbling about the short
rations. Each day's march is taking him further away from his
base of supplies. By following the Helvetii is he going to his
own destruction instead of to glory? Suppose Dumnorix man-
ages to arouse the country behind him, so that retreat is cut
off? Reluctantly he abandons the pursuit of the Swiss and turns
back.

And now the Helvetii make their fatal mistake. When they
see the Roman legions marching away from them, fired by the
desire to avenge the massacre of their comrades on the bank
of the Saone, and exultant with the thought that the Romans
have lost courage and are fleeing they in turn pursue. . . .
Cæsar's longed-for opportunity has come at last. . . . For
the Barbarians, charging in disorderly masses, are no match
for the disciplined legionaries who, taking up a position on

higher ground, repel with immense slaughter each successive wave of the attack, and finally, changing from defensive to offensive tactics, break through the Helvetii until they reach the main body of the wagons which they set on fire.

The Swiss, hopelessly demoralized, flee in all directions, the Roman cavalry, in small detachments, like bodies of mounted police, pursuing the wretched fugitives and cutting them to pieces until their arms ache with the weight of their swords. For miles the countryside becomes a shamble. The pursuit lasts for days. The Swiss who escape struggle on to Langres where they surrender. Of the three hundred and seventy thousand that left Switzerland, only ninety thousand are left—from these Cæsar exacts a large indemnity, takes children as hostages for their good behavior, and sends them home to their cantons—when the Helvetii finally stumble back into the blackened ruins of their miserable mountain villages, not fifty thousand, and these half-starving and in rags, are still alive.

But Cæsar is generous. He has promised these survivors of the ill-fated migration corn from his own province until they have rebuilt their villages, and grown new crops. He has praised the valor of the chiefs left alive, given them presents, and expressed hopes that in the future, should he ever need their help in a war with the Germans, they will be prompt in furnishing him with auxiliaries.

And already laurel-wreathed despatches are on the way to Rome to tell the burgesses how narrowly they have escaped destruction at the hands of a Barbarian horde outnumbering the Cimbrian invasion—the mighty army of the Helvetii, composed of the fiercest mountain tribes in Gaul, who have long meditated a raid on Rome—it was only the heroic valor of Cæsar's few legions, and his superior generalship, that managed to stem the flow of this otherwise irresistible human tide which unchecked would have poured over the Alps and swept away the whole of civilization.

In these despatches he tells also how after the great battle in which the Barbarian army was cut to pieces his soldiers jubilantly hailed him Imperator.

2

His recent slaughter of the Helvetii seems to Cæsar of excellent omen. The news of it is spreading, already has spread,
far and wide through Gaul. Distance will blur the details of
how the victory was actually achieved, and what the odds really
were. To the tribes which have never seen him but which he
expects to subjugate during his five years as proconsul in Gaul
the name of the triumphant Roman governor will be carried
with a dreadful significance magnified by rumor, inspiring in
the Barbarians, almost from the moment of his arrival in his
province, that terror of the very name of Cæsar which he is
relying upon to more than half-win his future battles for him
before they are fought.

And already a long chain of prisoners of war is crossing the
Alps to be sold into slavery in the capital.

This first of Cæsar's Gallic Wars has lasted exactly three
months—it began early in March and ended early in June. A
few weeks after sending the survivors home Cæsar hears that
a large body of Germans has crossed the Rhine with the intention of driving the Romans out of Gaul. Flushed with triumph, he sends a message to their king, Ariovistus, ordering
him to make immediate appearance at the Roman camp to explain his conduct.

Was not Ariovistus, he asks in his letter, officially declared
a "friend of Rome" during his recent consulship? Does he
realize that this is a signal honor not often conferred on a Barbarian chief? When the messenger has left he walks about the
camp preceded by his lictors carrying the laurel-wreathed
fasces. Here in Gaul he has a sense of power far greater than
ever he had in Rome. There, even when consul, he was over-
shadowed by the fame of Pompey and Crassus. Here he is supreme.

But instead of coming to the Roman camp as commanded,
Ariovistus sends a return message. If there were anything he
wished to discuss with Cæsar, he says, he would go to Cæsar.

Similarly if there is something which Cæsar wishes to discuss with Ariovistus he must come to Ariovistus.

Cæsar sends out his spies. They bring back very much the report he had expected. Like the Helvetian army the German army consists mainly of non-combatants. He decides to annihilate it as he did the Swiss migration.

He sets out for the Rhine. But as the distance between the vanguard of his army and Ariovistus decreases the legionaries grow nervous. For all their good discipline, they are very subject to panic when confronted by a novel situation. The Gauls they hold in contempt as they have seen and fought with them, and know how primitive is their science of warfare. But the Germans are a strange people, whom few of the soldiers have ever set eyes on.

Camp gossip says that they are a nation of terrible warriors, the men being of gigantic stature, each possessing the strength of half a dozen Romans, with arm and shoulder muscles so powerful that they can with ease uproot small trees, and eyes that dart an insupportable glare. And not only the common soldiers have the heart taken out of them by these rumors but the officers also. What lies ahead in the dark forest? Some find excuses to leave the army and return to the Province, others begin to murmur about the narrowness of the roads, the vastness of the forests which still separate them from Ariovistus, and the difficulty of bringing supplies up readily. The cheerfulness which followed the massacre of the Helvetii has been replaced by a sullen spirit of disobedience. One night Cæsar is warned that if, in the morning, orders for a further advance are given, the legionaries will mutiny.

He calls a council of his officers. The unanimous opinion is to go no further. Is he to be thwarted in his desire for a second great victory during his first year as governor? He seems to give serious consideration to the advice of his lieutenants. When the council has broken up he sits wrapped in thought. If he follows their advice will not a precedent be established? No matter if he commits a blunder, is it not better to stress the deeper discernings of his own judgment—even to make defeat seem part of a carefully laid plan?

His soldiers' trust in him must be absolute. As it is, they have no confidence in this march to the Rhine because they know that the victory over the Helvetii was the result of chance. But if the same good fortune attends him twice in succession will they not be inclined to see more than chance in the two victories—a proof rather of his invincibility as a general?

In the morning the Roman camp rings with the blare of bugles and cavalry trumpets. It is the *classicum*, the general's call to an assembly. Cæsar mounts the sodded mound of earth to the left of his tent, and addresses the legionaries. He mocks at their fear of the Germans. Have Barbarians ever challenged the might of Rome and been victorious? Do they forget that they are Roman soldiers—brothers in arms of those heroic warriors who under Scipio Africanus, under Marius, under Sulla, under Pompey the Great, have shown themselves unconquerable?

He comes to the mutiny. He has been told by some of his officers that the soldiers are unwilling to continue the march. But there are only two occasions on which a Roman soldier can, without dishonor to himself, refuse to obey the command of his general—the first is when continual reverses have proven that the auspices under which the general is conducting his campaign are unfavorable; the second is when by ungratefully appropriating to himself all the booty, and denying his soldiers their well-deserved share, he has broken faith with his army. But is there any soldier listening to him who can reproach him truthfully with either ill-fortune or avarice? Have they forgotten so quickly his great victory over the Helvetii? Did he not reward each of his legionaries with a substantial money-present?

His voice takes on a sterner note. These soldiers who are cowards—who allow themselves to be intimidated by idle stories told about the valor of the Germans—he does not want them in his army. He himself holds Ariovistus and his Barbarian followers in such contempt that he will go forward alone with a single legion. Here he pauses dramatically, to shout suddenly that this legion shall be the faithful Tenth! The rest of his army can go back to the Province. With a majestic wave of his arm he dismisses the assembly.

The soldiers surge to and fro in excited groups. Cæsar's speech has had its desired effect—there is a general feeling of shame, and also of envy for the legion trusted by the general. The centurions of the Tenth legion go to Cæsar and thank him for the honor he has paid the legion. The other legions send their centurions to him begging him to forget what he has heard, and for an equal chance with the Tenth to show their valor in a battle with the Germans. The whole army moves on towards the Rhine.

And Cæsar, as he rides with the Tenth legion, which he has made his praetorian guard, can see from the pride in the soldiers' faces and the worshipping glances they cast in his direction, that by diplomatically singling them out for distinction he has made himself their idol.

But what is Ariovistus doing?

He has arranged a conference with Cæsar. The meeting place is a tumulus midway between the two armies. The commanders are to come accompanied by bodies of cavalry. These will be stationed two hundred paces from the mound, each leader then riding forward protected by a personal bodyguard of ten men.

The Roman and the German meet. The king, sitting a magnificent black stallion, towers above the Roman general. He has long streaming hair, immense moustaches, and a skin bronzed by wind and sun. Unlike Cæsar he wears no tunic, his body being bare where unprotected by armor. Cæsar, pale-skinned, with thin body and hollow cheeks, looks frail and unhealthy by contrast.

Ariovistus opens the conference by stating that he has not crossed the Rhine to make war on the Romans but to solve the problem of over-population in his own kingdom. The migration is a peaceful one, and has the consent of the tribes living south of the Rhine—for years German families have been coming across the river and settling in Gaul, where they have intermarried with the natives. Cæsar replies that Rome has always looked upon the king as a friend, but that it cannot permit him to stay in Gaul—the Rhine is the natural boundary between Germany and Gaul and when Ariovistus crosses it he makes himself an enemy of Rome, which has guaranteed to protect the rights of the small helpless nations in Gaul.

Ariovistus laughs. If the Rhine is a natural boundary between Germany and Gaul why are not the Alps a natural boundary between Gaul and Italy? What right had the Romans ever to come north of the Alps and settle their province of Transalpine Gaul? And by what right is Cæsar at this very moment so far from the frontier of his province?

To these questions Cæsar makes no reply other than to repeat that the Rhine is a natural boundary between Gaul and Germany which Rome will not allow Ariovistus to cross—he must go back.

The face of the German king darkens. The Rhine is not a natural boundary, he repeats, raising his voice angrily, and he will not accept it as such. It is not a chain of mountains like the Alps. It is a river, up and down which both the Gauls and the Germans sail their boats. They have common occupations such as fishing which bring the people on either shore in almost daily contact. There are Gauls who speak the German tongue, and Germans who speak the dialects of the Gauls. The Gauls and the Germans have far more in common than have the Gauls and the Romans. Rome for a number of years has emphasized this point of the Rhine being a natural boundary south of which the Germans must not come, but not because of that friendship with the Gauls which it pretends—only in order that, without a rival, it may be free to continue its own conquests.

Cæsar's answer to this outburst is the brief statement that the Aeduii have appealed to him for protection against the Germans, and that he has promised to grant them this protection.

Then the German king, growing angrier, shouts in his deep guttural voice, "What Aeduan chief has asked Cæsar for protection?"

"Divitiacus"—Cæsar answers smoothly.

Ariovistus gives a huge scornful laugh. Who in Gaul or Germany does not know that Divitiacus is in the pay of Rome— that he is a traitor to his own country? Has Dumnorix asked for protection?

Cæsar is silent. The king's eyes flash triumphantly. No, Dumnorix has not, nor has any true Aeduan patriot. But more than once they have come to *him*, Ariovistus, and *asked him for protection against the Romans!* Is Cæsar aware of this?

Suddenly, gesturing towards the Roman cavalry, Ariovistus asks why Cæsar did not come to this meeting attended by the Gallic horse furnished him by Divitiacus—why that very morning he took the horses away from the auxiliaries and mounted his Tenth legion in their place, to bring this with him as his bodyguard? Was it, or was it not, because he feared the Aeduan cavalry would gladly betray him into the hands of Ariovistus?

Cæsar flinches. Ariovistus, well acquainted with Roman treachery, had been unwilling to trust himself on foot in the presence of Cæsar, but neither had Cæsar dared to meet Ariovistus with only Gallic auxiliaries to protect his person in case of trouble with the Germans.

When he remains silent, Ariovistus, who has been watching his face closely, leans towards him, and lowering his voice from its angry shout, suggests that they ride aside a few paces where they will be out of hearing of their personal bodyguards, as he has some confidential information to impart to Cæsar which is suited only for his own private ear. And as soon as they are quite alone, he tells Cæsar that he is not entirely unacquainted with the state of Roman affairs. He knows, for instance, that the Roman general has many enemies in the capital who would be grateful for news of his death. A chill runs through Cæsar as Ariovistus, dropping his mocking tone, adds that *Roman senators* have sent messengers to him offering him a huge reward in gold and the eternal friendship of the Roman state in return for the head of Cæsar.

Fury, which he has difficulty in dissimulating, follows. At this moment, listening to Ariovistus, his motives in wishing to conquer Gaul become transvalued for him. When in Rome, the plots and intrigues to betray generals had seemed to him a necessary and natural part of party politics—now that he is a general himself and in danger of assassination his viewpoint is different. Since leaving Italy for Gaul his colleagues, Pompey and Crassus, have sent him warnings that the Senate and the Barbarians are in communication with one another, but this is the first time he has been confronted with actual facts.

And suddenly he is not in Gaul to exploit the natives for his own personal advantage but to bring honor and glory to the Republic. A sentimental rage at the risks he is running while the senators safe on their magnificent estates plot against him sweeps through him. Dastardly is this betrayal not only of himself as governor, but of the gallant soldiers serving under him! Is it thus that the sacrifices being made by himself and his army—the hardships of the forced marches, the daily privations of a perilous military campaign in enemy territory, the risks run in battle—are appreciated?

Ariovistus, catching the expression of rage which convulses the Roman's face an instant, now speaks on in a more friendly tone. He would rather, he says, be Cæsar's friend than his enemy. . . .

Before he can say more, Cæsar has turned his horse and ridden back to his bodyguard. The king, realizing from the abrupt manner in which the governor has left him that he cannot make terms with Cæsar, and furious with himself for having divulged his secret to no avail, loses his temper again and launches into a violent denunciation of Roman hypocrisy and deceit.

He shouts that in Gaul the Romans shall go no further. If the Gauls are to pay tribute to any foreign people it shall be to the Germans, who are far more akin to them than are the Romans. And the day will come when the Gauls and the Germans, united to form a single great nation, will drive the

Romans back over the Alps into Italy where they belong!

Slowly, the German cavalry, alarmed by the shouting and the angry gesticulations of their king, has advanced towards the mound. Ariovistus having warned his officers of the Roman practice of breaking faith at parleys, they believe the Roman governor is about to make an attempt to kidnap the king. In a long menacing line they move nearer.

The Tenth legion rides forward to protect Cæsar.

But Cæsar has no inclination for a battle. He puts little trust in the fighting efficiency of the Roman soldiers when mounted. It is only in infantry formation that they are invincible. He rides at a quick trot back to the Roman camp, motioning to the Tenth legion to follow.

Only when far from the tumulus that was the meeting place does he rein in his horse, and face about. The king and his escort are vanishing into the forest to the north. Behind the dark eyes watching them lurks hate. *Ariovistus must be crushed!*

In camp he stirs up the passions of his soldiers by haranguing them on the theme of Ariovistus's insolence in daring to insult the person of a Roman commander.

The Barbarian chief had contemplated treachery. After defying the power of Rome to drive him back across the Rhine, he had signalled to his escort to ride forward and seize Cæsar. Only the valor of the Tenth legion had prevented this disaster.

While Cæsar is talking his eyes sweep the men's faces keenly. Has he traitors here in his own camp? Perhaps the attempted mutiny was the work of agents of the Senate serving under him. Perhaps among those officers who returned to the Province there are some who have already notified his enemies in Rome that Cæsar, like Cinna and Sertorius, has been killed by his own soldiers.

If Ariovistus is in league with the Senate to destroy him then the annihilation of the migration led by the German king will have a further justification. It is necessary now to his safety, to the safety of his army.

When Ariovistus, admitting he did unwisely by losing his

temper at the last meeting, tries to negotiate with him for a second, Cæsar refuses to grant it. He reads the king's message to his legionaries, citing it as proof that the defiance hurled at him by the Barbarian was nothing but vain boasting—Ariovistus dares not risk a battle with the Roman army.

Meanwhile his spies are investigating more thoroughly the strength of the Germans. They confirm their previous reports that the forces of Ariovistus are not greatly to be feared—there are too many women and children, and old men, encumbering the warriors. Though Ariovistus is recognized in a general way as the leader of the expedition this is composed of a number of tribes each of which in battle will fight under its own chief, and obey only his commands. The Germans lack completely the military organization of the Roman army, with its centralized control, and artillery equipment.

Cæsar, confident in his ability to win an easy victory, and susceptible already, if only subconsciously, to that conception of himself as a military genius which he wishes others to have, outlines briefly but authoritatively to his lieutenants a plan of campaign which will quickly destroy Ariovistus.

The army marches boldly forward. Suddenly news is brought that the enemy has established a camp between Cæsar and his base of supplies. *Ariovistus, the unscientific Barbarian commander, has outflanked Cæsar.* . . .

The officers are dismayed. Cæsar, masking his consternation, nods his head as though it were a move he had expected—Ariovistus, in his ignorance, has marched straight into the trap set for him by Cæsar. He drops his head, as though deep in thought, a slight smile playing on his lips. *But has his overconfidence changed victory into defeat?* The Cæsar behind the mask is appalled by the thought that where he himself is playing at being a great general Ariovistus may really be one.

But his officers, grouped around him, are watching his face closely, waiting to hear his decision. Before all else, he must keep up the pretense. Since he can think of nothing original, why not copy what Ariovistus has done? On his lips is the command to have the army discontinue its forward march, and turn back, when he sees that this may be considered a retreat.

Only two legions shall go. The other three shall remain here. If the two which return are successful in making the flank movement around Ariovistus and entrenching themselves in a camp lying between the Germans and the Province then his plan will seem to have been to surround the Barbarians and crush them between the two jaws of his army.

So he divides his army—and having done so realizes he has made a grave blunder. His officers would have advised him to the contrary, had they not believed that the move is part of a deeper plan they know nothing about. But Cæsar has no such plan. He is giving his orders blindly.

He has discovered that Ariovistus, handicapped though he is by the presence of so many non-combatants among the fighting men, is determined to take the aggressive. The Roman army undivided could have repulsed an attack, but now that the legions are separated, the German king, the greater strategist of the two, may be able to fall on either division and annihilate it before the other can advance to its reinforcement. The two legions, by making a wide detour of the German camp, have managed to get in touch with the train of supplies again, but the three between Ariovistus and the Rhine are still isolated; and the king, who has massed his cavalry, is watching these too carefully for them to dare an attempt at effecting a junction.

Cæsar feels the weakness of his position. And the skirmishes between the outposts of the Roman and German camps have made his soldiers lose confidence in their superior fighting ability. The Germans have a method of fighting which is new to the legionaries. While cavalry is their main arm, the cavalry do not fight alone—with each cavalryman goes a foot-soldier who runs beside his horse, comes to his rescue in case he is dismounted, and supports him in the charge—the agility and strength of these foot-soldiers, who keep up with the cavalry on the gallop by clinging to the manes of the horses, dismays the legionaries.

Each day Cæsar expects the German king to attack one of the camps. But the king, though Cæsar has been informed of his determination to take the offensive, stays in his camp. The uncertainty of not knowing which way he is going to strike makes Cæsar nervous. To feel out the king's plans he cautiously offers battle with some of his troops, but Ariovistus does not accept the challenge. The German cavalry can be seen by the legionaries lined up in front of the wagons with which Ariovistus has encircled his camp, but they refuse to advance to an attack, though the Roman soldiers, who usually have no difficulty in provoking an engagement with the Barbarians by this method, fling insults at them, and taunt them with cowardice.

Why does not the German king, who managed so cleverly to outflank Cæsar, seize the advantage put in his hands by the division of the Roman army? To Cæsar the suspense is unendurable. He pales at the only possible explanation he can think of—*Ariovistus is planning some master-move that will annihilate not either division separately but the entire Roman army!*

But one day Cæsar's spies bring into camp news of tremendous significance—news that dissipates all his fears and makes him exult in the knowledge that, once again as when the Helvetii made the mistake of pursuing, fortune has placed victory in his grasp.

Ariovistus, wishing to attack, has been prevented from doing so by the priestesses in his camp—they have warned him he will be defeated if he risks a battle with the Romans before the new moon—the German soldiers, who hold these "wise women," as they are called, in superstitious awe, have refused to follow their king into battle until the new moon rises.

The German camp must be attacked before the new moon! In both Roman camps a large red flag gives the signal for battle. The legionaries, told of the German superstition, march out confident of victory. The German warriors, with the screams of the "wise women" exhorting them not to give battle to the Romans as they will surely be vanquished ringing in their ears until the last moment, feel the battle is lost when the first German falls pierced by a Roman pilum. . . .

The legionaries break through the circle of wagons. . . .

Then, suddenly, Cæsar sees victory slipping away from him. The German women, their long hair streaming down their backs, stand on the wagons shrieking to their men not to let the Romans capture them and sell them into slavery—at sight of them being slaughtered by the legionaries, the Germans turn back from their flight and launch such a furious counter-offensive against the legionaries that the latter suddenly find themselves surrounded. Again Cæsar realizes he has blundered. His soldiers, outnumbered, and thrown into a panic, are beginning to flee in their turn. With two more legions he could stop this flight, and win victory. But he has left his third line with young Publius Crassus, the son of the millionaire, serving as one of his lieutenants in Gaul, and given strict orders that it is to be held in reserve for him to fall back on in case the attack on the German camp proves unsuccessful—on no account is it to take part in the attack. By blending caution with boldness he has lost the battle—had he risked all success would have been assured—by his very insistence that Crassus, no matter what may develop, obey orders and keep the third line from advancing, he has brought defeat on himself.

But suddenly he sees the Germans waver, then turn to flee again, while his legionaries, taking heart mysteriously, leap in pursuit, with shouts of triumph. At the critical moment, the needed reinforcements have arrived. Crassus, disobeying orders, has sent forward the third line on his own responsibility.

The battle now degenerates on the part of the Germans into a long and terrible fifty-mile flight towards the Rhine, with the Roman cavalry in pursuit. Before the pursuit ceases, the migration, though in numbers less than that of the Helvetii, has been even more utterly annhilated, a hundred thousand German corpses littering the south shore of the Rhine. Ariovistus, whose two wives and daughter are among those cut down by the cavalry, is one of the few who escape across the Rhine, but he dies of his wounds later.

Cæsar stands on the bank of the Rhine looking towards Germany. In the pale face the dark eyes glow with a fierce tri-

umph. Will the Germans ever again dare to challenge his authority in Gaul? Does the king Ariovistus still believe that the
Rhine is not the natural boundary between the two countries?

Under a sky angry with great clouds sweeping down from
the northern hills the water of the Rhine stretches away cold
and grey. Summer has passed. Soon winter will be here. The
wind already has a sharp sting as though coming from a land
of snow. Cæsar shivers. He stares at the water, at the forests
beyond. Into a little bay near his feet the river has washed the
bodies of several drowned Germans—one of them, a young
woman, lies on her back so close to him that by walking down a
few paces he could touch her face with his hand . . . his eyes,
with sensual interest, rest for a moment on the long wet hair,
the bare breasts, the large voluptuous hips.

War has sharpened his appetite for women—in his southern
province, to which he intends to return for the winter, leaving
Labienus in charge of the legions north of the Alps, he will
quickly forget in their embraces his self-denial on these two
campaigns.

Beside the woman lie an old man and a child. Cæsar scarcely
sees them. He notices them as little as he does the drift-wood
on the river, they are not the size of fly-specks on the vast window of his ambition. His glance has swept across them and
back to Germany. Some day, when he has subdued all Gaul,
he will throw a bridge across the Rhine and march his army
across it to new conquests. His stare is greedy . . . *what will
he find beyond those great dark forests?*

Then his lips tighten vindictively as he thinks of Ariovistus
again . . . of the Senate . . . of its secret offers of a huge
reward in gold and the eternal friendship of the Roman state
for his head.

He must hurry back across the Alps and get in closer touch
with Roman politics again. He must see Clodius. He must find
out what truth there is in the news sent him lately that Pompey
and Crassus are no longer as friendly towards him as when he
left Rome, because jealous of his popularity with the Roman
mob since the despatches telling of his defeat of the Helvetii

have reached the capital. He must know their feelings when they hear of this second great victory over the Germans. He must, above all, find out if it is true that there is a movement on foot to pardon Cicero, to have this bitterest, most dangerous, of his enemies recalled from exile.

Again the cold wind makes him shiver. Casting a last covetous glance in the direction of Germany, he turns away from the Rhine.

3

In sunny Macedonia, a thousand miles to the southeast of the great German forest, where the leaves are falling, a tall gaunt man paces the shore of the Ægean. The sky is blue, a warm breeze, so light that it scarcely ruffles the water of the little bay on which the town of Thessalonica is situated, caresses his haggard cheeks. But the calm beauty of the scene he contemplates, the remote loveliness of this sheltered spot in Greece which winter never invades, seem rather to exaggerate the misery of this man than to assuage it. He walks throwing out his arms as though to push back prison walls. He mutters, he gesticulates. He bursts into fits of passionate weeping. . . . As though fleeing from an eternal summer that is odious to him, from a sunlit peace that he detests, he enters a house, and covering his face with his hands, sits for a long time staring into darkness . . . the quiet of the house, where frightened slaves move noiselessly on bare feet in the rear rooms, is broken only by his groans . . . finally, with a deep sigh, and brushing the tears from his eyes, he draws parchment towards him and writes——

To Terentia, to my Dearest Tullia, and to my Son.
Imagine not, my Terentia, that I write longer letters to others than to yourself: be assured at least, if ever I do, it is merely because those I receive from them require a more particular answer. The truth of it is, I am always at a loss what to write; and as there is nothing in the present dejection of my mind, that I perform with greater reluctance in general;

so I never attempt it with regard to you and my dearest daughter, that it does not cost me a flood of tears. For how can I think of you without being pierced with grief in the reflection, that I have made those completely miserable whom I ought, and wished, to have rendered perfectly happy? And I should have rendered them so, if I had acted with less timidity.

I perceive you depend much upon the new tribunes; and if Pompey perseveres in his present disposition, I am inclined to think that your hopes will not be disappointed; though I must confess, I have some fears with respect to Crassus. In the meanwhile I have the satisfaction to find, what indeed I had reason to expect, that you act with great spirit and tenderness in all my concerns. But I lament it should be my cruel fate to expose you to so many calamities, whilst you are thus generously endeavoring to ease the weight of mine.

As to what you mention with regard to the area belonging to my house, I shall never look upon myself as restored to my country, till that spot of ground is again in my possession. But this is a point that does not depend upon ourselves. Let me rather express my concern for what does; and lament that, distressed as your circumstances already are, you should engage yourself in a share of those expenses which are incurred upon my account. Be assured, if ever I should return to Rome, I shall easily recover my estate; but should fortune continue to persecute me, will you, thou dear unhappy woman, will you fondly throw away in gaining friends to a desperate cause, the last scanty remains of your broken fortunes? I conjure you then, my dearest Terentia, not to involve yourself in any charges of that kind; let them be borne by those who are able, if they are willing, to support the weight. In a word, if you have any affection for me, let not your anxiety upon my account injure your health; which alas! is already but too much impaired. Believe me, you are the perpetual subject of my waking and sleeping thought; and as I know the assiduity you exert in my behalf, I have a thousand fears lest your strength should not be equal to so continued a fatigue. I am sensible at the same time that my affairs depend entirely upon your assistance; and, therefore, that they may be attended with the success you hope and so zealously endeavor to obtain, let me earnestly entreat you to take care of your health.

I know not whom to write to, unless to those who first write to me, or whom you particularly mention in your letters. As you and Tullia are of opinion that I should not retreat farther from Italy, I have laid aside that design. Let me hear from you as often as possible, particularly if there should be any fairer prospect of my return. Farewell! ye dearest objects of my most tender affection, farewell!

Thessalonica
October the 5th.

The humiliation of his exile is killing Cicero. If his sick wife, who is working night and day to secure his pardon, does not succeed in having the decree by which he was banished repealed within a few months he feels that he will die.

He does not eat, he cannot sleep. His letters to his friends are so abject, so woefully lacking in fortitude that many of them think he has gone out of his senses.

Is this broken-down philosopher the same man who used to sneer at the Greeks as a nation of weaklings? Who affected ignorance of their most exquisite statuaries as children's toys fit perhaps to amuse the trifling and effeminate minds of the Greeks but unworthy of interesting the more robust intellects of Romans? Who in his speeches to the Senate never missed an occasion to refer to the Greeks by the contemptuous diminutive *Graeculi*—little Greeks?

The weight of his own misery is crushing him. When he pours out his love for his family, it is self-pity that is tearing at his heart-strings. He is tormented by the thought that Terentia may die before she has obtained his pardon. He tells her to hope because he himself wishes to hope. The names of Pompey . . . Crassus . . . Cæsar . . . which he tries to efface from his memory, but which always return to taunt him, make him faint with rage; while at the thought of *Clodius . . . the destruction of his Roman palace . . . the erection of a temple dedicated to the Goddess of Liberty upon its site . . . and that most monstrous mockery of all, the erasure by Clodius of his name from the bronze tablet at the Capitol, and the substitution for it—as Saviour of his Country—of Clodius's name* . . . when this horrid phantasmagoria of mental images flits through the brain of Cicero, as it does many times a day, his veins seem on the point of bursting—his breath comes in long sobbing gasps.

Can he hope ever to be allowed to return? In this letter to his wife he has expressed optimism, he has tried to believe that Pompey at least may relent. A spark of courage flares up in him as he writes . . . his handwriting, a trembling almost illegible scrawl at the beginning, grows firmer towards the end. . . . But when the courier has departed with it, his spirits quickly slump again. . . . Yet his homesickness will not allow him to remain in Thessalonica longer—he must, even though he put his life in peril, creep a little nearer to Italy. He crosses the peninsula to Dyrrachium on the Adriatic.

Here he broods bitterly on his folly in having finally, when neither of the two consuls, nor Crassus, Cæsar, or Pompey, would interpose to save him, yielded to the advice of Cato and Hortensius to save himself by flight; and still more bitterly on not having joined the party of the triumvirate when his friendship was sought. News has been brought him of Cæsar's great victories in Gaul over the Helvetii and the Germans, and knowing that Cæsar is now this side of the Alps again in his southern province, he writes a long letter to him, seeking, as suavely as he knows how, to justify his opposition in the past, while at the same time promising obedience if allowed to return from exile.

4

In Cisalpine Gaul, this winter of 58–57, Cæsar is receiving disturbing news from the capital. Not only is there agitation to permit Cicero to return from exile, but worse still it is rumored that the senatorial party is coming back into power now that Piso and Gabinius are no longer consuls. Also there is a strong movement on foot to have Cæsar recalled from his command in Gaul so that he may be impeached for his unconstitutional acts when he occupied the consulship.

He writes to his daughter Julia, the wife of Pompey, urging her not to allow Pompey's friendship to be won away from him by his enemies. She answers that her husband is unquestionably jealous of her father's successes in Gaul, which are eclipsing the glory of his own victories in the East, but that she is doing what she can to keep him friendly. From Julia and from Clodius, whom he is keeping well supplied with funds, he learns that both Pompey and Crassus are trying to obtain the command of armies with which, if necessary, to hold their colleague in check; also that it is Pompey who has been most vulnerable to the petitions for Cicero's pardon.

He thinks the situation over. As long as he keeps sending abundant spoils back to the capital he will be popular with the people, no matter what political intrigues there may be against him. Clodius, who unites with the daring of Catiline the shrewdness of a practical politician, is his friend. He can rely upon him to fight to the last the movement to bring back Cicero. Once again, in this opposition, he himself will remain in the background.

He writes to Clodius to strengthen his party by continuing to gather around him all the bankrupts, gamblers, dissolute patricians, and ruined politicians whose allegiance can be bought with bribes; and as an additional precaution to secretly enter into friendly relations with Romans who have grudges against Pompey and Crassus. All this is to show on the surface as the work of Clodius, pure and simple, so that the more respectable burgesses will not draw away from Cæsar. But Cæsar, out of his Gallic spoils, will supply the money. What Clodius is to do in the name of Cæsar is to give huge public banquets, gladiatorial combats and wild-beast shows, and to adorn the city with new buildings, so that the people will be kept grateful to him for his generosity.

There are other things which he does not tell Clodius. He keeps to himself his intention of raising more legions at the first opportunity. Now that even Pompey, his daughter's husband, may turn against him, he puts all his faith in a large army. Only an army can make his words carry weight with his colleagues. When Piso, his father-in-law, who supported his interests while consul, leaves for his province of Syria, his grip on Roman politics will be immensely weakened; of the two new consuls, Lentulus is a friend of Cicero, while Metullus Nepos is devoted to Pompey. Not to appear the only member of the triumvirate who opposes Cicero's return, when he receives the exiled orator's letter he diplomatically, in case Cicero should be pardoned despite the opposition of Clodius, so phrases his reply as to put the burden of the propaganda against Cicero on the shoulders of Pompey and Crassus—he himself, he says, because of their life-long friendship, is necessarily grieved at the misfortunes that have overtaken Cicero, and, *if others are equally willing*, will be glad to take steps to ameliorate them. He hints broadly that where his colleagues want to keep Cicero in exile for political reasons, Clodius's zeal in this direction is animated only by personal animosity, and for this reason is perhaps the more to be feared—now that Clodius is the idol of the people, it may be difficult, even should Pompey and Crassus consent, and the new tribunes also, for them to over-ride the young demagogue's opposition. . . . The friendly tone of this letter to Cicero he keeps a secret from Clodius. Nor does he confide to anyone his determination to gradually build up his army until it is more powerful than any with which either the Senate or his colleagues can oppose his desire to be king.

A pretext to levy more troops, and to charge their expenses to the state-chest, is not long in coming. In the middle of the winter Labienus sends news that the Gallic tribes on the Atlantic, who have heard of the terrible fate met by the Helvetii and the Germans at the hands of the new governor of the Roman province, are combining to form a defensive alliance against the Romans, in case the latter should attempt to carry their conquests further westward.

On the strength of this message from Labienus, he immediately raises two fresh legions in Cisalpine Gaul, while writing to Rome that a new horde of Barbarians, surpassing in num-

bers even the two great armies defeated by him during the
year just past, is gathering in north-western Gaul with the intention of crossing the Alps and descending on Rome as soon
as the winter is over. With these additional eight thousand
troops he joins Labienus in the spring. The Roman army north
of the Alps, which when he went to his province a year ago
consisted of only a single legion, now numbers eight.

The confederacy of tribes, which Cæsar has painted in such
lurid colors in his despatches to Rome, is made up for the
most part of Belgians and Germans living at the mouth of the
Rhine. Appalled by the manner in which in a single year the
new Roman governor of Transalpine Gaul has pushed outward
from his province and virtually added the countries of the
Aeduii and the Sequani to the Roman dominions, these tribes
have drawn together, forgetting their own quarrels, to repel
a similar invasion. The massacres of the Swiss and the eastern
German tribes led by Ariovistus has united them in hatred of
the Romans.

This year Cæsar makes no pretense of being concerned only
with the safety of his own province, as he did when he refused
to allow the Helvetii to cross the Rhone. He takes his army by
forced marches into the country of the Remi, four hundred
miles to the north-west of the Province. He easily seizes all
the principal towns—most of these little larger than villages,
with pitiful barricades of felled trees that the Roman artillery
quickly brushes aside with its great battering rams. Having
seized the towns, he holds the wives and children of the chiefs
as hostages. At the same time he informs the chiefs that Rome,
having heard of the intended invasion of the land of the Remi
by the fierce Belgic and German tribes who occupy the territory between them and the ocean, has despatched him with his
army to help them resist the invasion. In the same way that he
compelled the Aeduii to furnish him with auxiliaries and supplies, so he now forces the Remi to contribute cavalry and
corn. The Gallic auxiliaries—who are made to fight with their
right shoulders bare, so that the legionaries can distinguish
between friend and foe in battle—may be sullen and un-

dependable, but the sight of them lined up with the Roman army should help to demoralize the Belgians.

The confederacy knows of Cæsar's arrival. That, as soon as the grass was green, he should have brought his army so far from the Province with no regard for the rights of the tribes whose territory he has marched through—compelling these to sustain his legions on the march, and finally occupying the land of the Remi—confirms their belief that the Romans mean to subjugate the whole of Gaul. From all directions the tribes hasten to concentrate for mutual protection, until three hundred thousand people, of which as in the case of the Helvetii and the Germans under Ariovistus four-fifths are incapable of bearing arms, are collected in a huge encampment on the western bank of the Aisne.

Cæsar fortifies the eastern bank, choosing for his camp a plateau having the river on one side and marsh on the flanks— to the rear is firm ground over which his supplies can come safely.

Here he simply waits. That the Barbarians will have to break up their immense camp before many weeks is a foregone conclusion. Already sickness and starvation are killing them off rapidly. The chief of the confederacy, King Galba, is daily having greater difficulty holding them together. And a month has scarcely passed when his patience is rewarded, the starving tribes beginning to scatter and go back to their homes.

Now he gives his orders to attack. The red *vexillum* replaces the white flag at his headquarters. The legionaries summoned to an assembly show their enthusiastic approbation of his harangue on the certainty of victory by loud shouts, raising of their right hands, and beating of their shields with their spears. They leave the camp, cross the river, and pursue the dispersed confederacy, cutting to pieces each tribe in turn.

From the survivors he chooses hostages, telling the miserable remnants of the confederacy that any further attempt to make war on the Romans will be crushed with even greater severity.

One tribe, the Nervii, has escaped the slaughter. Realizing

how completely at the mercy of the Roman army would be the divided confederacy, it had been the first tribe to leave the encampment, and had marched night and day to put distance between it and the Aisne. Fifty thousand strong, it now lies concealed in the forest forty miles above Namur.

Gallic deserters from the Roman army come to it and urge a surprise raid on Cæsar's baggage train. They describe to the Nervii the customary manner in which the Roman army marches—a single legion in the van as advance guard, then the baggage-wagons, and after these the main body of soldiers. Knowing that the Romans are advancing towards them to complete the overthrow of the confederacy by their destruction and feeling that the attempt will have more than a chance of success as they will outnumber the four thousand legionaries in the vanguard, the Nervii accordingly take up a hidden position in the forest on the right bank of the Sambre, at a point on the road along which the Roman army is approaching.

Cæsar comes riding along the forest road.

He is with the van of the army, which today, to make more rapid the clearing of a route for the baggage train through the difficult country his army is advancing across, *he has unexpectedly increased to six legions,* leaving two legions to act as rear-guard for the baggage.

The reconnaissance party that goes ahead to pick out a site for the camp has found a good location on high ground near both wood and water. The scouts have already drawn at right angles to each other the two bisecting lines that mark the four gates, and are staking out the camp.

The sun is sinking over the forest. The gleam of water can be seen ahead of the army. On an open slope is the reconnaissance party black against the sky-line. The legionaries, who have marched seven hours since morning, covering fifteen miles, sigh with relief as they realize they are nearing the spot selected for the camp. It lies on the side of a hill, having at the foot a small river, with thick forests beyond.

The reconnaissance centurion reports to Cæsar that some

Barbarians have been seen along the stream on its far side, but that they were few in number, and immediately took to flight, vanishing into the forest—it was not worth-while pursuing.

The march is halted. The legionaries, who never sleep in the open—the success of Roman arms in hostile countries is largely due to this custom of always guarding against surprise by building fortified camps—lay aside their helmets, shields and spears and begin digging in for the night.

Cæsar remains on his horse, dictating letters to his two secretaries. Now and again his eyes roam with satisfaction over his busy little soldiers, but his thoughts are elsewhere. He does not fear an attack by the Nervii. Since his defeat of the confederacy he feels himself invincible. And his legionaries have caught the same spirit—usually when building the camp a guard of cavalry is stationed near the diggers, but tonight on account of the extra legions, this precaution has been dropped —officers and centurions alike have relaxed their discipline— the Nervii are believed to be miles away.

He finishes the letters begun on the march in the late afternoon, and the secretaries withdraw to a respectful distance. He sits on his horse alone, the slanting sunlight swirling in glittering rays from the immense jewel in the heavy gold ring on one of the hands holding the reins, whereupon is engraved that image of his ancestress Venus which his soldiers have already come to regard with superstitious reverence.

Thoughts of Rome weave in and out through his mind. . . . The opposition there against him seems to be growing more pronounced. . . . Clodius has stopped the recall of Cicero, but he had to use force to do it. . . . The Senate now has a tool equally dangerous, an enemy of Clodius's named Milo, who displays the same audacity. The two rivals, whose gladiators cross swords every day on the streets of Rome, have brought the city into a state of anarchy. There was a pitched battle in the Forum when Cicero's pardon was under discussion the like of which had not been witnessed by the capital since the days of Sulla. The sewers were choked with corpses, the Tiber floated hundreds of dead bodies, an army of slaves had to wash the Forum with sponges to clean away all the blood and gore. . . . There is no question now but that Pompey and Cicero are in friendly communication with each other—in a few months, writes Clodius, despite all he is doing to prevent it, Cicero will most likely have been allowed to return from exile. . . .

And in Egypt Ptolemy has been driven from his throne, the natives having revolted against the monstrous taxation under which the whole country has groaned since the extortion by the triumvirate of their 6000 talents for officially recognizing the Flute-player as ruler. Ptolemy is coming to Rome to persuade Pompey and Crassus to put him back on his throne. If, as a "friend of Rome," he gets a Roman army to help him, there will be another huge bribe. Will he, Cæsar, far away in Gaul, get his proper share of this bribe?

Sudden shouts dispel abruptly these thoughts of Rome and Egypt. He is suddenly in Gaul again. Out of the forest opposite Barbarians are swarming across the river.

In an instant, it seems, they are everywhere among the legionaries. Before the Roman soldiers have time to drop their digging tools and seize their arms the Nervii are slaughtering them. He stands dazed, unnerved by the same hollow feeling of disaster he experienced on realizing he had marched too far from his base in pursuit of the Swiss, when Ariovistus intercepted his supplies.

But this time with his legionaries dropping right and left around him the feeling is more acute than ever before. He shouts for his armor-bearer, but the latter has been separated from him in the confusion. He snatches a shield from one of his soldiers—the legionary obediently gives it up to his general, then falls dead, his body transfixed by a Barbarian spear.

The onslaught of the Nervii seems irresistible. They have driven the two left legions, the 12th and the 7th, back in panic on the approaching baggage train, they are swarming into the unfinished Roman camp. The troops around Cæsar are in hopeless disorder. He is caught up and carried back with them in their flight like a leaf in a storm. Only the legions commanded by Labienus manage to rally, form their lines, and finally drive back a wing of the Nervii which they pursue across the river into the forest.

The slaughter is worst in the neighborhood of Cæsar. Taller than the average Roman, and distinguished by his cloak as an officer of importance, he becomes singled out for attack. His bald head, lacking its helmet, shines whitely conspicuous. The oak-wreath that he wears to conceal his baldness has fallen over his eyes, and is wet with blood from a dart that grazed his temple. He tears it off and dashes it to the ground.

Wherever he looks he sees Barbarians hacking their way towards him. Following Roman custom they have set fire to the baggage wagons. Dense smoke blinds his eyes a minute. When it clears away he notices a mysterious lull in the fighting. The nearby Barbarians have ceased attacking and are looking up at the hill-top, upon which a large body of horsemen has suddenly appeared.

His heart swells with hope. These, he knows, are Gallic auxiliaries from Trèves commandeered by him recently, and whose arrival he has been expecting for several days. He gives a triumphant shout, waving his hand to them to ride down. The Gauls sit their horses motionless a moment, surveying the situation—then glad to leave the Romans to their fate ride back again the way they have come.

His heart sinks. Is all lost?

With renewed ferocity, now that the auxiliaries have turned their backs on the Romans, the Nervii are back at the charge. Cæsar is surrounded. Another instant, and they will have broken through the thin guard of legionaries desperately trying to protect him. But suddenly a short sturdy Roman, blood streaming down his face, bursts their ranks apart. It is Labienus, who seeing Cæsar's peril, has crossed the river again with the Tenth legion in time to save the life of his general.

The Nervii, contesting each foot of ground desperately, begin to give way. Had the Roman marching order for the day not been changed their surprise attack would have been a success, but faced by six legions instead of one the odds, now that the legionaries are recovering from their panic, are against them. When a few minutes later the Roman rear-guard comes up they realize the day is lost and take to flight.

The Romans pursue, scouring the forest until they find the Barbarian camp. Furious at how near this single tribe came to annihilating the whole Roman army, Cæsar has issued orders to spare not a single member of the tribe. When the butchery of the women and children in the camp ceases, and the Roman cavalry has hunted down the refugees, not five hundred of the original fifty thousand Nervii are still alive.

The campaign against the Belgian confederacy ends with a march to exterminate the Aduatici, a German tribe which had been advancing to join forces with the Nervii, but which on hearing of their massacre, had shut itself up in the town of Namur.

Namur holds out against the Romans for several weeks. Cæsar, the memory of his near defeat on the bank of the Sambre still rankling, and his ill-humor increased by the latest news from Rome—not only is Cicero back in the capital, but the candidate for next year's consulship, Domitius Ahenobarbus, Cato's brother-in-law, who has every chance of being elected, openly favors recalling Cæsar and repealing his laws, —treats the Aduatici, when the Roman artillery finally makes a breach in the town walls, as mercilessly but more profitably than he did the Nervii. He destroys Namur and sells the whole population of sixty thousand inhabitants into slavery to the contractors of Crassus.

Then, as winter is once again approaching, he leaves Labienus in command of the army, and crosses the Alps to his southern province.

5

On the 4th of August, after being in exile sixteen months, Cicero, pardoned, had left Dyrrhachium for Rome. Crossing the Adriatic, he had landed at Brundisium on the heel of Italy, and from there had proceeded by land to the capital.

The Senate, to drum up feeling against Cæsar, has prepared for him a tremendous welcome. Cicero forgets the dismal months in Greece. The triumph of his return restores his faith in himself as the greatest Roman of his age. A friend of his, Lucius Lucceius, the historian, is at work on a history of the Republic—Cicero writes to Lucceius urging him not to treat the Catiline conspiracy (and the noble part played by himself in suppressing it) as a mere incident in this history, but to make a separate book of it. (Appendix, p. 301.)

But trouble is brewing. No sooner has Cicero, taking advantage of Clodius's absence one day, gone to the Capitol, and inscribed his own name again on the tablet commemorating him as "Saviour of His Country," also carrying off another tablet on which Clodius had engraved the decree of his exile—than the "pretty boy" resumes his persecutions.

A few weeks after requesting the historian "not to confine himself to the strict laws of history," but to give a greater latitude to his praise of Cicero than Lucceius may possibly think his actions merit, Cicero is writing to his friend Atticus of the following outrages recently committed by Clodius——

"November the third, the workmen were driven by armed men from my land; the portico of Catulus was pulled down, which in accordance with a decree of the Senate, by arrangement of the consuls, was being rebuilt and had been raised as far as the roof; they shattered the house of my brother Quintus by throwing stones at it from my land, then set it on fire by order of Clodius, in sight of the city, by hurling firebrands amid the clamor and uproar of, I shall not say the good men, as perhaps there are none, but of nearly all men. Clodius rushed about in a fury; after this burst of rage he meditated nothing but the slaughter of his foes; he went from street to street, and openly offered the hope of freedom to the slaves. . . . November the 11th, when I was going down the Sacred Way, he followed me with his men; shouting, they suddenly attacked me with stones, clubs, and swords; I retreated to the vestibule of the house of Tettius Damio. Those who were with me kept his men from entering. . . . November 12th he made an attempt to burn the house of Milo on the Germalus, openly leading up men with shields and drawn swords, and others with flaming torches. . . ."

Rome is convulsed with factional strife, the result of competition to put Ptolemy back on his throne and claim the reward. Pompey, trying with might and main to get the appointment, is entertaining the Flute-player lavishly at his Roman palace. A delegation of a hundred principal citizens from Alexandria which sailed for Rome to implore the Roman people not to force the tyrant back upon their country, has been intercepted and murdered by a band of assassins in the pay of Pompey.

But Clodius has suddenly turned against Pompey, and is vigorously opposing his appointment——

"It seems to me" (writes Cicero a few weeks later to his brother Quintus) "that we have great storms beginning to brew. Pompey makes no secret of it to me that plots are being hatched against his life . . . that *someone* is supplying Clodius with funds!"

And in the same letter to Quintus he describes the scene which took place when at a recent public meeting the party of Crassus, who is being supported by Clodius for the appointment, and that of Pompey, quarreled over which of the two leaders should command the Roman army that is to reinstate the Flute-player.

"Pompey spoke—or rather intended to; for as soon as he rose, the hired rowdies of Clodius made such an uproar lasting too throughout his whole speech, as to drown his voice with their interruptions, and even with insults and abuse. When he had made his peroration, up got Clodius; whereupon such an uproar was raised by our side—for we had determined he should get as good as he gave—that he lost all control of his thoughts, his voice, and his countenance. This scene, though Pompey had all but finished speaking at eleven, lasted till quite one; people meanwhile shouting all sorts of abuse, culminating finally in the filthiest doggerel about Clodius and his sister. Furious and white with rage, he appealed to his partisans above the shouting to say who it was that was starving the people to

death? His rowdies shouted back, Pompey. Who was it that
wanted to go to Alexandria? Pompey, they answered. Whom
would they vote for to go instead? Crassus, they replied—he
was in the assembly at the time. . . . About two the Clodi-
ans began, apparently at a given signal, to spit upon our
party. . . ."

6

Cæsar, wintering in Hither Gaul, is keeping in close touch
with the excitement in Rome. Since he himself cannot go with
Ptolemy to Alexandria, he has instructed Clodius to support
Crassus's ambition in this direction.

Like himself, the fat millionaire views with suspicion Pompey's friendliness with Cicero. With Pompey aspiring to control of the capital's corn supply and endeavoring to dictate the
military policies of the Republic, the balance of power in the
triumvirate is threatened. Cæsar knows that Cicero is trying to
turn Pompey against him, but he hopes that the orator's loose
tongue will in the end be his undoing.

Clodius's brother, Appius, who crosses the Alps to see Cæsar,
tells him Cicero is making himself unpopular right and left in
Rome by talking too much. Swelled to bursting with vanity
over his home-coming, and Pompey's flatteries, he is busily
revenging himself on those political enemies who helped send
him into exile by flinging personalities at them. Too cautious to
aim his insults at any member of the triumvirate, he attacks
mercilessly the underlings.

After Clodius, Piso and Gabinius, during whose consulship
he was banished, come in for the choicest abuse. Cæsar's father-
in-law, who has a high meaningless forehead and a pompous
manner, he attacks sometimes by the method of irony.

For Piso! O ye gods how unwashed, how stern he looked!
—a pillar of antiquity, like one of the old bearded consuls; his
dress plain plebeian purple, his hair tangled, his brow a very
pledge for the Commonwealth! Such solemnity in his eye,
such wrinkling of his forehead, that you would have said the
State was resting on his head like the sky on Atlas. Here I

thought I had a refuge. Here was the man to oppose the filth of Gabinius—his very face would be enough!

But on other occasions—when Piso is in the Senate to hear him—he abandons humor for more vigorous invective.

When all the good were hiding themselves in tears, when the temples were groaning and the very houses in the city were mourning over my exile, you, heartless madman that you are, took up the cause of that pernicious animal, that clotted mass of incests and civil blood, of villainies intended and impurity of crimes committed.[1] Need I speak of your feasting, your laughter, and handshakings—your drunken orgies with the filthy companions of your potations? Who in those days saw you ever sober, or doing anything that a citizen need not be ashamed of? While your colleague's house was sounding with song and cymbals, and he himself was dancing naked at a supper-party, you, you coarse glutton, with less taste for music, were lying in a stew of Greek boys and wine in a feast of Centaurs and Lapithæ, where one cannot say whether you drank most, or vomited most, or spilt most!"

Gabinius he has inveighed against in terms equally uncomplimentary.

Behold him, as he appeared when consul at a meeting called by the arch-thief Clodius, full of wine, and sleep, and fornication, his hair moist, his eyes heavy, his cheeks flaccid, and declaring, with a voice thick with drink, that he disapproved of putting citizens to death without trial!

What worries Cæsar more than Cicero's garrulousness is the growing power of the senatorial party. Some day he intends himself to break with Pompey and Crassus, but the right moment has not arrived yet. Is it not still to the interest of each member of the triumvirate to stay united against the Senate? If Ahenobarbus is elected consul, not only will Cæsar be recalled, but the Senate will also make every effort to ruin his colleagues.

This second winter in Cisalpine Gaul he sees how serious

[1] Clodius.

would be the consequences of such a rupture. By quarreling among themselves they are giving the oligarchy an opportunity to regain control of the government. The time has not yet come when any one of the triumvirate is strong enough to stand alone.

And both Pompey and Crassus realize how dangerous will be their situation if Ahenobarbus is elected consul. In a year they will be running for the consulships themselves, and they need Cæsar's support. In face of the common peril they must forget for the time being their private differences. Through the winter Cæsar keeps in continual communication with his colleagues, and the result of this correspondence is a decision that before he goes north over the Alps again the three must meet in a personal interview.

Since Cæsar cannot come to Rome, no Roman governor being allowed to return to the capital until his term of office has expired, the meeting place fixed upon is the little town of Lucca, on the frontier of Cæsar's southern province, a hundred and seventy miles north-west of Rome.

Crassus leaves Rome for Lucca on the first of April. Pompey, under pretense of discharging his new duties as corn administrator (which he gives out necessitate a tour of the Mediterranean provinces), follows secretly on the eleventh.

Cæsar meets Crassus in Ravenna, from which they proceed together to Lucca. Crassus has grown fatter. Underneath the surface cordiality of their greetings, the meeting is strained.

Cæsar, since Crassus saw him last, has leaped into fame as a general. For his great victories in Gaul the Senate has been forced by public sentiment in Rome to decree him a public thanksgiving of fifteen days. No Roman general has ever previously enjoyed this honor, Pompey, on the conclusion of the war with Mithridates, having only been given ten days, the longest *supplicatio*, however, up to this time. Crassus feels pushed into the background, and Cæsar reads the jealousy in his furtive glances.

But the strain wears off when Crassus begins to gossip about

Pompey. He hints that Pompey cannot forget that he is the general who defeated Mithridates. He mentions Cicero's nickname for Pompey—*Sampsiceramus*—and laughs spitefully at it. As they journey to Lucca he grumbles about the manner in which Pompey, when they were consuls together, stole the triumph which he, Crassus, should have been granted for suppressing the slave insurrection led by the ex-gladiator Spartacus; it was *his* army, he maintains, which really defeated Spartacus, but Pompey, coming up with reinforcements towards the end of the battle, took the credit for the victory.

Cæsar smiles and nods. He seems to agree that Pompey is intensely egotistical, but implies that he and Crassus ought to be able to smooth out all difficulties so that the triumvirate will once again be able to function smoothly in opposition to the oligarchy. He praises the valor of Crassus's son, Publius, and Crassus is especially interested when he hears it was Publius who commanded the cavalry that drove the Germans back to the Rhine. He is thinking that he will take his son with him when he goes East after his consulship.

He discusses this matter of his province with Cæsar. Suppose, when they draw lots for provinces, Pompey gets Syria instead of himself? Will he be allowed to keep it? If so, then Crassus has no interest in attending the Lucca Conference. He must be guaranteed Syria as his province. But this means that Pompey will have to be satisfied with Spain. And Pompey wants Syria as badly as he does. What is the solution? Cæsar suggests Egypt. If Pompey is allowed to have a free hand in Egypt he will probably let Crassus have the East to exploit. And he himself is willing to abandon his rightful claim to take part in the restoration of Ptolemy if there is no attempt to interfere with him in Gaul.

Pompey arrives in Lucca.

Cæsar's meeting with him is even more strained than was that with Crassus. A grimace of a smile twitches the lips of Pompey the Great as he embraces his now celebrated father-in-law. Cæsar affects not to notice the older man's ill-concealed jealousy. He postpones the discussion of politics awhile to talk about family affairs. At first Pompey answers his questions about Julia and their child with a haughty aloofness, then his genuine love for his young wife makes him more genial.

But, as they talk on, coming to the subject of Cæsar's successes in Gaul, it is only too plain to Cæsar that Pompey's pride will not permit him to recognize any merit in his father-in-law's military achievements. The Roman mob may applaud the Gallic campaigns, but in Pompey's eyes they do not constitute war in the grand manner such as he himself conducted against Mithridates in Asia. Cæsar, in his opinion, has done nothing to entitle him to be called, like Pompey, "the Great." The quick night marches which the governor of Gaul tells him about, make no impression upon a mind full of fond memories of the slow and imposing procession-like marches of the Asiatic army; they may be effective but they lack dignity.

Like Crassus, Pompey, after wine has increased his amiability, gossips to Cæsar about his colleague. He sees Crassus as devoured with jealousy of his military honors. Crassus, he says, has never ceased brooding over the imaginary injustice done him by Pompey at the time of the servile war with Spartacus—yet the whole world knows that it was only the arrival of Pompey which saved Crassus from overwhelming defeat. He comes to the matter of Clodius's recent conduct, telling how only a short time before he left Rome, one day as he was being carried through the streets in his litter, a bucket of swill had been thrown down on his head from some upstairs window. There is no question in his mind but that it was Crassus at whose instigation Clodius had committed this assault.

Cæsar looks deeply concerned. His eyes meet those of his illustrious son-in-law sympathetically as Pompey the Great, his aristocratic nostrils quivering in recollection of the insult, flutters a perfumed handkerchief in front of them. He makes no attempt to justify Clodius's conduct on this occasion, but he does put forth the mild excuse that Clodius, as Pompey well knows, has always been hopelessly irresponsible and erratic.

Meanwhile Rome talks of nothing but the Lucca Conference.

In the Senate Cato and Hortensius make speech after speech denouncing the "three kings." The wits of the senatorial party, reviving the story of Cæsar's affair with King Nicomedes, write satires in which Pompey is featured as king of Rome, and Cæsar as queen.

But gradually one senator after another leaves the capital on some excuse—important business in the provinces, the sickness of a relative at Pompeii, a villa at Baii perhaps that is in need of repairs. They slip out of Rome by different gates, but all the roads seem to lead to Lucca, which, for the time being, has taken the place of Rome as the capital of the Republic. Here, in the Big Three, is concentrated all its power and wealth, and here, to their mutual astonishment and embarrassment, all the senators meet again.

Never, indeed, has the little town of Lucca been the setting for such a glittering gathering as the one now assembled here.

Two hundred senators, accompanied by over a hundred lictors, are in obsequious attendance on the triumvirate. The narrow streets are blocked with the litters and carriages of distinguished Romans jostling each other for the privilege of paying court to the three virtual rulers of the Republic. Metullus Nepos, now proconsul of Hither Spain, and Appius Claudius, propraetors of Sardinia, are both here to take orders. And to Lucca also, at the advice of Clodius, have hurried all the bankrupts, gamblers, tavern and brothel keepers, soldiers of fortune, penniless patricians, and Romans weighed down with debt, who are being collected by Cæsar for the nucleus of his own private party.

After the preliminary gossiping and backbiting is over, the three members of the triumvirate, meeting no longer in twos, manage to forget their personal differences, and to make equitable division of the Roman empire.

Pompey and Crassus are to be consuls again. When their year ends Pompey is to have Hither and Further Spain for

his provinces, and Crassus, Syria. Cæsar's governorship in
Gaul is to be extended an additional five years—then ten years
will have elapsed since his consulship, so that he, also, in 49
when he returns to Rome can be consul again. In case of trouble at the coming elections, he is to allow a number of his
soldiers to go to Rome on furlough under Crassus's son, Publius. The soldiers will be in Rome not only to cast their votes
in favor of Pompey and Crassus, but also to carry the elections
by force if the Senate tries to block their re-election.

The military support which Pompey and Crassus may need
later for regulating the affairs of the capital is to be found in
new legions which they will raise for their Spanish and Syrian
armies, but will keep in Italy until no longer necessary to force
Rome to obedience. Each is to hold his governorship for five
years. Gabinius, Pompey's henchman, and at the present time
governor of Syria, is to be allowed to march his army across the
Egyptian border and reinstate Ptolemy. Cæsar is to have the
prerogative of increasing his legions in number from eight
to ten, and of charging the pay for the troops on the state-
chest.

Nor is Cicero forgotten. Though willing to overlook Pompey's treachery in assisting the orator to return to Italy, Crassus and Cæsar have no intention of allowing Cicero to make
trouble for them in the future. And Pompey has already been
told of things said by Cicero which make him doubt the sincerity of the latter's gratitude and protestations of friendship. But there is no question of banishing the orator again,
and giving him the advantage of being able to pose as a martyr.
It is deemed best to put him under such heavy obligations to
the party that he has no alternative but to do its bidding. Cæsar
has already lent him large sums of money. Now Pompey is to
obtain for him the governorship of Cilicia. And when Cæsar
crosses the Alps again, he is to take with him as a hostage for
Cicero's good behavior, his brother Quintus.

So the Lucaa Conference breaks up, a big success. All present
difficulties have been smoothed out. The hopes entertained by
the Senate that there would be a split in the triumvirate have

been dashed to the ground. The three joint rulers of Rome part on the friendliest of terms.

Cæsar stands watching a carriage vanish into the distance. It contains Pompey the Great and Crassus. Through the bright sunshine of a spring morning they are driven away from him. And neither of them will he ever again see alive.

7

When Publius Crassus came to Lucca on his way to Rome with the soldiers, he had told Cæsar that the tribes in Brittany were forming a confederacy with the object of revolting against the Roman rule (while Cæsar, the previous year, had been crushing the Belgians, Crassus had conducted a less successful campaign against the maritime tribes further to the south); and he had advised his commander to have a fleet built, as these tribes, particularly the Veneti, the most important of the coast clans, could never be effectively subjugated without a navy. Cæsar had accordingly given orders that a large fleet should be built in the mouth of the Loire, to be ready not later than the beginning of summer, when he would be back in Gaul to continue his conquests. The Lucca Conference over, he goes to the Loire and finds a hundred galleys waiting for him; manned by crews imported from Marseilles and pressed into service from the coast tribes. But as the weather is too bad for these to venture out into the open sea as yet, he decides to ignore the advice of young Crassus, and to start the campaign without waiting for the fleet.

The Veneti inhabit the coast forty miles north of the mouth of the Loire. They are a fishing people who live on headlands which at high tide are cut off from the mainland; their ships, propelled by leather sails, have flat keels so that they can be navigated in very shallow water. They make scarcely any attempt to resist the legions in battle, but when Cæsar has captured one of their wretched villages he finds his victory meaningless as the inhabitants, abandoning their miserable huts, have simply taken to their ships and sailed off to another headland.

The legionaries, accustomed to great gaudy victories, begin to murmur. They dislike the scrambling over the slippery rocks when the tide is low, and the same vista of great grey ocean with the Barbarian ships sailing away from the headland which always meets their eyes when they have finally reached the fishing village which is their destination. Swift and dangerous currents move between the headlands and the mainland at high tide, and crossing these channels a number of the legionaries are drowned. Cæsar, thwarted in his desire to succeed where Crassus had failed, finally resigns himself to waiting for the arrival of his fleet.

And one day, to the joy of the legionaries, the weather changes . . . the wind drops . . . the dark storm clouds vanish . . . for the first time since their coming to Brittany a warm sun shines down on them out of a clear sky. The army is in good spirits again immediately the news spreads that the Roman fleet has left the mouth of the Loire, and is on its way north.

The Veneti have heard the news also. That sky, so dark and stormy, which had depressed the spirits of the Romans, had been for them a mantle of protection; it is this sunshine which is ominous with the menace of the Roman invasion. From headland to headland is passed the message that the galleys are coming. The chiefs of the clans meet and decide that they must risk a naval battle with the Roman fleet. They believe that their own ships, sturdily built to weather storms in the open sea, and having sails, will be more than a match for the Roman triremes with their oars.

The fleet arrives. The Roman army, from the cliffs on which the camp is situated, watches its approach, stirred by the sight of the many oars flashing in the sunlight and the sharp armored prows cutting through the water.

Each galley has a hundred and seventy rowers, and will carry a hundred fighting men besides. The galleys have a smart military appearance which the sailing ships of the fishers, with their patched leather sails, and motley crews, lack altogether. But Cæsar, after the arrival of the fleet, changes his mind about commanding it in the naval battle. He had been ambitious to own a navy as well as an army since a navy is all he needs to be able to claim complete equality with Pompey, who was admiral in the naval war against the pirates. But he has a dread of the water. Once as a youth he had nearly drowned in the Tiber—it was a friend, Caius Cassius, whom he had over-confidentially challenged to a race after they had been exercising together in the Campus Martius, who had rescued him and dragged him ashore. From the cliffs he surveys the rocky coast where the ocean, even in fine weather, swirls and eddies treacherously around the headlands. The naval battle will in all probability take place here in the Bay of Quiberon with the army watching from the cliffs. He likes the picture of himself, as admiral, leading this navy to victory over the ragged Barbarian fleet under the admiring eyes of his soldiers. But can he be sure of victory?

The doubt gnaws at his ambition to be admiral. Suppose a storm should spring up suddenly? In rough water his triremes for all their fine fighting appearance may prove quite unmanageable. And individual encounters between the galleys and the fishing boats have given indication that in many respects the latter, inelegant though they may be to look at, possess certain advantages. They are so massively constructed that the rostrums of the triremes—beams projecting from the prows below water, and topped with sharp iron points or an iron figure of a ram's head—seem unable to do them damage. Also they stand too high out of the water for the turrets erected on the galleys to be effective as points from which to hurl missiles down upon them.

He imagines his army looking on not at the spectacle of victory, but at the destruction of his fleet by the Barbarians—at his flagship being sunk, and himself ignominiously drowned. He reflects further that since all the wars in Gaul, whether on land or water, are being conducted under his auspices (so that in case of victory by a subordinate officer he receives the credit while defeat reflects not on his own ability but on that of the lieutenant), for him to command in the coming naval battle would be a foolish and unnecessary risk. He decides to let Decimus Brutus have charge of the fleet, while he himself will stay with his army and watch the battle from the cliffs.

Decimus Brutus—who will later be one of the band of conspirators that assassinates Cæsar—is the cousin of Marcus Brutus, reputed the illegitimate son of Cæsar by Servilia, the sister of Cato.

A strong courageous young soldier, he feels Cæsar is doing him a great honor when he gives him command of the fleet. To test the fighting powers of the triremes he sends out several of them, one by one, to skirmish with detached vessels of the fishing fleet. In every one of these duels the fishing boat, mainly because of its sail, comes off the winner. This being the case, he conceives the idea of furnishing each galley with long poles having sharp curved knives at their ends, which, reserved as a surprise for the day of the big battle, can then be used to cut the ropes holding up the sails, thus crippling the Barbarian ships.

Meanwhile the Veneti, elated by the superiority of their ships in the individual encounters, and hopeful that the Romans, seemingly so invincible on land, may be poor fighters on the water, have assembled all their vessels for the battle. As Cæsar had hoped, it takes place in the Bay of Quiberon, a hundred miles to the south-east of the modern port of Brest.

On the cliffs all the legionaries who are not serving as marines in the war-galleys line up to watch the outcome, while hovering on the outskirts of the fishing fleet are smaller boats containing the families of the Veneti, come to pray for the defeat of the hated Roman invaders.

The fishing boats sail to and fro, their crews shouting defiance to the Romans. The galleys remain motionless, except when now and again the oars of a trireme flash like a single blade and the sharp cruel beak darts forward across the water. To the Veneti, whose sail-boats are built for long seagoing journeys—many of them have been to the coast of Britain and back—the Roman galleys, because propelled by oars, are by comparison, for all the glitter of the armed men on board, little more than large gaudy water-toys. The battle begins.

To encourage the Veneti in their over-confidence, Brutus has given orders that in the beginning the Roman fleet shall seem to be worsted. The captain of each galley has been instructed to make his boat seem unwieldy and slow by contrast with the Barbarian ships. And the Veneti, as the Roman galleys seem unable either to keep pace with them or to change direction with the same ease, become increasingly audacious. When they have approached close enough for the two fleets to be thoroughly intermingled, Brutus gives his signal, and the Romans, reaching across with their sharp hooks, cut the sail ropes of the enemy ships.

From ten in the morning till sunset lasts the battle. The spectators on the cliffs roar out their applause much like an audience in one of the Roman amphitheatres as ship after ship of the fishing fleet is boarded by the legionaries in the galleys, whose short deadly swords make quick work of the fishermen, armed only with crude spears and axes. The bay becomes full of drowning Barbarians, whom the soldiers on the galleys push down with the points of their long pilums.

By three o'clock the Roman onlookers know the battle has been won. But the Veneti, urged on by the shrieks of their women, and made desperate by the realization that their only hope of escaping subjugation by the Romans lies in their fleet —if this is defeated, all is surely lost—fight on. The ships that still have their sails put trust in the wind, which usually does not die down until the late afternoon—when there is no longer any chance for victory they believe they can always make their escape.

Cæsar, from the cliffs, is watching the progress of the battle with sharp eyes. Will the Barbarians suddenly realize that the odds are against them and take refuge in flight? It is his ambition to destroy the fishing fleet as entirely as he destroyed the Helvetii, the Germans, and the Belgian confederacy.

And the Veneti, lured into continuing the unequal combat by the shouts of derision hurled at them from the heights, and believing that their sails will carry them to safety whenever they choose to retreat, wait just too long—they are on the point of sailing away, when an hour earlier than usual, the wind suddenly drops.

The sun keeps sinking, until, a round red disk, it stands balanced on the horizon to seaward. With its red horizontal rays it lights up the Bay of Quiberon, made redder by the light of burning ships. Except for a few vessels that have managed to escape, the whole fishing fleet of the Veneti, numbering more than a hundred ships, has been destroyed.

On the still surface of the bay the Roman galleys, low and sinister, and flashing red glints from the armor of the legionaries, lie clustered like fantastic water monsters. The shore is strewn with corpses.

Cæsar stands watching the last fishing boat being boarded and sunk. The blood-red sun lights up his face and hands. From the spot on the cliffs, where, a small black figure with head bent forward slightly, he stands silhouetted against the western blaze, his shadow, far-flung and gigantic, stretches away eastward across Gaul.

The particular crime of the Veneti, as distinguished from their more general one of having resisted the Roman invasion, had been their detention of several Roman cavalry officers sent out the previous year by Crassus to procure corn and provisions. The Veneti, from whom Crassus had already torn children as hostages, had detained these supply officers, and sent a messenger to Crassus, saying that they would release them only when the Romans had given them back their children.

In the third book of his Commentaries on the Gallic Wars Cæsar explains that it was largely this "open insult offered to the Republic in the detention of the Roman knights" that had "urged him into the war." And in the same book he tells in what manner, after the battle in the Bay of Quiberon, he punished the survivors of the tribe for this crime.

"By this battle the war with the Veneti and the whole of the sea coast was finished; for both all the youth, and all, too, of more advanced age, in whom there was any discretion or rank, had assembled in that battle; and they had collected in that one place whatever naval forces they had anywhere; and when these were lost, the survivors had no place to retreat to, nor means of defending their towns. They accordingly surrendered themselves and all their possessions to Cæsar, on whom Cæsar thought that punishment should be inflicted the more severely, in order that for the future the rights of ambassadors might be more carefully respected by barbarians: having, therefore, put to death all their senate, he sold the rest for slaves."

8

The winter of 56–55 he spends like the two previous ones in the north of Italy on the frontier of his southern province. In Rome Pompey and Crassus have been elected consuls, but after more stubborn opposition from the Senate than the triumvirate had expected. Clodius lets him know that the fury of the Senate, led by Cato, reached white-heat when in the people's assembly it was proposed that Cæsar's governorship in Gaul be prolonged the agreed-upon five years. Cato talked for two hours against the proposition—finally, when he refused to sit down and keep quiet, Clodius had rushed up and dragged him off the rostrum. When all the adherents of the Senate had been driven from the assembly, the party of the triumvirate had passed the decree giving Cæsar his additional five years, and also that which made Pompey and Crassus governors respectively of Spain and Syria for the same term. But as the meeting was breaking up Cato had returned at the head of a body of armed men—taking the party of the triumvirate by surprise, he had driven it from the Forum, and the senatorial faction had then pronounced the decrees just passed illegal, and were voting Cæsar's recall when Pompey appeared leading the troops on furlough in the capital.

A pitched battle had been fought, in which Cato was wounded, and the triumvirate had been victorious. To insure the legality of the decree extending Cæsar's term as governor Clodius had had the vote for it taken a second time.

Since his election Pompey has been trying his best to eclipse Cæsar's popularity with the people. He is building the first stone amphitheatre in Rome, which will hold fifty thousand people. Also he is spending enormous sums of money on games and wild-beast shows. At a recent big show given by him which lasted five days a hundred lions were killed each day. He also exhibited a number of elephants, but to Cæsar's delight—as he recalls the great success of his own elephant hunt in the Circus—this attempt on Pompey's part to win favor with the populace by entertaining them with a similar spectacle proved a complete failure.

For the elephants could not be made to fight. Instead of charging the soldiers wounding them with spears, they had thrown up their trunks and trotted around the Circus whimpering. And suddenly, through the blood-thirsty Roman audience, which had been looking forward to the elephant hunt, reserved for the last day, as the most exciting number on the program, had swept a wave of superstition. It was said that the elephants had been seduced on board the African transports by Pompey with a promise that they would not be ill-used—that now they were appealing to the gods. By loud angry shouts the mob had expressed its disapproval of the slaughter, until finally the hunt had been abandoned and the still living elephants, amid great applause, had been driven out of the Circus.

In the spring of 55, the beginning of his fourth year in Gaul, Cæsar hears that at the invitation of the Belgians the Germans living across the Lower Rhine are migrating to the territory south of the river depopulated by him in his campaign against the Belgian confederacy. In numbers this migration is said to be even larger than the one led by Ariovistus.

He goes to the Ardennes, where envoys of the tribes meet him, the Germans having already crossed the Rhine. He tells them that no matter whether the Belgians want them to come or not, it is his order that they return where they came from. Then, when the envoys have departed, he follows with his army until only twelve miles from the German encampment, situated on the isthmus formed by the confluence of the Meuse and the Rhine.

He has the ground reconnoitred, for his promise to the envoys that he will give the tribes plenty of time in which to leave Gaul means nothing—his object in marching towards the camp has been to find a pretext for another successful war.

He rides forward in person with the scouts. From the hill-top which the Romans take as their observation post the German encampment can be seen stretching away along the isthmus. In it are nearly half a million people. His eye gleams as it rests on the tapering strip of land hemmed in by the two rivers. He imagines the Barbarian camp suddenly attacked from the wide end of the wedge. He sees the Barbarians flying in thousands down the isthmus, with the land, growing narrower, huddling the fleeing crowds ever closer together, pressing them tighter and tighter, until finally at that glittering spot ahead of him where the Meuse and the Rhine unite to form a single stream, the point of the human wedge is pushed off the land into the water.

His quick march has put the Germans in a panic. Again they send envoys. Their own land has been occupied by tribes who for years have been pressing on them from the north—they beg the Roman general for three days' time in which to find where to go. Cæsar says he will give them twenty-four hours. No sooner have the envoys gone than he devises his pretext for war. He knows that there will be many among the younger hot-blooded Germans in the camp who will bitterly resent the intolerance of his latest order. By what right, they will surely ask, do the Romans dictate affairs in Gaul more than four hundred miles away from their province? He therefore sends out a body of cavalry with orders to approach as close as possible to the German camp and, while not themselves attacking, to goad the Barbarians by the general insolence of their manner into an engagement.

Later in the day the news spreads quickly through the Roman camp that the Barbarians, ignoring the twenty-four hours' agreement, have treacherously fallen upon the cavalry advance guard, killing seventy-four legionaries.

He harangues his soldiers on the perfidiousness of the Barbarians. In the morning the German camp is to be attacked. But when morning comes, accustomed as he is to fortune smiling on him, there occurs an event which takes his breath away —*the chiefs of all the German tribes appear at the Roman camp in a body to apologize for the hotheadedness of the warriors who had attacked the Romans the day before!*

Cæsar listens to their apologies, smiles, and seems to forgive. But he says he must detain the chiefs in his camp as a guarantee that the same outrage will not again occur. Under the mask of equanimity triumphant thoughts whirl madly through his brain. Fate having delivered the German chiefs into his hands, *and with the river to help him,* should he not within the next few hours achieve a victory so glorious that all his previous ones will pale into insignificance beside it?

He marches with his army against the Barbarian camp. The leaderless Germans flee in panic when the Roman cavalry suddenly emerges from the forest and comes thundering down on the wagons.

Behind the cavalry is the infantry, deployed over the country like a great drag-net. Down the isthmus goes the stampede. Crazed with fear, men, women and children rush madly away from the horror that follows behind leaving the ground in its wake a shambles of dead and dying, the tree-trunks spattered with blood.

Suddenly the van of the fleeing thousands sees ahead of it *water*—desperately, but too late, realizing the trap in which it is caught, it tries to turn back—the swords of the legionaries, rising and falling in the rear, press the horde forward into the confluence of the two rivers, until, with the exception of the chiefs detained in the Roman camp, and a few thousand survivors who escape drowning, this second great German migration has become like the first, extinct.

The survivors find refuge across the river in Westphalia. Cæsar orders the German tribe sheltering them, to give them up. The Sigambri refuse. His chance to cross the Rhine, to show the Barbarians how far-reaching is his arm, has come. The forest rings with the axes of the legionaries. In ten days a bridge is built, across which he marches his army.

But, to his disappointment, the Sigambri have not awaited his coming. While the bridge was being built they had collected their possessions and fled into the north. The summer is nearly over—what remains of it he wishes to employ otherwise than in pursuing them through their forests. Having, therefore, "remained in their territories long enough to burn all their villages and houses, and to cut down all their corn," and having "spent altogether eighteen days beyond the Rhine, and thinking he had advanced far enough to serve both honor and interest," he returns into Gaul, cutting down the bridge behind him.

9

It is the mysterious island lying off the west coast of Gaul that he wishes to visit before the summer is over. In a single year to be the first Roman general to cross the Rhine, and also to go to Britain—how Rome will ring with his exploits when this news reaches it!

Since his first year in Gaul he has been curious about this island where the men's skins are reported to be blue, and which is said to abound in gold mines, and with pearls. Now he has a legitimate excuse for invading it. For, like the Sigambri across the Rhine, the island has been guilty of the crime of giving refuge to the wretched homeless survivors of the massacres perpetrated by the Roman army in Gaul during the four years Cæsar has been governor.

He hurries from the Rhine to the French coast. The fleet that defeated the Veneti has been brought up from Brittany to take across the expeditionary force. But his fear of the ocean returns when he stands on the shore of the Atlantic. He stares westward across this stormy sea, so different in its cold forbidding aspect from the blue Mediterranean. The mystery in which the island is wrapped makes him, now that he is ready to sail for it, uneasy also.

"For neither does any one except merchants generally go thither, nor even to them was any portion of it known, except the sea-coast and those parts which are opposite to Gaul. Therefore, after having called up to him the merchants from all parts, he could learn neither what was the size of the island, nor what or how numerous were the nations which inhabited it, nor what system of war they followed, nor what customs they used, nor what harbors were convenient for a great number of large ships."

Conflicting with the desire to be the first Roman to land in Britain is fear of the unknown. In the same way that he appointed Decimus Brutus commander of his fleet, so he now decides to let a subordinate run the initial risk. He sends Caius Volusenus, one of his lieutenants, over with a ship of war to briefly explore the near coast of the island.

Volusenus is gone five days. When he returns he has little information to give Cæsar about the island, as he had thought it unwise to go ashore, but he has found a possible landing place, and the fact that he has made the round trip without mishap gives his commander confidence. Having sent messages to the Britons by Gallic ships that he is coming not as an enemy but as a friend, Cæsar sets sail with eighty warships, carrying two legions, and eighteen transports on which are the cavalry mounts.

Following the custom of his land marches to travel whenever possible under cover of darkness he starts his journey about midnight. The night is clear, with the moon approaching fullness. Fine weather, with a mild westerly wind blowing, has been chosen for the sailing, but as soon as the land is well behind the legionaries are ill at ease. Though they have been in Gaul several years, they seem to notice for the first time, now that they are on shipboard with nothing to do but to stare out into the night, how different is this northern sky to the familiar one of Italy. They see different stars, the moon too looks different. To quiet their uneasiness they try to talk. The conversations are troubled, and die away.

But the sound of the sea never ceases. The rising and falling of the ships, the vista of dark water stretching away in all directions, steadily increases the nervousness of the legionaries. The unfamiliar environment brings them to the verge of a panic like that which disorganized the army on its first march against the Germans.

They miss the substantial feeling of *terra firma*. On this treacherous fluid heaving under their feet they lose the sense of superiority which on land their industry with shovel and mattock gives them—the sea itself is hostile—in case of trouble there can be no seizing of their digging tools and intrenching themselves snugly behind the walls and ditch of a neat Roman camp.

Cæsar shares his soldiers' disquietude. Like them he cannot sleep. He stands on deck caught up in a strange mood of loneliness. It is not remorse for the monstrous reign of terror he has established in Gaul, for the hundreds of thousands killed by his soldiers and the equally large number made homeless since he has been governor, for he has the Roman viewpoint towards the Barbarians—they are no better than animals, and their sufferings mean nothing. Nor, as he looks up at the innumerable stars in the sky, is he troubled by any superstition that these may be the eyes of gods looking down at him, for he has remained and always will remain essentially irreligious. It is a sudden sense of his distance from Rome that disturbs him, a nameless fear of the alien depths of space above him, of the ocean restless, unstable, shifting, a dread of the darkness, the Unknown, the Infinite.

The sky begins to lighten. Shadows take shape in the darkness ahead. The vague fears of Cæsar and his legionaries vanish as over Gaul the sun rises.

Nearby, to westward, are white cliffs—the chalk cliffs of Dover. Though nothing moves, something strange about the outlines of these cliffs makes the legionaries crowd to the bows of the ships to stare.

And as the Roman fleet moves closer to the shore of the

island and they are able to see details, the mysterious terrors
of the dark sea voyage return to them suddenly for a moment
in the bright light of day. For the cliffs are lined with people
staring down at them. On every height are painted warriors
on horseback and in chariots. Silently and enigmatically these
watch the approach of the Roman fleet . . . rigid as sentinels
who have been awaiting its arrival the whole night long. . . .

They give no answer when the Romans, through interpre-
ters, shout up what Cæsar had said in his written messages—
that the Romans have come not as foes but as friends.

As the natives seem determined to oppose his landing,
Cæsar, at the advice of Volusenus, takes the fleet a short distance up the coast to where this is more open. But when the
fleet arrives at the beach selected by Volusenus it is found to
be lined with the cavalry and charioteers of the Britons who
have followed along the land.

The ships anchor as close to shore as possible. The legionaries are then ordered to leap into the water and drive back
the Barbarians. But once again, for all their good discipline,
the Roman soldiers, dismayed by the sight of the tatooed
Britons riding their horses into the waves, and dreading the
water, are on the point of mutiny.

Their officers urge them on, but they continue to hold back.
Cæsar, however, has measured the odds. He is sure that the
uncouth Britons, formidable though they may be in appearance, can be no match for his eight thousand trained soldiers,
once these are through the waist-deep water and on shore. Besides the transports carrying the legionaries he has a number
of ships equipped with catapults and rock-throwing engines,
and with these he forces the natives to retreat while his army
makes its landing.

Having driven back the Britons the legionaries immediately
set to work building a camp. Other parties raid the countryside for food and forage. The Britons, meanwhile, amazed
at the quickness with which the Roman camp springs into existence, and looking upon the invaders with their terrible war

engines as more gods than men, have decided to make any terms with Cæsar that he desires. They send envoys to him. These he lectures severely, telling them that after their treacherous attempts to keep him from landing, when they knew he was coming as a friend, he would not be doing wrong if he laid waste their whole country.

He asks them why the Britons have given refuge to his enemies from Gaul, and why they have not obeyed him when he has sent messages to them ordering them to surrender these Gauls. Do they wish to be called friends of Rome and have extended to them all the privileges which the term implies, or do they mean to be enemies? Terrible to her foes, Rome is a great mother to her allies. To become one of these, the Britons must promise never again to shelter rebellious Gallic chiefs, they must deliver up to him those now in the island, and as a guarantee of good faith they must give him the children of all their own principal chiefs as hostages for him to take back with him into Gaul.

The envoys go back to their tribes. Cæsar is well satisfied with the interview. From their manner he has guessed there will be no further resistance. Like all Barbarians who for the first time enter a Roman camp, they have been awed by their strange surroundings. He guesses rightly that they look on the Romans as superhuman beings.

And his own soldiers have regained their confidence. The Britons, like the Germans, having been proven to possess no war machine comparable with that of the Romans, are now to them no different from any of the other despised Barbarians.

It is Cæsar's fourth day in Britain. The envoys left the camp in the afternoon. When night comes, he enters his tent and goes to sleep feeling that already, in so short a space of time, he has made the island his.

Midnight approaches.

A round golden moon shines down on the Roman camp. And suddenly, as though driven by a tempest—though the air is quite still—great waves begin to break on the beach near the camp.

They crash down with thunderous force. Like furious hands they reach up for the Roman warships that have been dragged up on to the beach and dash these to pieces. The part of the fleet that is riding at anchor they tear loose and likewise destroy.

Bewildered, the awakened legionaries run to and fro in the camp, scarcely able to believe that this mysterious destruction of their fleet is not part of a terrible nightmare.

The panic spreads to the officers, to Cæsar himself. Little as he puts faith in the supernatural, this strange storm on a calm night inspires him with an irrational terror—what other explanation can there be than the one of the legionaries that it is the work of an angry deity who has the island under his protection and is wrathful at the Roman invasion?

From the nearby heights the Britons watch the Roman fleet being destroyed. They see the consternation in the Roman camp. And a suspicion enters their minds that these little dark men who are thrown into such dismay by what to them is a quite natural event cannot after all be gods. For would gods be so ignorant as not to know that off the coast of Britain the full moon brings a high tide and heavy swell? Even they, who are only Barbarians, are aware of this. Had the fleet been theirs, such a catastrophe would never have happened. They would have known it was necessary to drag the ships higher up on to the beach when the moon became full, and to anchor those in the water further off shore. They watch the frightened legionaries running helplessly about on the beach while the waves complete the destruction of the fleet. *The Romans did not know!*

In the morning the Romans, terror-stricken—"for there were no other ships in which they could be conveyed back, and all things which are of service in repairing vessels were wanting, and corn for the winter had not been provided in those places, because it was understood by all that they would certainly winter in Gaul,"—hurry to see by daylight the damage done the fleet. They find ships piled one against the other along the beach; some have been destroyed beyond repair, others are in a less hopeless condition. But the morale of the troops has been broken. Cæsar decides to get out of the island as soon as possible. He sets the soldiers to work repairing the less damaged ships with the timber and brass taken from the ones completely wrecked, and sends to Gaul for more ships. Since the disaster to the fleet the Britons have again opened hostilities; they make several attacks on the camp, and he hears that in the interior of the island a large force is gathering against him. . . . He will leave Briton now, but return the following year with a much larger army to complete its conquest.

So as soon as the damaged ships have been repaired, and enough new ones have arrived, he crosses the channel back to Gaul. Before going over the Alps for the winter in his usual manner, he sends messages to the Britons reminding them of the hostages promised, but these messages produce little effect, only two tribes sending hostages.

Again he leaves Labienus in charge of the army, commanding him, in preparation for next year's raid on Britain, to build as many new ships as possible during the winter, and to have the old ones thoroughly repaired. Then he hurries south. He has written to Rome telling of his tremendous victory over the second great German army, of the bridge across the Rhine, of his trip to Britain. Clodius is busy exciting the mob to a frenzy of enthusiasm for the general who can accomplish such wonders in a single year.

On that frontier line between Hither Gaul and the north of Italy which he may not cross as long as he is governor, he hears echoes of the wild jubilation in the capital. He is showered with congratulatory letters; each day more carriages leave Rome bound for his province. And pressure on the Senate from that idle greedy rabble profiting most by the miseries of the Barbarians—every month luxurious new villas are springing up in the countryside around Rome and along the Bay of Naples, the property of once penniless Romans made wealthy by Cæsar's generosity with his Gallic spoils—brings him the unprecedented official recognition of a twenty-day thanks-giving.

10

All winter he looks forward to his second expedition to Britain in the spring. When he re-crosses the Alps in April he finds that Labienus has six hundred transports ready for him.

While the fleet is being assembled at Boulogne he tours western Gaul to make certain all the tribes are quiet. He passes through a country desolate everywhere with black remains of burnt villages standing out as landmarks of his campaigns. But Gaul seems quiet. Nowhere does he find any evidence to indicate that a general uprising is planned. The tribes show little love for the invaders, but they seem to be making no attempt to concentrate their forces at any single point. His policy of depopulating Gaul of its patriots, leaving only those too weak to resist or who can be bought over, seems to be working out well; he has slaughtered the natives in such a whole-sale manner that with his ten legions of professional soldiers he feels that he will have no difficulty in keeping the whole territory between the Alps and the Atlantic firmly under control. He returns to Boulogne confident he can make the second trip to Britain in safety.

The embarkation is held up by contrary winds. While waiting for fine weather he increases the number of Gallic hostages he is taking to Britain with him, for to safeguard his base in Gaul he is compelling all the hostile chiefs to accompany him on the trip. Among these is the Aeduan chief, Dumnorix, who, from Cæsar's first appearance in Gaul, has been one of his most bitter enemies—again and again Cæsar has tried to buy his friendship, but always unsuccessfully.

Dumnorix seizes the opportunity afforded by the delay in starting to induce some of the other Gallic chiefs to make with him a desperate attempt to regain freedom. One morning when

Cæsar is in good humor as the wind has veered to the east so that the expedition can now start, news is brought him that Dumnorix, taking with him some of the Gallic auxiliaries, has escaped from the camp. He frowns. Has a pursuit party been sent out? He orders a second larger party to leave the camp immediately. In a loud voice he tells the commanding officer to bring back Dumnorix dead or alive. He instructs the officer privately to be sure that Dumnorix is killed.

The day draws to a close. While his face gives no sign of his irritability, he is furious that the embarkation fleet has been held up. But with Dumnorix alive on the continent, can he feel safe in Britain?

Towards evening the Roman cavalry returns, and a bloody head is flung at Cæsar's feet. He feigns indignation with his soldiers for having killed the chief. But inwardly he smiles. For now, free from anxiety, he can sail.

Two days later, at sunset, he leaves Boulogne with eight hundred ships, carrying twenty-five thousand foot-soldiers, and three thousand cavalry.

This time the white chalk cliffs of Dover are deserted, the Britons, who have heard of the departure of Cæsar's immense plundering expedition, having all fled into the interior of the island. Leaving six thousand legionaries to guard the camp on the coast, Cæsar sets out with the rest of his army for the interior. He hopes to draw the natives into one of those large pitched battles where the Roman legion functions at its best as a machine. To induce the islanders to abandon their guerilla warfare he sends his cavalry out in every direction to burn villages, destroy crops, and kill cattle.

And the Britons fall into the trap set for them. They concentrate to resist the Roman advance, barricading themselves behind felled trees. The Romans, bringing up their battering rams and catapults, easily take the camp by assault, and cut the army of the Britons to pieces.

But just when Cæsar is congratulating himself on the victory a messenger arrives from the Roman camp on the coast with the news that once again the Roman fleet has been destroyed by a storm.

He rides back to camp. This time it was not the high tide, but a sudden tempest that had wrecked the fleet of transports. Forty of these are completely destroyed. He sends word to Labienus, whom he has left in Boulogne with two legions, to have new ones built, then rejoins his army. The legionaries crowd around him, all discipline forgotten in the superstitious fear with which this second catastrophe has filled them. He tells them the reports of the damage were greatly exaggerated, in a few weeks the fleet will be intact again. The march forward into the interior recommences.

Each day he hopes to emerge from the forest into a more prosperous country, but the wilderness continues to hem in his army. He reaches the Thames, where the tribes of the interior, combined under the leadership of Cassivellaunus, are drawn up on the further bank, confident that the Roman army will not dare attempt the crossing. But to the legionaries who have bridged the Rhine, crossing the Thames is a small matter. When he realizes that the river is no obstacle to the Romans Cassivellaunus falls back without a battle to St. Albans, the principal town of the Cassi, of which he is chief.

This is situated deep in the forest, with marshes on every side. The Britons cannot believe that the Romans, with their small knowledge of the island, will dare to follow so far inland. To St. Albans, as a safe retreat, they have driven all their cattle, and carried all their possessions.

The Roman army marches on, making its own roads, building bridges, leaving behind it a smooth highway through the forest, with milestones marking the distance. One day the tramp of the legions is heard in St. Albans.

The town is taken, and the Romans kill all the cattle that they do not need for their own commissary. The Britons, who have fled to the marshes, starve here until Cassivelaunus sends envoys to the camp asking for peace.

In St. Albans the legionaries impatiently await orders for

the return march. Britain is to them a dark and dismal country. Where are the great rich cities they had expected to loot? At night they feel they are camped in the very heart of darkness. The weather is growing cooler. From the great elms and oaks, autumn leaves flutter down through the forest. A white mist shrouds the marshes.

In Gaul, even when they had reached the Atlantic, they had the feeling of solid land behind them across which they could march back to Italy; here, with winter approaching, they become increasingly conscious of the water which separates them from the mainland.

Cæsar, hearing their murmurs, reluctantly abandons the attempt to penetrate the interior further. His expedition has been only an empty gesture. He has found neither gold nor pearls. His only booty consists of several thousand prisoners —who on account of their blue skins, dyed with woad, will be interesting as curiosities to the Roman burgesses—and some British chariots, which will also be exhibited in his triumph.

The new transports sent over by Labienus have arrived. As the white cliffs of Dover recede, he stands in the stern of his flag-ship, watching the mysterious island, which has so bitterly disappointed his hopes, grow smaller and smaller to westward, until it finally vanishes.

When he lands in Gaul a courier from Rome gives him a letter from Pompey telling him that his daughter Julia is dead.

PART 4

Vercingetorix, The Civil War and Cleopatra

I

THE news of his daughter's death comes as a great blow to Cæsar. Who will be Pompey's next wife? He is not yet ready for a rupture, and Julia had been invaluable in holding Pompey's friendship. He feels it is vital that he cross the Alps immediately and see Pompey personally. Perhaps he can persuade him to marry again into the Cæsar family. And he himself will agree to divorce Calpurnia in order to marry Pompey's only daughter, now the wife of Faustus Sulla, son of the Dictator.

His anxiety to return to his southern province increases when this same year the only child of Pompey and Julia dies, and as a further calamity, his own mother, Aurelia.

But the expedition to Britain is now to be paid for dearly. Gaul, during his absence, has been planning a general uprising. The murder of Dumnorix had determined the tribes to make a concerted effort to annihilate the Roman invaders in case Cæsar was not—as they prayed—drowned in a storm on the way to Britain, or killed on the island. If he returns unharmed, then the uprising shall take place as soon as he has gone back over the Alps.

Cæsar's spies warn him when he returns from Britain of this restlessness throughout Gaul. They tell him the Germans have been invited to come across the Rhine and help in the rebellion. They emphasize how the hopes for the success of the rebellion are all based on the belief that he himself will be absent when it takes place, having gone south as usual to Hither Gaul. For Cæsar the situation is made worse by the fact that this winter the legions will have to be quartered at considerable distances apart from each other—the harvest has been poor, as the Gauls, weary of planting crops for the Romans either to seize or to destroy, are living miserably as best they can without farming the land, the Roman reign of terror having driven them to seek safety in the mountains and marshes.

Much as he longs to, he dare not leave Gaul. His eight legions having been placed in winter quarters in as many different camps, he pretends to leave as usual, but secretly remains in the camp of Trebonius—another of his generals who ten years later will figure prominently in the assassination. Meanwhile the Gauls and Germans, believing he has crossed the Alps, are preparing to put their plans into execution. The first Roman camp to be attacked will be the one nearest the Rhine—Induciomarus, the leader of the rebellion, is trusting that if the Roman reputation for invincibility can once be broken down by the capture of a single camp, then those states in Gaul which still fear the Romans too much to take part in the rebellion will join the confederacy and the seven other camps can be likewise destroyed in the winter before Cæsar's return.

One day in midwinter a messenger arrives at the camp of Trebonius. He comes from the camp at Charleroi, a hundred and twenty miles away, commanded by Cicero's brother, Quintus. Cicero, it seems, is in desperate need of help. For several days his camp has been besieged by a large Barbarian army.

Cæsar marches north quickly, arriving in time to raise the siege. That the camp has been attacked with a determination never before exhibited by the Barbarians is evident from the heaps of dead lying around the wall. In Cicero's legion not one man in ten is unwounded.

Following his usual custom, Cæsar mounts an improvised turf rostrum, and addresses the legionaries. He praises their valor, and he tells Quintus Cicero that his gallant defense of the camp will cement for all time that friendship he has always felt for him and his brother. But the tremendous losses of the Barbarians, the persistence they had shown in assaulting the camp, puzzle him. They seem to have been animated by a confidence in their ability to take the camp by storm that refused to weaken even in face of the appalling slaughter inflicted upon them by the legionaries. What gave them this confidence? Was it only the belief that Cæsar was hundreds of miles away across the Alps?

An officer who has been examining some of the Barbarian prisoners breaks excitedly into the presence of Cæsar. One of the prisoners has confessed that a few weeks ago the Roman camp at Aduatuca, near modern Liège, seventy miles to the north-east of Cicero's camp, was stormed by the Germans, and every soldier in the legion killed.

After the first shock of the news has passed, Cæsar sees it not altogether as a catastrophe. The legion commanded by Cotta and Sabinus which has been wiped out was not, as he first believed, defeated in an assault on the camp. It had unwisely, at the advice of the German chief Ambiorix, who had professed friendship for the Romans, marched out to join Cicero at Charleroi, Ambiorix having come to the camp with information relating to the contemplated general uprising throughout Gaul, when the Roman camps were to be destroyed one after another. As soon as the legion was on the march the Germans, and several Gallic tribes, had made the surprise attack which had ended in its annihilation.

There are elements in this disaster which Cæsar realizes he can turn to profit. He can play up the treachery of the Barbarians in a manner that will justify his past and future cruelties. He now has an excuse to deal more mercilessly than ever with the tribes that will not submit to Roman rule.

Clodius can so emphasize the perfidiousness of the Barbarians who lured the legionaries from the safety of their camp and then massacred them, that his enemies in Rome— Cato at the time of his own abominable treachery in holding the German chiefs in his camp, and then falling on the helpless tribes, had risen in the Senate and urged that instead of voting Cæsar a twenty-day thanksgiving the Republic should hand him over to the Germans for them to do what they wanted with—will have to be silent. Also his repeated victories without a single serious reverse have introduced doubts whether these huge "armies" he constantly defeats are really armies at all. Pamphlets and satires are being circulated in which he is alluded to as "Great Cæsar," and "The Unique General"; and in which he figures as a pirate committing atrocious crimes in the name of the Republic. But now four thousand Roman soldiers have been killed in a single battle with the Barbarians. These soldiers, however, were under the command, not of Cæsar, but of subordinates. Cæsar's reports then will have to be accepted as true—Rome actually *has* again and again been in peril of a great Barbarian invasion—his Gallic wars *have* really been conducted in defense of the Republic—the Barbarians *are* dangerous enemies who have only been held at bay by Cæsar's matchless generalship—when Cæsar is absent his officers are powerless to achieve the same victories.

To counteract the effect on the morale of his soldiers produced by the disaster of Aduatuca he stirs them up to vengeance. He goes into mourning, letting his hair and beard grow long, and swearing they shall not be cut until he has avenged the dead legionaries who have fallen not in honorable war, but were treacherously murdered—until every man, woman and child of the tribes which took part in the massacre are killed.

He raises two more legions in Italy, and borrows one from Pompey. With these more than filling the gap in his army left by the loss of Sabinus's legion, he, in the spring, commences to retaliate.

He soaks western Gaul in blood. One tribe after another is either put to the sword, or sold into slavery. The Nervii, the Treveri, the Senones, the Carnutes and the Menapi are all exterminated, and their lands laid waste. All day the smoke from burning towns and villages streams away over the forest, all night the horizon is ringed with fires.

Once again he crosses the Rhine to carry the Roman reign of terror into Germany, returning to Gaul only when he has destroyed all the villages along the river and the Germans have fled into the interior as far as the Harz mountains.

The Eburones, the tribes which had taken the most active part in the destruction of Sabinus's legion, he leaves until the last, finally surrounding their country with ten legions and five thousand cavalry, while issuing an invitation to every tribe which had not joined in the uprising to take part in the hunt of this outlawed tribe and help pillage their land in concert with the Roman legionaries. For weeks the Eburones are hunted like wild beasts, the cordon of legionaries tightening, and the cavalry scouring the forest, until the sixty thousand members of the tribe have been killed.

And the massacre of Aduatuca has also given him an opportunity to *formally* change the status of the Gauls. The captured chiefs are no longer treated as prisoners of war, *but as rebels guilty of high treason against the Roman Republic.* There are solemn trials of one chief after another,—the most important of these being Acco, the leader of the Carnutes,— each of whom, found guilty, is beheaded by Roman lictors.

Thus the rule of the *fasces* is ceremoniously ushered by Cæsar into Gaul—the natives who persist in fighting for liberty after this will be considered traitors instead of patriots, since as subjects they no longer have the right to make war on Rome.

So at the close of the summer Cæsar comes out of mourning. The sacredness of the lives of Roman citizens has, he hopes, been sufficiently impressed on the Barbarians. He has a stronger army than ever before. He can this winter leave Gaul in safety again and arrange to see Pompey in the north of Italy.

He is preparing to cross the Alps when he receives news that Crassus and his entire army of seven legions—which he had taken with him to Syria at the expiration of his consulship— have been destroyed by the Parthians in the East.

2

The fat millionaire, whose lifelong ambition had been to

He lives in a voluptuous paradise.

lead a triumph in Rome for the conquest of the Far East, has had his army annihilated at the first battle.

He is dead, and Publius is dead—the bones of twenty thousand legionaries whiten the Mesopotamian desert, while ten thousand others have been made prisoners by the Parthians.

Crassus had left Rome to plunder the East as Cæsar is plundering Gaul. There had been opposition in Rome to his declaring war on the Parthians unprovoked. Attempts to keep him from going to Syria as governor had been made. Cæsar, through Clodius, had given Crassus his support. As he rode out of Rome, his intention to involve the Republic in more wars in the East being known, he had been publicly cursed by a tribune of the people, and unfavorable auspices for his expedition invoked.

But fat Crassus is not disturbed. He sees himself as a second Alexander setting out to conquer the East. As soon as he reaches Syria he begins plundering the temples. With his seven legions, four thousand slingers and archers, and four thousand cavalry, he sees himself as invincible.

He lets his army wander on in a vaguely north-east direction, content to know that he is headed in a general way for that great country of inexhaustible wealth which lies beyond the mountains over which the sun rises. He is intoxicated with the novelty of being able to rob directly instead of having to employ the more tedious ordinary business methods.

He weighs with his own hands the gold and silver vessels taken out of the temples of Derceto at Hierapolis Bambyce and of Jehovah at Jerusalem. He levies immense new tributes from tribes already crushed by the weight of the indemnity exacted by Pompey. He crosses the Euphrates and marches eastward towards Parthia.

He has paid as little attention to the Parthian protests that no state of war exists between Parthia and Rome as to those of the smaller Syrian tribes he has plundered. Cæsar, with no authority from the Republic, had commenced his Gallic wars; Gabinius, acting for Pompey, had crossed the Egyptian border, and taken the first Roman army to the Nile to reinstate

Ptolemy, with equally little authority; now Crassus, similarly, makes his own war with the Parthians.

The latter, as the Roman army continues to advance, decide to use guile. They send Crassus a guide—an Arab prince, named Abgarus, who pretends to be an enemy of the Parthians—he advises the Romans not to march on Parthia by the circuitous route of Armenia as they intend doing, but to take the short-cut across the Mesopotamian desert—only a forced march by this quickest route will enable the Roman army to catch up with the Parthians who have already evacuated their western provinces and are carrying away with them all their gold and silver.

The thought of all this treasure that may escape him is too much for Crassus. He orders the direction of the march to be changed, and the Roman army, led by Abgarus, turns away from the Euphrates . . .

Weighted down with their heavy armor, the Roman infantry stumbles on day after day through the deep sand of the desert. At last the first Parthian horsemen are seen in the distance. Abgarus is sent forward with his Arabs by Crassus to reconnoitre. The Parthian squadron vanishes over the sand-hills, Abgarus apparently in hot pursuit. Hours pass, and he does not return. Finally the Roman army has to continue its march without him.

And suddenly, from all sides of the desert, the Parthian army, which has been collecting on the horizon, closes in. To give the impression of a ragged horde that can easily be defeated they have covered their armor with skins of animals. The Romans, confident of victory, go forward to meet them. As the legions approach, the Parthians pull off the skins and appear before them in coats of shining mail.

Before the legionaries can recover from their surprise the Parthians are attacking them furiously. In previous wars with the Romans they have learnt the folly of attempting to defeat the legions with infantry. Their present army consists exclusively of cavalry; the mass of the troops being mounted archers, the rest cavalry armed with long lances. To disorganize the legions the Parthians gallop up and down creating clouds of dust. Publius, leading a charge of the Roman cavalry, gets separated from the main body of the army, and his cavalry detachment is cut to pieces. The Parthians gallop with his head to where the legions are making their stand, and, jeering, hold it up on the point of a lance for Crassus to see.

Night comes, and they gallop away. Crassus sits dazed. His eyes stare at the ground, his immense body seems to have lost the power to move. He sees only the bleeding head of his son, hears only the derisive shouts of the mailed Parthians. His officers have to take command. They march the remnant of the army to the town of Carrhae. Here Crassus pulls himself together somewhat. But, though the town is fortified and has a Roman garrison, he will not remain in it,—terrified at the thought of being so close to the desert where two thirds of his legionaries have already been destroyed, he leads out the survivors and tries by forced marches to reach the Armenian mountains—on the way he is again surrounded by the Parthian army and this time himself perishes with the rest of his army.

To celebrate their great victory, the Parthians, so many of whose people have in the past been dragged captive through the streets of Rome, and then strangled at the foot of the Capitol, give a mock Roman triumph. One of the fattest of the Roman prisoners is dressed up to resemble Crassus. He has to ride in a triumphal car from the sides of which hang the heads of the Roman officers. And in his hand, as the car passes through crowds of jeering and hooting Parthians, he is made to hold, and to appear to be reading, one of the obscene romances of which several hundred had been found by the Parthians among Crassus's personal belongings, and which he was taking with him for the entertainment of himself and his officers during the years he intended to conquer the Far East.

3

The death of Crassus is a serious loss to Cæsar. The fat

capitalist had been jealous enough of Pompey to side with Cæsar when there were internal quarrels within the triumvirate. Now he will have to rely altogether on Clodius. Since Julia's death, the personal relation existing between her husband and her father has been broken—to Cæsar's mortification Pompey has made no effort to have his daughter divorce Faustus Sulla in order to marry Cæsar, and Pompey himself has not married again into the Cæsar family; his new wife is the daughter of Quintus Metullus Scipio.

The annihilation of Crassus and his army occurred in June. Cæsar, back in Cisalpine Gaul for the winter of 53–52 after taking revenge for the massacre of Aduatuca the winter before, tries hard to postpone the inevitable split between Pompey and himself. But on the thirteenth of January there occurs for him an unprecedented calamity—Clodius, his faithful henchman, is killed by his rival Milo in a brawl on the Appian Way.

The details of his death are brought to Cæsar in his southern province. The two rivals had met by accident on the road near Rome one night. Their attendants had started to fight. Clodius, wounded in the shoulder by a sword-cut, had sought refuge in a nearby house. Milo, thinking the moment a favorable one for getting rid of his rival, had had him dragged out and killed. His body, left lying in the road, had been found the next morning by a passing Roman patrician and brought in to the city.

Each day brings more startling news. Rome is in a state of anarchy. When Clodius's body was exhibited in the Forum, the mob, believing the murder of their favorite to have been premeditated on the part of the Senate, broke into the Senate-house, made a pyre of the benches and seats, and burnt the body here. The fire not only burnt down the senate-house but also several nearby temples. Pompey, lying outside the city with the legions meant for Spain, has been called into Rome to restore law and order. He has been offered the dictatorship. This he has declined, but he has allowed himself to be elected consul without a colleague.

Furious at the death of his henchman, Cæsar, in the interval between the burning of the senate-house, and the offering of the dictatorship to Pompey, meditates marching on Rome with his army. But will his troops follow him? Has he yet a strong enough case against the Republic to assure him of his soldiers' sympathies?

And at this moment news of vital importance comes over the Alps—the Gauls, led by a young chief named Vercingetorix, believing that with Clodius, Cæsar has lost his only ally in Rome, that his enemies in the capital will now be able to effect his recall, are planning an insurrection more widespread than any of the previous ones.

Shall he take his army to Rome, or cross the Alps to fight Vercingetorix?

While he is still undecided which to do, he hears that Pompey's army is in occupation of the capital, and of Pompey's election to the sole consulship. He realizes that the opportunity for seizing Rome under pretext of restoring law and order has passed.

But he writes angrily to Pompey that the murderer of Clodius must not be acquitted. Pompey, afraid to challenge Cæsar at the moment, agrees that Milo shall either be put to death or banished. He also suggests to Cæsar that he give up his governorship of the two Gauls, and return to Rome, to become his consular colleague. In this apparently generous offer Cæsar discerns a trap—he knows too well how quickly Roman generals are pushed into the background once they have resigned command of their armies. He writes back refusing the offer.

Pompey may be all-powerful now, but the day shall come, Cæsar resolves, when, the trouble in Gaul over, he will be able to challenge his right to supreme power in Rome. Brooding darkly on Clodius's death he hurries back across the Alps to crush the insurrection of Vercingetorix before it gets a foothold in Gaul.

Vercingetorix, like Induciomarus—who during the previous uprising had been killed in a cavalry skirmish with Labienus—feels it vital to strike while Cæsar is still south of the Alps.

A young Gaul, thirty-three years of age, and chief of the Arvernian tribe, he has seen Gaul under the iron heel of Cæsar for six years. Before Cæsar's arrival, Roman governors had come and gone, with Gaul beyond the province scarcely aware of their existence. No one of the proconsuls had stood out as a personality; their names were not even remembered; they were only Romans in each of whose persons was invested for the time being the power of Rome. Now the situation is reversed—it is Rome that has faded into the background, and Cæsar's name that looms up in the foreground gigantic and terrible. The Gauls tremble at the sound of it, and Vercingetorix knows that Cæsar's mere presence with any Roman army convinces his countrymen that a battle is lost before it has been fought.

But through the Roman traders who have followed in the wake of Cæsar's conquests the Gauls as far even as the Atlantic have become familiar with affairs in the capital. They know, as well as did Ariovistus, that Cæsar has many enemies in Rome. They have heard of his alliance with Pompey and Crassus—they hear of Crassus's death in the East, and the destruction of his army by the Parthians—of the rumored split between Pompey and Cæsar now that Cæsar's daughter is dead, and Pompey has re-married—of the killing of Clodius, and Pompey's present control of the capital. And Vercingetorix himself has been approached by agents of the senatorial party who assure him that the Roman people have given Cæsar no authority to make war on the Gauls; these tell how strenuously Cato opposed voting him a thanksgiving for the second massacre of the Germans; they paint Cæsar as an adventurer-general exploiting the Gauls for his own profit; they mention the immense sums he sends regularly to Rome to bribe magistrates, and tell how his party in the capital is made up entirely of the riff-raff of the city—all the worthless Romans that money can buy; they state that Cæsar's wars in Gaul are being conducted by him solely for the purpose of training a large army with which some day to return to Rome and make himself king.

And there surges through Vercingetorix as he listens an ungovernable fury against this smiling monster who with false
promises had duped the Arvernians into becoming his allies
when he first came to Gaul. For the Arvenians had been won
over by Cæsar's graciousness. They had put faith in his assurances that he was not leaving his Province for purposes of
conquest, but only to champion the rights of the small Gallic
nations. They had allowed themselves to be influenced by his
propaganda against the Germans. . . . Arvernian auxiliaries
have fought side by side with the Roman legions. . . . They
have helped Cæsar to conquer Gaul. . . . Before the eyes of
Vercingetorix there rises a dreadful picture of the havoc
wrought in Gaul by Cæsar, who during his six years as governor has killed over a million people, destroyed thousands of
towns and villages, laid the land waste in every direction.

His blood boils as he listens to stories of Cæsar's dissolute
private life. Who, ask the agents of the Senate stirring up the
young Gallic chief to revolt against Cæsar, have been his
companions and friends since childhood if not wastrels and
profligates? Clodius, Cæsar's lieutenant in Rome, had been
guilty of criminal intercourse with his three sisters. Mark Antony, long a friend of Cæsar, and now one of his generals in
Gaul, was for years as a young man a male prostitute who
hired himself out to the Roman millionaires. Cæsar himself
has been guilty of unnatural sexual crimes—Vercingetorix is
informed of the time when he was the favorite of the depraved
king of Bithynia, Nicomedes.

Is this the man who has censured some of the Gallic chiefs
for having more than one wife? The soul of Vercingetorix recoils from Cæsar's infamous hypocrisy. Cæsar, who, guilty of
every conceivable form of treachery himself, yet can lecture
the Gauls upon the subject of honor. Who seizes children as
hostages, yet solemnly pronounces sentence of death upon
Gauls who lay hands on Roman cavalry officers pillaging the
country for supplies, but called "ambassadors." Who, an enemy
of the Republic himself, has had the Gallic chief Acco, fighting for the liberty of his tribe, beheaded as a criminal guilty

of high treason against the Roman Republic. . . . Whose officers are said to have debauched many of the Barbarian boys seized as hostages.

Vercingetorix sees Gaul the prey of a band of monsters who win their battles not because they are braver than his country-men but because they are better armed, and have a superior military science. In the name of civilization they commit every atrocity. Yet they come from Rome, the world's cesspool of crime, viciousness and corruption. Will no patriot arise to throw off this intolerable Roman yoke?

Yes, he will be this patriot! And if he cannot supply the Gauls with the superior arms of the Romans he can at least get them to adopt the Roman methods of warfare. He will in-duce his countrymen to destroy their own harvests and burn their own villages so that the legions as they advance will find themselves in a land of famine. He will refuse to come to any pitched battle with the Roman infantry but harass it with cavalry. And meanwhile he will be teaching the Gauls how to intrench themselves in camps and to march and manœuvre in the formation of the Roman legion, so that while carrying on his guerilla warfare he will at the same time be training an army capable of some day taking the offensive against Cæsar.

He submits his plans to the other Gallic chiefs. All his eloquence is useless. They are willing to rise against the Ro-mans now while Cæsar is over the Alps, but, should the in-surrection fail, they say their peoples would never consent to take the drastic measures of destroying their own villages and crops suggested by Vercingetorix. They will fight under his leadership, but he must devise some other method of warfare.

All are optimistic that the Romans will have been driven out of Gaul before spring comes. For is not Rome on the brink of civil war? Gaul, say the chiefs, has seen Cæsar for the last time. There are rumors he has been captured by an army sent out by the Roman people, that he has been taken in chains to the capital. There are other rumors that he has already been put to death. In the Roman camps the legionaries are panic-

stricken now that they have lost their general. There will be
no need to adopt the terrible measures recommended by Vercingetorix. Cæsar will never return to Gaul, and before the
snow is off the ground the tribes will have fallen on the camps
separately and destroyed them.

But suddenly he is among them. He has crossed the Alps
in wintertime while the tribes are still making their plans. He
defeats them in several pitched battles, which against the advice of Vercingetorix they risk with the Roman infantry. Now
the chiefs, rather than lose Vercingetorix as their leader,—he
has refused to take part in any further war with the Romans
unless he can have the same supreme command over the Gallic army that Cæsar has over the Roman,—agree to the sacrifice.

And the Roman army, marching in pursuit of the fleeing
Gauls, sees night after night burning villages lighting up the
sky. As far as the Roman foraging parties can reach, the land
has been laid waste, and all food that could not be carried off
destroyed by the retreating army of Vercingetorix. Impotent
fury rages in the Roman camp. For the Barbarians have never
fought in this manner before. They have always been so reluctant to leave their homes and to see them injured that a
single Roman pillaging expedition could make a whole countryside sue for peace. Now, in their turn, they are starving the
Romans.

Cæsar, himself, is worried. Will this young chieftain be
willing to abandon even the larger towns such as Avaricum,
Gergovia, and Alesia? The whole of his own military success
in Gaul has been the result of inducing the Barbarians to concentrate their forces, which are then inevitably defeated with
tremendous losses by the Roman war machine. If Vercingetorix persists in guerilla warfare, what can the Romans, a
mere handful compared with the native population of Gaul,
accomplish? If the Gauls will not plant crops, where is his
food supply to come from? He cannot convert his legionaries
into farmers. He depends upon Gaul to support his troops.

Have his ruthless methods not sufficiently intimidated the

Gauls? To spread more terror, he again gives his officers orders to lay waste the countryside and massacre the Barbarians, but he is powerless. In this land he is marching through everything has already been destroyed, and the inhabitants have all fled.

He presses on towards Avaricum. Will Vercingetorix sacrifice the town, and cheat him of the opportunity of pillaging it and putting the defenders to the sword? He does not doubt the ability of his siege engines to break through the walls. But as each day's march only shows him more burnt villages he dreads finding Avaricum in flames. He knows what a bad moral effect this will have on his army, already disheartened by the desolate country being marched through. Their hopes are fixed on Avaricum which he has promised to let them plunder. Will he find it only a heap of ashes?

Meanwhile the Gauls, in their retreat, are nearing Avaricum. Vercingetorix has sent messengers to the town to tell of the Roman advance and to order that it be abandoned. The chiefs of the Biturige tribe serving under him remonstrate with him against including the capital of their country in the general burning of the smaller villages. The sacrifice is bitter but the young patriot leader insists it must be made. To defend the town would be making the mistake of concentrating his forces, and giving Cæsar the opportunity for certain victory.

Avaricum comes into sight. On three sides it has river and marsh—there is only a single narrow ridge along which it is vulnerable to assault. The chiefs of the Bituriges declare emphatically that the town is impregnable; for the inhabitants themselves to destroy it would be a monstrous crime. The town, they say, is well enough supplied with corn and provisions to stand a long siege. A meeting is held to decide the fate of the city.

And at this meeting the pleadings and threats of Vercingetorix are alike in vain—the Bituriges resolve, with or without the assistance of the allied tribes, to defend Avaricum against the Romans.

The Roman army, sixty thousand strong, approaches Avaricum.

Cæsar's scouts have sent back word that the town has not as yet been destroyed but he is uneasy until his own eyes supply him with proof; until he is looking at Avaricum, not in smoke and flames, but lying tranquil behind its wall in the afternoon sunlight.

He camps on the ridge. The legionaries, in good humor again now that they have reached their destination, set to work industriously preparing for the siege.

For a Gallic town Avaricum is strongly fortified, having a wall forty feet thick; the marsh and river prevent the building of a line of circumvallation around this wall; Cæsar decides to reduce it by erecting an agger or tower upon the ridge from which, when level with the wall, the legions can enter the town.

But Avaricum puts up a more determined resistance than he had anticipated. The defenders, many of them iron miners, are as skillful at digging as the Roman soldiers. They undermine the agger, and set it on fire. They catch with nooses the *falces murales*—metal hooks used by the Romans to tear the stones out of the wall—and draw them into the town. They keep raising their own towers on the wall as fast as the Romans increase the height of the agger. They embarrass the besiegers by throwing boiling pitch and stones down on their heads.

Nor can Cæsar induce Vercingetorix—who, unwilling to risk losing his army in case the siege is successful, has not entered the town but is lying nearby safely protected by the woods and marshes—to fight him in the open.

The days pass into weeks and still the Roman eagles have not been carried into Avaricum. Cæsar's supplies are getting low. All the country within reach of his foraging parties has been devastated by the cavalry of Vercingetorix. The bitter cold and wet—it is still winter—is telling on the health of his legions.

His situation becomes desperate. But dare he abandon the siege? Will not all Gaul be in arms against him as soon as the news spreads that Avaricum has held out successfully—that he has commenced his retreat? Yet to continue the siege many days longer may mean starvation.

But while Avaricum's prolonged resistance against the Romans is putting heart into the rest of Gaul the inhabitants of the town itself are losing their confidence. They are deceived by the apparent optimism in the Roman camp. They do not know that Cæsar is almost ready to abandon the siege. They only know that week after week with menacing persistence the great Roman siege engines have battered at that short strip of wall which alone protects them from the legions. They have thrown every possible obstacle in the way of the building of the agger but gradually this has risen in height until it is level with the wall. They pass each night dreading that on the morrow the Romans will be in the town.

Vercingetorix, though Avaricum is still holding the Romans at bay, has not changed his mind about the folly of risking a severe defeat at the hands of Cæsar. He believes the town will fall eventually. There is a way of retreating from it through the marsh to his army that the Romans do not know of, and he advises the garrison to leave Avaricum secretly and join him, so that even though the town and the non-combatants fall into the hands of Cæsar the army will still be free to continue the war. The garrison finally decides to take his advice. But on the night arranged for the evacuation the wailing of the women being left behind gives the alarm to the Romans, and makes the attempt fail.

Again fortune has favored Cæsar. Uncertain as to the state of hope or despair existing within the walls of Avaricum, and inclined to believe that the failure of his army to take the town has given the garrison confidence, he now knows that the Barbarians feel themselves in as desperate a situation as he himself does. Would the Bituriges be deserting their families unless driven by necessity? Shall he abandon the siege when perhaps one last determined effort may bring success?

In the morning he assaults the town more furiously than

ever before, and Avaricum falls. His soldiers, he tells in his Commentaries, "being excited by the fatigue of the siege, spared neither those worn out with years, women, or children." Of the forty thousand Gauls in the town only eight hundred escape the butchery and find refuge in the camp of Vercingetorix.

Avaricum has fallen, but Vercingetorix is still undefeated. The capture of the Biturige capital has only strengthened his conviction that the science of war is as yet far too elementary among his countrymen for them to dare to resist the Romans in any concentrated position. The loss is not irretrievable. The Biturige tribe has paid dearly for not following his advice, but with the rest of his army he can still harass the Romans with guerilla warfare. Not yet has he lost hope of uniting Gaul against Cæsar, and eventually driving him back across the Alps.

The eventual capture of the town has not banished the effect upon the whole of Gaul of its prolonged resistance to the Romans. Even the Aeduans, who stand in greater awe of Cæsar than most of the other Gallic tribes as for seven years he has made their country the base of his operations against the rest of Gaul, now secretly negotiate with Vercingetorix. When Cæsar orders them to provide him with all their cavalry for auxiliaries, and also with ten thousand infantry, they feign obedience, but the first serious reverse met with by the Roman army will mean the desertion of these troops. For since the murder of Dumnorix and Acco there is scarcely a Gaul, even among those once won over by promises and presents, who does not mistrust Cæsar. If he has appeared a friend to some, and encouraged them to nourish grievances against and make war upon neighboring tribes is it not because he wishes them to fight his battles for him? When he has completed the conquest of Gaul will this friendship continue? Once Gaul has been subjugated will it not be exploited as are the other Roman provinces?

Cæsar, since taking Avaricum, has divided his army, sending Labienus with four legions against the Senones and the

Parisii, western tribes south of the Seine who have joined the insurrection, and with six legions himself preparing to march against Gergovia, the principal town in Arvernia.

For unless Vercingetorix is captured or killed within the next few months will not the whole of Gaul be in arms against him? From every direction his *speculatores*—the spies belonging to his highly organized intelligence system—bring news of fresh risings among the Barbarians.

In Rome his enemies are jubilant over reports of the reverses he is meeting with. To Cicero, now governor of Cilicia, a friend, Marcus Coelius, requested by the orator to keep him informed of happenings in Rome and Gaul, writes——

"As to Cæsar, we have frequent and no very favorable reports concerning him; however they are at present nothing more than rumors. Some say he has lost all his cavalry, and I believe this is the truth of the case; others that the seventh legion has been entirely defeated, and that he himself is so surrounded that he cannot possibly receive any succours from the main body of his army."

He knows how eagerly the senatorial party—Pompey also —awaits his destruction. And once he is no longer victorious will not the fickle populace quickly transfer its loyalty to another general?

After these seven years in Gaul is he on the verge of failure? Must the name of CÆSAR dwindle and give way to that of VERCINGETORIX?

It has been his purpose to make this name of his stand out in huge and terrible letters. To increase its significance he has at all times dwelt upon his descent from a goddess. But for the first time the name of a Gallic chief is now catching hold of the imagination of the Barbarians in a similar way. Where the names of many chiefs have in the past confused the minds of the Gauls, so that the various tribes have seemed to be carrying on independent wars against the Romans, that of Vercingetorix is becoming a symbol of liberty around which all the tribes of Gaul are rallying against the common enemy.

It is a name that is coming to stand not for the welfare of any individual tribe, but for the welfare of a united Gaul. It must be erased from Gaul before it overshadows that of CÆSAR.

So he will march against Gergovia, the capital of Vercingetorix's homeland.

Will Vercingetorix, he wonders, allow sentiment to overcome his judgment and attempt to defend Gergovia?

Vercingetorix, knowing it to be Cæsar's intention to lay siege to Gergovia, is retreating in this direction. He will not depart from his policy of never meeting the Roman general in open battle but he means to harass the legions mercilessly with his cavalry.

He hopes for no immediate victory over Cæsar. His aim is mainly to win time. Time in which to discipline the Gauls, and to teach them that battles are won not by valor but by superior science. Time in which to train them to protect themselves at night by digging camps like the Romans. Time in which the tribes who still hesitate to rise against Cæsar may be induced to join the confederacy. And time mainly in which to conquer in his countrymen their dread of Cæsar as an invincible general.

To the young Arvernian chief, Cæsar's advantages are only too apparent. The Roman commands an army of professional soldiers, unencumbered by women and children. He is not fighting in his own country, so does not hesitate to pillage and to destroy in order to win his victories. Above all, he is in supreme command—the legions are military units which unquestioningly obey his orders—his army is not made up of many tribes each of which wishes to fight under its own chief. To be strong Gaul must have an army in which all power is likewise centralized in a single commander.

Shall Gaul, with its millions of people, submit to conquest by a small expeditionary force of fifty thousand soldiers? Vercingetorix sees it a single great nation from the Alps to the Atlantic. A nation powerful enough to expel the Roman invaders, to drive them back across the mountains into Italy.

And time to effect this unity in Gaul is what he is fighting for. Until he feels certain of victory he will not abandon guerilla warfare. And if the Romans are eventually driven out of Gaul will not the sacrifice of towns and villages have been worthwhile?

He approaches Gergovia. And once again, when he orders the town to be destroyed, he is brought face to face with the bitter realization that he will not be obeyed.

Gergovia stands on the top of a high hill. The Arvernians, like the Bituriges, believe their capital to be impregnable. That Avaricum has fallen is to them no proof that Gergovia, defended, will finally meet the same fate. Has not Gergovia, on its hill-top, a much stronger natural position than Avaricum, which could be approached by the ridge?

They refuse to destroy the town. Neither will Vercingetorix yield to their pleadings to increase the garrison with his army, and assist directly in the defense. Never will he allow himself to be trapped within walls. He pitches his camp on a neighboring hill, ready to harass the Romans with his cavalry during the siege, but ready also at any moment to save his army by retreating.

The Roman army draws near. Cæsar, who during the march has feared as when on the way to Avaricum that he will find the town destroyed, is again relieved when he sees it untouched upon its hill-top. He hopes that the fall of Gergovia will so undermine the influence of Vercingetorix that the spread of the insurrection will be stopped. But again day after day passes and still the defenses of Gergovia have not been broken down. Nor will Vercingetorix allow himself to be lured into a fixed battle outside the town. The legionaries, impatient at the delay, and grown over-confident since the capture of Avaricum, begin to make mistakes. In one rash assault seven hundred of them are killed. The corn and cavalry promised by the Aeduans fail to arrive. Cæsar finds his retreat cut off by hostile Gauls encouraged to rise against him by the town's successful resistance. The legions under Labienus are in an equally desperate situation. The day comes when he realizes that Gergovia has vanquished him—his soldiers are starving—the cavalry of Vercingetorix intercepts all his supplies—the Aeduans have now become his open enemies—tremendous as will be the moral effect on the whole of Gaul, he has no alternative but to abandon the siege.

And it is the very fact that Gergovia can claim the distinction of being the first and only town in Gaul to successfully withstand a siege by Cæsar which brings final and overwhelming defeat to the Gauls in their struggle for liberty.

For in the mad joy which sweeps through the whole of Gaul at the news that the legions have abandoned the siege, firing the tribes with an exultation which destroys all caution, even Vercingetorix is caught up. The Gauls, made overconfident in their turn by the victory, clamor for battle with the retreating Romans. Has the moment come in which to destroy Cæsar?

Blinded by the desire to drive the hated Roman invaders out of Gaul Vercingetorix forgets his carefully planned policy of never engaging in a fixed battle with Cæsar until his own army is better disciplined and equipped. . . . He follows Cæsar. . . . The Gauls, as confident of victory as had been the Helvetii seven years ago, rush headlong upon the legions. . . . The battle ends with the complete rout of the army of Vercingetorix.

The survivors retreat to the town of Alesia. Vercingetorix sends messengers to every state in Gaul pleading with the tribes for reinforcements, as the fate of Gaul hangs in the balance. But the relief army arrives too late—the legions have had time in which to make their position impregnable—again the disorderly charge of the Gauls is repulsed with immense slaughter . . . and Alesia surrenders.

Vercingetorix calls all the chiefs who have not been killed or captured to a meeting at which, assuming the whole responsibility for the war, he offers to die or to surrender himself to Cæsar as they see fit, so that the Roman vengeance will not fall on the Gallic peoples.

When Cæsar demands that he be given up alive, he puts on his finest armor, and mounting a magnificent stallion, richly caparisoned, rides proudly out from the gates of Alesia to where the Roman is sitting in his tribunal. Three times he makes the circuit of Cæsar, then, dismounting, takes off his armor, and, as a sign of submission, seats himself at the feet of Cæsar.

And here he sits in silence until Cæsar, with a little movement of his hand, orders him to be led away and reserved for his triumph.

Vercingetorix's surrender marks the end of the strongest opposition met with by Cæsar during his nine years in Gaul.

But Gaul, if no longer united, is still not entirely crushed. His eighth year is spent suppressing independent uprisings. His ferocity is now at times almost that of a madman. His epileptic fits, from which he has been free for several years, have returned with greater severity than ever before. When he broods over the thought that the unrest in Gaul may cheat him of his ambition to be king his fury against the Gauls is ungovernable. Were Gaul quiet he might be in his southern province watching the political movements in Rome, and counteracting the influence of his enemies here. With bloody strides he crosses and recrosses Gaul depopulating it of those who refuse to submit to his will.

But he has not dropped his mask of good-nature and kindliness. The blame for the atrocities committed by his army he lays on the legionaries. Writing in his Commentaries, he tells, for instance, how, "contrary to his natural humanity," he was forced to punish Guturvatus, one of the captured Gallic chiefs, "because of the clamors of his soldiers, for they alleged that all the dangers and losses incurred in this war against the Carnutes ought to be imputed to Guturvatus. Accordingly, he was whipped to death, and his head cut off."

The last stand of the Gauls is in the mountain-town of Uxellodunum, which falls only when Cæsar diverts by means of subterranean drains the spring from which the besieged obtain their water. With grim fury, "especially as he knew that all the Gauls understood that his command was to continue but one summer longer, and if they could hold out for that time, that they would have no further danger to apprehend," he waits for the town to surrender. And when at last it does, he crowns his eight years of murder and pillage in Gaul with an act of deliberate and monstrous cruelty that will distinguish as long as they live these last champions of the cause of freedom.

"Cæsar, being convinced that his lenity was known to all men, and being under no fears of being thought to act severely from a natural cruelty, and perceiving that there would be no end to his troubles if several states should attempt to rebel in like manner and in different places, resolved to deter others by inflicting an exemplary punishment on these. Accordingly he cut off the hands of those who had borne arms against him. Their lives he spared, that the punishment of their rebellion might be the more conspicuous."

4

Meanwhile, in Rome, his enemies have steadily increased in power. The Senate and Pompey are now working in harmony to bring about his downfall. He is to be recalled from his command, and is never under any circumstance to be consul again.

Pompey's legions, raised for the Spains, still lie in the suburbs of the city. To weaken the army of the governor of the Gauls he is asked to contribute a legion for an expeditionary force to be sent against the Parthians to avenge the death of Crassus. Pompey has expressed his willingness to lend a legion, so Cæsar must naturally do likewise. At the same time Pompey asks for the return of the legion lent by him to Cæsar a year ago, as this is the one he wishes to send to Parthia. If Cæsar sends the two legions he will weaken his army by eight thousand men, if he refuses he will make himself unpopular with the people.

The tribunes Bursa, Rufus and Crispus, who had led the

mob which set fire to the senate-house following the killing
of Clodius, have all been banished. Cicero had been active in
the prosecution, his eloquence being mainly directed at Bursa,
who, besides trying to induce the mob to fall upon Cicero as
the avowed friend of Milo, has in other ways elected himself
to fill the position, left vacant by the "pretty boy," of Cicero's
most hated enemy. In a letter written to a friend, Marcus
Marius, shortly after Bursa has been sentenced to banishment,
the orator indeed becomes almost sentimental over the merits
of Clodius as compared with the unpardonable and odious
viciousness of Bursa.

"To speak truth, I had openly declared war against the
former; whereas I have been the advocate and protector of
the latter. Besides, there was something enlarged at least in the
views of Clodius, as he aimed by my destruction at overturning
the whole commonwealth; and even in this he acted less from
the motions of his own breast, than by the instigations of a party
who were sensible they could never be secure, whilst I had any
remaining credit. But the contemptible Bursa, on the contrary,
singled me out for the object of his malice, in mere gaiety of
heart; and without the least provocation, offered himself to
some of my enemies as one who was entirely at their service
upon any occasion wherein they could employ him to my
prejudice."

Cicero goes to Cilicia as governor. It irritates him that his
friend Marcus Coelius, who has promised to keep him in touch
with affairs in the capital, fills his letters almost entirely with
news of the latest trivial happenings in the capital, and also
bothers him continually about some panthers which he has
asked Cicero to send him from Cilicia (Coelius being a candidate for the ædileship, and wishing to exhibit the panthers in
his wild-beast shows), and a debt in Cilicia that the orator has
agreed to collect for him. But at last, in Coelius's letters, some
important political news begins to trickle through the repeated
allusions to the panthers and "the sum of money which is due
to me on the bond of Sittius."

Cicero hears of "a meeting of the Senate, holden in the

temple of Apollo, at which, upon a debate relating to the payment of the forces commanded by Pompey, mention was made of that legion, which, as appeared by his accounts, had been lent to Cæsar; and he was asked of what number of men it consisted, and for what purpose it was borrowed. In short," says Coelius, "Pompey was pushed so strongly upon this article, that he found himself under a necessity of promising to recall this legion out of Gaul."

He hears how Pompey, though growing bolder in his opposition to his former colleague in the triumvirate, is still keeping up a pretense of great affection for the governor of Gaul. "Your friend Pompey," writes Coelius, "openly declares that Cæsar ought not to be admitted as a candidate for the consulship, while he retains his command in the province. He voted, however, against passing a decree for this purpose at present."

Cæsar's ninth year in Gaul is drawing to a close. The Senate is determined that his command shall be taken away from him by March 1st, 49, if not before. In September of the year 50 Coelius details to Cicero certain preliminary decrees recently passed by the Senate to this end. He adds, "In the debates which preceded these decrees, Pompey let fall an expression that was much observed, and gave us very confident hopes of his good intention. 'He could not without great injustice,' he said, 'determine any thing in relation to the provinces under Cæsar's command, before the first of March; but after that time, he assured the Senate, he should have no sort of scruple.' Being asked, 'what if a negative should then be put upon a decree of the Senate for recalling Cæsar?' he declared, that he should look upon it as just the same thing, whether Cæsar openly refused to obey the authority of the Senate, or secretly procured some magistrate to obstruct their decrees. But suppose, said another member, Cæsar should pursue his pretensions to the consulate, and retain his command abroad at the same time. 'Suppose,' replied Pompey, with great temper, 'my own son should lay violent hands upon me?' From expressions of this kind the world has conceived a notion that a rupture will undoubtedly ensue between Pompey and Cæsar."

Coelius warmly praises a Roman named Curio, who, it seems, is "preparing most strongly to oppose Cæsar's demands. What he may be able to effect, I know not; but sure I am, that a man who acts upon such patriot principles, must gain honor at least, if he gain nothing else."

Apropos of Curio, Cicero's correspondent continues, "He treats me upon all occasions with great generosity. He has presented me with some African panthers which he had procured for his own games. I must therefore remind you of what I have often mentioned already, and entreat you to send me some of these animals from your part of the world; and I again likewise recommend to your care the bond of Sittius."

Impatiently dismissing from his mind the panthers and the bond of Sittius, Cicero eagerly awaits further developments. Nor is he to be disappointed. Soon there arrives a letter from Coelius which contains the interesting if startling piece of information that the worthy Caius Curio, "the man who acted upon such patriot principles," has indeed gained more than honor—Curio has sold himself to Cæsar, who in return for his support in the capital has agreed to pay Curio's enormous debts, amounting to more than 60,000,000 sesterces ($3,000,000).

Shocked as he is by the news, Cicero will not admit to Coelius that this recent triumph of Cæsar comes as a surprise to him. In the rôle of an aloof and disinterested spectator he writes, "Is Curio really then become a convert to Cæsar? But extraordinary as this event may appear to others, believe me it is agreeable to what I always expected. O ye immortal gods! how do I long to laugh with you at the ridiculous farce which is acting in your part of the world!"

But bitter envy of Cæsar consumes him as the subsequent correspondence of Coelius relates how successfully the wealth of the governor of Gaul is blocking legislation. Can it be, after all, that in the eyes of posterity Cæsar, and not Cicero, will be the great Roman of the age?

The thought makes him sick with rage. Nor is his peace of mind increased by the note of pessimism which he detects creeping into his friend's accounts of proceedings in the capital. Coelius has always been a faithful partisan of the senatorial party. Now he seems to put little faith in its future. In one long letter, greedily perused by the orator, he writes——

"As to political affairs, the general contest still is in re.ation to the provinces. Pompey now seems to unite with the Senate that the 13th of November be limited for Cæsar's resigning his government. Curio, on the contrary, is determined to oppose this to the utmost; and accordingly has relinquished all his other schemes, in order to apply his whole strength to the affair in question. As to our party, you well know their irresolution; and, consequently, will readily believe me when I tell you they have not the spirit to push their opposition to the last extremity. The whole mystery of the scene in short is this: Pompey, that he may not seem to oppose Cæsar, or to aim at anything but what the latter shall think perfectly equitable, represents Curio as acting in this affair merely upon his own authority, and with no other view than to create disturbances. It is certain, at the same time, that Pompey is much averse to Cæsar's being elected consul, before he shall have delivered up his government, together with the command of the army, and indeed he seems to be extremely apprehensive of the consequences, if it should prove otherwise. In the meanwhile he is severely attacked by Curio, who is perpetually reproaching him with deviating from the principles upon which he acted in his second consulship. Take my word for it, notwithstanding all the difficulties they may throw in Curio's way, Cæsar will never want a friend to rise up in his cause; and if the whole turns, as they seem to fear, upon his procuring some tribune to interpose his negative to their decrees, I will venture to pronounce that he remain in Gaul as long as he shall think proper."

But suddenly, for the time being, Cicero's interest in the affairs of Cæsar vanishes. For he has seen an opportunity to win glory for himself in his province. Like Crassus, the orator has always secretly longed for a triumph. Since the annihilation of Crassus's army in the East, Rome has lived in fear of a Parthian invasion—the governor of Cilicia now busies himself harassing the mountain tribes in his province, while sending reports to Rome to the effect that he is heroically holding back the van of the Parthian hordes. Puffed up with self-importance after capturing a small backwoods town named Pindenessum, he makes haste to inform Coelius that he has "just had employment enough of the military kind to entitle him to a triumph."

The crisis facing the Republic in the west dwindles for him into insignificance. He sees all Roman eyes turned not to Cæsar in Gaul but to himself in Cilicia. With naïve child-like conceit he babbles on about himself to Coelius, explaining how much the reputation of his name had helped him to win his great victory.

"For you cannot imagine of what importance it is, in places of this kind, to have the populace ask, *Is this the consul that saved Rome? Is this he that was so honored by the Senate?* together with other questions of the same import, which I need not add."

5

Gaul is at last quiet.

During his eight years as governor Cæsar has killed over two million of the inhabitants. The losses to his own army have not been more than a few thousand legionaries.

With the fall of Uxellodunum the tribes from the Alps to the Atlantic accept the Roman conquest. From village to village wander Gauls without hands and with their eyes battered in—they are members of the last Gallic garrison to whom their own countrymen dare not openly show pity except at the risk of incurring the displeasure of Cæsar, who has not let this last handful of patriots live to be honored as heroes, but to check further revolt by their dreadful appearance as they go begging along the highroads until they die.

The time has come at last—for he may need auxiliaries to help him in the coming war against Pompey—when he can afford to be merciful . . . generous. . . . He invites all the chiefs in Gaul to an impressive conference. He tells them of the glorious future that awaits Gaul now that it is part of the Roman empire. He gives them magnificent presents. . . . His gracious smiles tell them that Cæsar, terrible to his enemies, is the soul of magnanimity to his friends. . . . Let them be loyal to him in the impending crisis and before many months are over they shall no longer be merely chiefs of petty barbarian tribes but shall sit in the Roman Senate and take part in the government of the empire.

From his southern province he watches Rome. All depends now on his army, for despite the immense sums he is spending buying over the tribunes, he knows Pompey is all-powerful in the capital. Galba, an officer who has served under him in Gaul, sent back to stand for this year's consulship, received a majority of votes but the election was set aside by the Senate on the grounds of bribery. Lentulus and Marcus Marcellus, the consuls, have pledged themselves to break Cæsar's power by having him recalled. The consuls-elect, Lucius Paulus and Caius Marcellus, are likewise for Pompey and the Senate.

He has sent Pompey the two legions asked for, but he still has nine left. And if he is recalled in disgrace, the soldiers will not receive the presents which he would otherwise distribute at his triumph. By reminding them of this, and laying stress upon the Senate's ingratitude in trying to bring about the downfall of a general who for eight years has been adding to the glory of the Roman arms, can he not insure himself of their loyalty?

He will not, however, put himself in the wrong by marching against Rome without every apparent justification. Though he aspires not to be consul, but to be king, he will make his whole quarrel with Pompey and the Senate their refusal to allow him to serve his second term as consul. And he will seem to his soldiers to be demanding only his rights when he insists that he retain his command in Gaul until after the elections; for, before his split with Pompey the latter had obtained the passage of a decree permitting him to be a candidate for consul while still governor of the Gauls, which decree has since been made invalid by a more general law—sponsored by Cicero, and aimed as specifically at Cæsar as Clodius's law regarding putting Roman citizens to death without trial had been aimed at Cicero—which annuls all previous decrees making exceptions to the law that candidates for the consulship must be present in person at the elections.

The invaluable Clodius is dead, but besides the officers who served under him in Gaul and now sent to Rome to obtain political positions—among these is Mark Antony, who commanded the cavalry of Gabinius when the latter took the first Roman army to the Nile to reinstate Ptolemy, and subsequently became one of Cæsar's cavalry officers in Gaul—his Gallic spoils shall buy for him the other tribunes of the people, so that when the civil war breaks out he will seem to be leading his army against Rome not to destroy the Republic but to champion the cause of the people against the tyrannies of Pompey and the Senate.

Nearer and nearer, as the year 50 draws to a close, does the dark cloud of civil war approach Rome.

Meanwhile Cicero's chief correspondent in Rome, Marcus Coelius, now ædile, has been having private troubles which have prevented him from sending the orator much political news. Having quarreled with Appius, the censor, the latter and several friends have tried to have him arrested for violating one of the Roman blue laws relating to the seduction of boys.

"Towards the close of my Circensian games," writes Coelius, "these shameless confederates caused me to be indicted on the Scantinian law. But Pola, whom they had spirited up to be the informer, had scarce entered his action, when I lodged an information against our worthy censor himself, for the very same crime."

His honor cleared on this score, Coelius becomes more communicative upon the matter of public affairs——

"As to the political situation; I have often mentioned to you that I imagined the public tranquillity could not possibly be preserved beyond the present year; and the nearer we approach to those contentions which must inevitably arise, the more evident this danger appears. For Pompey is determined most strenuously to oppose Cæsar's being consul, unless he resigns his command; and Cæsar, on the contrary, is persuaded that he cannot be safe upon these terms. He has offered, however, to throw up his commission, provided Pompey will do the same. And thus their very suspicious friendship and alliance will probably end at last in an open war."

As Cicero reads on, an expression first of bewilderment, then of dismay, comes into his face.

Thoughts flit through his mind. Curio's infatuation for Mark Antony, whom he had kept for years as his favorite—Coelius's similar taste for boys—Cæsar's large following of degenerates —the African panthers so generously bestowed on Coelius by Curio—his own remissness, as one of the most prominent members of the senatorial party, in failing to supply Coelius with an equal number of Cilician panthers for his games (he has sent none at all).

He carefully re-reads the closing paragraph of the letter——

"For my own part, I shall be extremely perplexed in what manner to act in that conjuncture; and I doubt you will likewise find yourself under the same embarrassment. On the one hand, I have an interest and connexion with Pompey's party; and on the other, it is Cæsar's cause alone, and not his friends, that I dislike. You are sensible, I dare say, that so long as the dissensions of our country are confined within the limits of debate, we ought ever to join with the more righteous side; *but that as soon as the sword is drawn, the strongest party is always the best.* With respect to our present divisions, I foresee that the Senate, together with the whole order of judges, will declare in favor of Pompey; and that all those of desperate fortunes or who are obnoxious to the laws, will list themselves under the banners of Cæsar. As to their armies, I am persuaded there will be a great inequality. But I hope we shall have time enough to consider the strength of their respective forces, and to declare ourselves accordingly. . . ."

His surmise is correct. Soon afterwards he hears from other friends in Rome that Marcus Coelius, like Curio, has sold himself to Cæsar.

Cæsar stands by the Rubicon, the little river which separates his southern province from Italy. How often, during the past nine years, has he gazed across it in the direction of Rome, a hundred and fifty miles away! The Rubicon he may not cross as long as he retains command of his army. Can he be sure that the legions will follow him to Rome?

He has made the fortunes of all his generals so should they not remain loyal? Without exception the officers who have served through the Gallic wars were either penniless or heavily in debt when they commenced their careers under him. Now Decimus Brutus is worth over two million dollars, while Labienus, Antony and Trebonius have received equally large shares of the Gallic spoils. And no Roman commander has ever been more generous to his legionaries.

In Rome, Pompey and the Senate are counting upon disaffection in Cæsar's army should he violate the law by attempting to bring it into Italy. Their agents are in Gaul sounding the generals. They report that Cæsar is unpopular with his officers because during the Gallic wars, though in his letters to Rome he praised their personal valor at every opportunity, he took to himself always the credit for the generalship that made the Roman arms victorious. Labienus especially is bitter as it is he who every winter commanded the legions while Cæsar returned over the Alps to look after his personal affairs.

And the agents of the Senate are right when they aver that Labienus will never help to make Cæsar king. For Labienus is himself ambitious. He knows that as long as he remains with Cæsar he will never be more than a subordinate. He knows also that time and again Cæsar has only been saved from defeat by that very initiative of his officers which he has tried so hard to crush. He has grown to hate Cæsar's colossal vanity—his emphasis upon his descent from the ancient kings of Rome and the Goddess Venus—his conceit in his unique generalship. Why should he help Cæsar become king when by going over to Pompey and the Senate he may some day be king himself?

But the other generals and the legionaries?

Cæsar is in constant correspondence with Cicero, whose two

years' term as governor of Cilicia has just expired, and who is now returning to Rome. Can he induce Cicero to come to the Province before going to the capital? If so, and he is able to buy over the orator, he will have besides his army—eloquence! With Cicero to make magnificent speeches in his defense, how can his cause fail to impress posterity as a just one?

Pompey is likewise in the market to hire the orator's golden tongue. Each of the rivals flatters Cicero and promises him a triumph for his military exploits in Cilicia. His vanity immensely gratified by such competition for his services, Cicero nevertheless feels himself on the horns of a dilemma. His jealousy of Cæsar makes him eventually decide to go with Pompey.

He writes to Atticus, however, that he intends privately to advise Pompey to come to terms. Of Cæsar he says, "We have to do with a man full of audacity and completely prepared. Every felon, every citizen who is in disgrace or ought to be in disgrace, almost all the young, the city mob, the tribunes, debtors, who are more numerous than I could have believed, all these are with Cæsar."

With civil war imminent, Cicero is still mainly interested only in the matter of his triumph. But the Senate is in no mind to grant him such an honor for his petty scuffling with the Cilician tribes. It does, instead, award to Bibulus, the general in command of the Roman army fighting against the Parthians, a twenty-day thanksgiving. "Pardon me!" exclaims the philosopher in a letter to Atticus, "but this is more than I can bear!"

He now more than half wishes he had thrown in his lot with Cæsar. But Pompey soothes his ruffled feelings with promises. Marcus Tullius shall have his parade—let him only be a little patient.

Pompey, who for weeks has been openly expressing his contempt for Cæsar as an adversary, has suddenly grown uneasy. He is calling in the veterans of the war with Mithridates. Can he muster an army as large as that of Cæsar?

The week of the crisis arrives—the first week in January of
the year 49 B.C.

Cæsar, that his cause may appear in every way a just one, has
sent a message to the Senate saying that he will disband his
army provided Pompey will do the same. He knows that Pompey's pride will never permit him to make such a concession.

The Senate refuses to negotiate further with the defiant
governor. It orders a general levy throughout Italy. The consuls make Pompey commander-in-chief of the army. Cæsar's
province is taken away from him and given to Domitius Ahenobarbus, one of his most bitter enemies. To all of these measures,
the veto of the tribunes, known to be in Cæsar's pay, is disal-
lowed.

From Rome Cicero writes as follows to his favorite slave
Tiro (with whom, after his death, he will be accused of having
had homosexual relations) of the event immediately leading
up to the civil war—the flight of the tribunes——

"Cæsar has written a very warm and menacing letter to the
Senate. He has the audacity, notwithstanding their express prohibition, to continue at the head of his army, and in the government of his province. Curio, in conjunction with Quintus
Cassius and Mark Antony, without the least violence being offered to them, have withdrawn themselves to Cæsar."

Cæsar's moment has come.

The flight—prearranged—of Mark Antony, Curio and the
other tribunes to his camp has taken place. To obtain a theatri-
cal effect that will properly impress the legionaries they have
left Rome disguised as slaves—they cross from Italy to Hither
Gaul in carriages driven at a mad gallop as though the pursuing forces of the Senate were only a few miles behind—
while the legionaries, recognizing in Antony and others of
the refugees their former generals, crowd excitedly around the
foam-lathered horses, the tribunes rush to Cæsar and throwing themselves at his feet implore him, in the name of the
people, to come to Rome and protect the citizens against Pompey and the Senate.

Cæsar addresses his soldiers. He points to the tribunes of

the people who have fled to him for protection. Are not the rights of Roman citizens being trampled beneath the feet of a despotism? Will the legionaries turn a deaf ear to the entreaties of their fellow-citizens?

He reminds them that for nine years they have been battling bravely with the Barbarians, performing deeds of valor which eclipse those of all previous Roman armies. Are they not the legionaries who first crossed the Rhine, who first went to Britain? And is such service to go unrewarded? For months the Senate, with promises of pensions, has tried to persuade them to desert the general under whom they have fought all these years, but do they not know that once no longer in the army, the Senate, jealous of their successes, will fulfill none of its promises? Cæsar, on the contrary, has always thought first of the welfare of his soldiers. Has he not raised their pay from 480 sesterces ($25) a year to 900 sesterces ($45)? Did he not wear mourning until he had fittingly avenged the massacre of their comrades at Aduatuca?

And every legionary he cries, as when addressing his army at the time of the threatened mutiny on the march against Ariovistus, who does not feel his cause to be a righteous one is free to leave the camp and join the forces of Pompey—but to each of those who are willing to follow him and the tribunes to Rome and fight to uphold the sacred rights of Roman citizenship he promises the sum of 5,000 sesterces ($250).

The legionaries beat on their shields, raise their right hands, and cry *Hail Cæsar!*

On the eighteenth of January he crosses the Rubicon.

6

"Labienus is a hero. Never was act more splendid. If nothing else comes of it, he has at least made Cæsar smart."

Thus writes Cicero to Atticus of the desertion to Pompey and the consular army of Cæsar's most trusted general, his right-hand man through the Gallic wars.

But if Labienus is the hero of the hour, even his arrival in

the capital cannot stay the panic which sweeps through it when
it is known that Cæsar has really crossed the Rubicon. To Tiro,
on January 29th, Cicero writes——

"You will easily judge of our distress when I tell you that
myself and every friend of the Republic have abandoned
Rome, and even our country, to all the cruel devastations of
fire and sword. Our affairs, indeed, are in so desperate a situation, that nothing less than the powerful interposition of some
favorable divinity, or some happy turn of chance, can secure
us from utter ruin. It has been the perpetual purpose of all
my speeches, my votes, and my actions, to preserve the public
tranquillity. But an invincible rage for war had unaccountably
seized not only the enemies, but even those who are esteemed
friends of the Commonwealth; and it was in vain that I
remonstrated that nothing was more to be dreaded than a civil
war. Cæsar, in the mean time, unmindful of his former character and honors, and driven, it should seem, by a sort of frenzy,
has taken possession of Ariminum, Pisaurum, Ancona, and
Arretum."

Pompey the Great, on whom all had relied, has bitterly disappointed the senators. He seems to have no plans other than
that of flight to Asia. All his boastful promises have collapsed.
Once the news arrives that Cæsar has actually commenced his
march upon Rome, he is one of the first to leave the city. "The
consuls are helpless," writes Cicero to Atticus early in February. "There has been no levy. The commissioners do not even
try to excuse their failure. With Cæsar pressing forward and
our general doing nothing, men will not give in their names.
Pompey, miserable and incredible though it be, is prostrate.
He has no courage, no purpose, no force, no energy. . . .
Caius Cassius came on the 7th to Capua, with an order from
Pompey to the consuls to go to Rome and bring away the
money from the treasury. How are they to go without an escort, or how return? The consuls say he must go himself first
to Picenum. But Picenum is lost.—Cæsar will soon be in Apu-
lia, and Pompey on board ship. What shall I do? I should not

doubt had there not been such shameful mismanagement, and had I been myself consulted. Cæsar invites me to peace, but his letter was written before his advance."

Anticipating that Cæsar, when he takes the city, will be as merciless to his enemies as was Sulla, the senators are hurrying across the peninsula to Brundisium, from which, with Pompey, they will sail for Asia. But Cæsar's policy, as he marches south along the Adriatic, is to undermine Pompey by kindness. He pardons the garrison of every town which resists him. And the huge sums of money sent back by him while in Gaul, with his fame as an invincible general, have done their work well. His army, consisting of a single legion only when he crossed the Rubicon, but subsequently increased to three by the addition of two more he had sent for to join him, is swelled to thirty thousand men by the garrisons which go over to him.

Cicero, who, when Italy was being divided into districts for the various proconsuls to defend, had prudently chosen a section of the coast near Capua which he knew would lie south of Cæsar's line of march to the capital, is in an anguish of indecision. Shall he stay in Italy with Cæsar, or go to Asia with Pompey? Pompey's power is still strong in the East, and he controls the Mediterranean fleet with which he intends to blockade Italy, thus to starve Cæsar into submission. But Cæsar unquestionably has the stronger army, and also the greater popularity. Which side is the safe side?

"My connections, personal and political, attach me to Pompey," he writes to Atticus, "but Pompey has shown neither conduct nor courage, and he has acted throughout against my advice and judgment. I pass over his old errors: how he himself armed this man against the constitution; how he supported his laws by violence in the face of the auspices; how he gave him Further Gaul, married his daughter, supported Clodius, helped me back from exile indeed, but neglected me afterwards; how he prolonged Cæsar's command, and backed him up in everything; how in his third consulship, when he had begun to defend the constitution, he yet moved the tribunes to carry a resolution for taking Cæsar's name in his absence, and himself

sanctioned it by a law of his own. Let us forget all this:
but what was ever more disgraceful than the flight from
Rome?"

He prays to the immortal gods that before Pompey can
escape there will be a battle which will spare him the necessity of making a decision. When he hears that Cæsar has arrived at Brundisium too late to prevent Pompey's departure, he
makes up his mind to leave Pompey to his fate, justifying his
change of attitude with the excuse that Pompey is no better
than Cæsar—he too wants to be king. "The prospect is fright-
ful. The fleets from Alexandria, Colchis, Sidon, Cyprus, Pam-
phylia, Lycia, Rhodes, Chios, and Byzantium will be employed
to cut off our supplies, and then Pompey himself will come
back in his wrath!—I, whom some have called the Saviour
and parent of my country to bring Getes, and Armenians, and
Colchians upon Italy! I to famish my fellow-citizens and
waste their lands!"

Cæsar, aware that the orator has not yet left Italy, sends him
urgent messages begging him not to sail until they have had
an interview. Cicero agrees to meet him on the road to Rome.

No sooner has he made this decision than he regrets bitterly
not having crossed the Adriatic with Pompey. Insupportable is
the thought of himself, the great Cicero, taking orders from
Cæsar! He feels a sudden rush of hatred against Pompey for
having, unprepared, entered the war. Carried away by his
emotion, he gives in a letter to Atticus, his true reasons for
having played the part of a benevolent peace-maker, and advis-
ing Pompey privately to come to terms——

"Cæsar, I reflected, was but mortal; and there were many
ways in which he might be got rid of!"

7

Cæsar is on the road to Rome. Victory has slipped from his
grasp. The flight of Pompey has disarranged all his plans.
With Pompey have gone the two consuls, and most of the senators. Now that the entire government has removed itself from

Italy, will he not appear in the light of a usurper rather than in that of a liberator?

And unless he carries the war into Macedonia after Pompey, will not the latter, whose authority on the Mediterranean is immeasurably greater than his own, eventually be able to return and destroy him? His dream of a quick decisive battle which would make him master of Rome has come to nothing because of Pompey's cowardice.

Under his mask of clemency and geniality he is bitterly resentful. He is popular in Italy now, but how long will this popularity last? Seen from a distance Pompey and the Senate are sure to arouse sympathy. They can pursue his own tactics when in Gaul of indirectly moulding public opinion. Sooner or later the worthlessness of his own followers is going to militate against him.

For this reason he feels it vital to win over Cicero. If, when he enters Rome, and convenes what is left of the Senate, Cicero will speak in his defense and justify his contemplated carrying of the war into Macedonia against Pompey, his position will be immensely more secure.

So, as arranged, they meet on the road. And of this meeting Cicero writes later to Atticus:

"My language was calculated rather to make him respect than be grateful to me. Where I was deceived, was in having expected to find him yielding; I have never seen anything less so. My decision about not going to the town he said was a censure on himself; others would be more inclined to hang back because I had refused to come. I replied that their case was not the same. After much of this, 'Well, come then and prepare a peaceful ceremony,' he said. 'And,' said I, 'with full discretion?' 'Am I,' said he, 'to dictate to you?' 'This,' say I, 'is what I shall propose: that in the opinion of the Senate, it is inexpedient that you should proceed to Spain, and that troops should be conveyed to Greece; and I shall—' I add, '—fully express my sympathy for Pompey.' Then he, 'But that I cannot approve of your saying!' 'Just what I was thinking,' say I. 'But the very reason that I do not want to be here, is that I must either speak in this way and about many things which

I could not leave unsaid on any terms if I were there, or else not go at all.' In the end, as if he were anxious to quit the discussion, 'Would I then take time to think over it?' This could not be refused. So we parted."

Cæsar goes on to Rome alone. His feeling of impotence has increased now that Cicero has refused to talk to order. The acclamations of the mob brought together by his henchmen in the capital to greet him on his arrival in Rome after more than nine years' absence cannot banish his ill-humor. Underneath the smiles he gives the shouting crowds lurks baffled rage.

News has been brought him that Marseilles, the main seaport of Gaul on the Mediterranean, has revolted against the garrison he left there, and declared for Pompey, and that Pompey is sending a fleet to its support. After all these years of war is he now to lose Gaul? Pompey has several legions in Spain which threaten to invade it. He decides to march himself against this Spanish army before attacking Pompey in Macedonia.

In Rome he makes an empty gesture of conducting the government in a constitutional manner. The consuls being absent, two of his officers, Mark Antony and Cassius Longinus, convene the Senate—to the handful of senators who assemble he justifies his march on Rome as a measure necessary to the safety of the Republic. To conduct his Spanish war he demands the keys of the public treasury in the temple of Saturn.

He goes to the treasury. Metullus, a tribune faithful to Pompey, bars the way. Cæsar's suppressed fury leaps suddenly to the surface. He draws his sword, and stepping close to Metullus, with a glance at his soldiers, hisses through clenched teeth, "It is as easy to do this as to say it!"

Metullus stands aside. Cæsar enters the treasury and takes the money. Next day he is on his way to Spain.

The year 49 draws to a close. Cæsar is still besieging Marseilles. Cicero is still in Italy trying not to compromise himself by accepting a command under Cæsar or Pompey.

Even though the news from Spain is not encouraging, the

orator-philosopher has become hopeful of Cæsar's approach-ful downfall. To Atticus he writes, "Pompey will not lay down his arms for the loss of Spain. And Cæsar cannot stand long. He will fall of himself if we do nothing. When his affairs were most flourishing, he became unpopular with the hungry rabble of the city in six or seven days. He could not keep up the mask. His harshness to Metullus destroyed his credit for clemency, and his taking money from the treasury destroyed his reputation for riches."

After a strenuous campaign, lasting through the winter, Cæsar manages to triumph over Pompey's Spanish legions. Marseilles surrenders. But Curio, sent to Africa to win this province away from Pompey who has a number of garrisons here, has been killed and his whole army annihilated by the Pompeians and their ally, Juba, King of Mauretania.

Cæsar hurries back to Rome, where he finds that the popular sympathy has already gone over to Pompey. Mark Antony, left in charge of Rome when he went to Spain, has brought civil affairs into a state of hopeless confusion. And Cicero has at last made up his mind and gone to join Pompey in Macedonia.

He has himself appointed Dictator in order to be able to refuse the title. Until he has inflicted an overwhelming defeat upon the consular army in Macedonia he will stifle his desire to be king, in order to claim only what seem his rights. It is the beginning of the year 48, the year in which except for Pompey's treachery he should, without opposition, have been allowed to return from Gaul for his second consulship. He goes through the form of being elected consul. When his officers try to make him sole consul he refuses this honor also, so that he may seem reluctant to violate the constitution as Pompey has done. He takes Servilius Isauricus, one of his generals, as his colleague.

A year has passed since he crossed the Rubion. He stays in Rome eleven days, then goes to Brundisium, from which on the 4th of January he sails with 15,000 men for Macedonia.

He lands safely on the eastern shore of the Adriatic, having managed to slip by Pompey's fleet. But Antony, scheduled to follow with the other half of his expeditionary force, is block-aded in the Italian port by the Pompeian squadron. Cæsar marches north along the coast until he is near Pompey's camp at Dyrrachium; while awaiting Antony's arrival he keeps up the pretense of having been forced into the war.

He sends a messenger to Pompey, urging peace. Pompey, purpling with fury at the artful manner in which his former colleague is trying to put him in the wrong by hiding his own ambition under disinterestedness and love of country, inter-rupts the messenger to shout grandiloquently— "What care I for life or country if I am to hold both by the favor of Cæ-sar? All men will think thus of me if I make peace now. . . . I left Italy. Men will say that Cæsar has brought me back."

He encourages his legionaries to fraternize with Pompey's soldiers across the narrow river which separates the two armies. Labienus, familiar with his late commander's methods of break-ing down resistance by means of propaganda, disperses these meetings, telling the soldiers of the expeditionary force as they recross the river, that— "There can be no peace till you bring us Cæsar's head!"

Pompey's army, assembled by him while Cæsar was in Spain, numbers more than forty thousand men. Cæsar, though he has withdrawn all his legions from Gaul, has less than thirty thou-sand troops in his expeditionary force even after Antony man-ages eventually to join him in the spring. But his inferiority numerically is more than compensated for by the lack of unity of command in the enemy camp. Pompey is nominally com-mander-in-chief, but the consuls, the senators, and Labienus, are all giving him advice.

Though the soldiers facing him are now legionaries instead of Barbarians, Cæsar's star of good fortune will continue to protect him against his own mistakes—in its many leaders the consular army is still in essence the same sort of disorganized gathering which he was wont to find opposite him in Gaul.

And no sooner does Antony join him than he makes two

blunders, either one of which, had Pompey won the war, would have been sufficient to destroy his reputation as a military genius. He first weakens his army, already too small to accomplish its purpose of driving Pompey out of Dyrrachium, by sending part of it against Pompey's father-in-law, Metellus Scipio, who is bringing reinforcements to Pompey from Syria —he then goes through the absurd motions of trying to shut Pompey up in Dyrrachium, without a fleet.

Pompey's navy controls the Adriatic. He can escape at any moment by putting his army on board the transports lying in the harbor. But Cæsar sets his legionaries to work industriously digging trenches around the town. His officers, as these trenches increase to miles in length, look at one another askance. Suppose Pompey should make a sally? Cæsar's army is now so spread out that at no point are the siege fortifications defended by more than a few men. Had their commander no deeper plan the siege of Dyrrachium from the landward side would seem to be the work of an arrogant child.

What is this plan? There is none. One June day the Pompeian army issues from Dyrrachium and falls on the scattered forces of Cæsar—in the resulting battle his army is routed with a loss of more than a thousand legionaries killed.

And two things only, as he retreats into Greece, save him from overwhelming defeat—the arrival of Calvinus, who, hearing of the disaster at Dyrrhacium, rejoins him without orders with the legions he had imprudently detached from the main body of his army, and the failure of Pompey to keep up the pursuit.

The Pompeian camp is a chaos of conflicting opinions.

Pompey has three alternatives—he can follow Cæsar into Greece, he can take his army back to Italy and engage the legions left by Cæsar here, or he can stay where he is.

For all his apparent indecision and cowardice at the outbreak of the civil war Pompey the Great had left Italy not because he was as altogether lacking in a plan to oppose Cæsar as Cicero at first thought. He has been trying to put into execution a

policy determined on by him two years before Cæsar crossed
the Rubicon. After the deaths of Crassus and Julia, when it
had been obvious that it was only a question of time until there
would be war between himself and Cæsar to decide who should
rule Rome, realizing he could not keep an army in Italy large
enough to contest the issue with Cæsar's Gallic legions, he had
decided when the crisis came to let Cæsar occupy Italy, and to
rely on his fleet and the dissensions which would divide Rome
once Cæsar had come into authority to bring him eventual victory.

Now he advocates letting Cæsar wander about Greece among
the hostile tribes until his supplies fail and his army is worn
out by marches. Both Cicero and Cato are of this opinion that
it is best to avoid a battle. But the consuls, Scipio and Lentulus,
and most of the senators, want to finish the war quickly. The
victory at Dyrrhacium has filled them with over-confidence.
When they might have annihilated Cæsar's army directly after
the battle had a vigorous pursuit been instituted, they had
chosen instead to look on Cæsar's cause as already lost—the
Pompeian army in their opinion has nothing to do now but follow leisurely and cut to pieces the survivors.

Pompey's warning not to risk all in a fixed battle with Cæsar they will not listen to. The consuls accuse him of deliberately attempting to protract the war so that he can remain
commander-in-chief. There are murmurs that he like Cæsar
aims to destroy the constitution. Already in the Pompeian camp
the war is seen as ended—the whole talk is of who shall profit
most by Cæsar's downfall. Intriguing and plotting has begun
to decide who shall now be Pontifex Maximus—who shall
have his Roman palace and gardens by the Tiber—who his
country estates and villas on the Bay of Naples.

So approaches the fateful battle of Pharsalia, fought on the
9th of August, 48.

Cæsar has crossed Greece from the Adriatic to the Ægean,
and is now fifty miles south of Thessalonica, where Cicero
spent his exile. The news of his defeat at Dyrrachium has preceded him; everywhere, on his line of march, the towns have

closed their gates to him. But he has had time in which to re-organize his army. When Pompey catches up with him he is camped near the town of Larissa, on the plain of Pharsalia.

The consular army no longer has any leader who can give orders that will be obeyed by the whole army. Pompey, his father-in-law Scipio the consul, the other consul Lentulus, each one of the three hundred senators and senators' sons who are with the army, all have different opinions about how the battle should be fought. Labienus, the one competent general with the Pompeian forces, who from his nine years of service under Cæsar in Gaul knows best what tactics to employ to defeat his former commander, has no voice at all. The idol of the hour when he left Cæsar at the Rubicon, he has long since been pushed into the background by the many illustrious person-ages surrounding Pompey. Cicero, anticipating the coming dis-aster, has feigned sickness and remained at Dyrrhacium where Cato has been left in command.

And at Pharsalia the consular army, though outnumbering Cæsar's forces two to one, advances to attack in such hopeless confusion because of this quarreling among the leaders that when the battle ends fifteen thousand of the Pompeians lie dead on the plain while Cæsar has only lost two hundred le-gionaries.

"I must confess my own opinion always was, that the battle of Pharsalia would be decisive; and I imagined that the victors would act with a regard to the common preservation of all, and the vanquished to their own; but both the one and the other, I was well aware, depended on the expedition with which the conquerors should pursue their success: and had they pursued it immediately, those who have since carried the war into Africa, would have experienced (and experienced too, if I do not flatter myself, by my intercession) the same clemency with which the rest of our party have been treated who retired into Asia and Achaia. But the critical opportunity (that season so important in all transactions, and especially in a civil war) was unhappily lost; and a whole year intervening, it raised the spirits of some of our party to hope they might recover the victory, and rendered others so desperate as not to dread the reverse. Fortune, however, must be answerable for the whole train of evils which this delay has produced: for who would have imagined either that the Alexandrine war could have been drawn out to so great a length, or that the paltry Pharnaces could have struck such a terror throughout Asia? . . . As I imagined that Cæsar would immediately after the battle of Pharsalia have returned to Italy, I hastened hither in order to encourage and improve that pacific disposition, which he had discovered by his generosity to so many of his illustrious enemies; by which means, I have ever since been separated from him by an immense distance. Here, in truth, I sit the sad witness to those complaints that are poured forth in Rome, and through all Italy; complaints which both you and I, according to our respective powers, might contribute somewhat to remove, if Cæsar were present to support us."

Cicero is writing to Caius Cassius of the "lean and hungry look."

A year has passed since the battle of Pharsalia, which should have ended the civil war. In Spain and Africa, Pompey's two sons, Sextus and Cnaeus, his father-in-law Scipio, his son-in-law Faustus Sulla, and Cato and Labienus have rallied around themselves new armies. A state of anarchy exists in Rome where Mark Antony rules.

Cicero sits in Brundisium devoured by doubts. After Pharsalia he had refused to take part in any further resistance to Cæsar. He had written to his son-in-law, Dolabella, who at the outbreak of the civil war had joined Cæsar's party, begging him to effect a reconciliation between himself and Cæsar. Cæsar had answered with a curt note telling him to return to Italy.

At that time the cause of the Pompeians had seemed to Cicero a lost cause. But now, a year later, he is less certain. And should the Pompeians triumph in the end he knows that his desertion of the party at Dyrrhacium will make him one of the first victims of their revenge.

Week after week, month after month, he has awaited Cæsar's arrival in Italy. He has seen Rome, wholly Cæsar's when news of the great victory at Pharsalia reached it, gradually alienated by Antony's misrule. Antony, sent to Rome after Pharsalia to take charge of the capital as Cæsar's master of horse, has spent the year in riotous debauchery, and in confiscating property to increase his own wealth. The other local Cæsarians, with the army to enforce their will, have made equal abuse of their power.

With Cæsar's continued absence, his past pretensions when he crossed the Rubicon of coming to Rome, not as an adventurer-general, but as a Liberator interested only in making Rome safe for democracy, have had time to be revealed in their true light.

Where has he been all these months—where is he now?

In Egypt with Cleopatra.

8

After the overwhelming defeat of the Pompeian forces at Pharsalia Cæsar had ridden through the Pompeian camp towards the tent that had been occupied by his former son-in-law and colleague in the triumvirate. Among Pompey's personal effects is found his private correspondence. The letters are brought to Cæsar. But does he not already know well enough who are his enemies? If he reads the letters will he learn anything new? But on the other hand does he not here have an opportunity to help build up his reputation for magnanimity and clemency? In the presence of his officers, and a number of the prisoners, he burns the letters, unread.

For days his cavalry scour the hills to which the survivors of the battle have fled, but Pompey the Great is not among the prisoners brought in. The battlefield is carefully searched for his body—it is not found there. He has escaped, but where? The Pompeian army is no more, but as long as Pompey remains at large Cæsar cannot rest easy. At last he learns that Pompey has taken ship for Egypt.

Cæsar follows. Crossing the Hellespont, he suddenly finds himself surrounded by the Pompeian fleet, cruising in the straits. As he is rashly making the passage accompanied by only a few warships, while the Pompeian fleet numbers more than a hundred vessels, it would seem that only a miracle can save him from destruction. The miracle happens. Caius Cassius, Pompey's admiral, without striking a single blow, surrenders with the whole fleet to Cæsar.

The reason for this extraordinary action is to be found in the same letter from Cicero to Cassius wherein the orator laments Cæsar's lengthy absence from Rome after Pharsalia.

"It was the hope that peace would be restored to our country, and the abhorrence of spilling the blood of our fellow-citizens, that equally induced both you and myself to decline an obstinate perseverance in the civil war. But though these sentiments were common to us both, yet as I am considered as having been the first to inspire you with them, it is more my part, perhaps to render you satisfied with having adopted them, than it is yours to perform the same friendly office towards me. But to say the truth (and it is a circumstance upon which I frequently reflect), we mutually convinced each other, in the free conversations we held upon this subject, that a single battle, if it should not wholly determine our cause, ought to be the limits, however, of our particular opposition."

This agreement between Cicero and Cassius that if Pompey meets with a single serious defeat they will support his cause no further has saved Cæsar. . . . He now goes on to Egypt. The great white lighthouse of Alexandria appears in the distance. The shore is seen lined with a huge crowd of Egyptians who seem overjoyed at his arrival.

A deputation of Alexandrians comes to meet him when he lands, bringing him a welcome offering. And suddenly, as this is brought forward, Cæsar's composure deserts him. For the welcome offering is the head of Pompey the Great.

In a quick rush all the events of his life-long association with Pompey go by. Incidents of their youth together when they were friends. Sulla—the formation of the triumvirate—his marriage with Pompeia—Pompey's marriage with his own dead daughter, Julia—the Lucca Conference, and that carriage

which bore fat Crassus and Pompey away from him throug'.
the sunshine of a spring afternoon.

He has turned aside to hide his genuine agitation. Pompey's
signet ring has been put into his hands. His fingers twist it
nervously. The Egyptians, and his own escort of legionaries,
stand silently by.

He still sees the severed head, the neck hideous with its clots
of dried blood, the face with its terrible dual resemblance to
Pompey and some strange old man. He, who has bathed a continent in blood, recoils for the first time from the grim mystery
of death. Is he not himself fifty-four?

The shock of the gruesome surprise passes. He becomes
conscious of the many eyes fixed upon him as he stares at the
ground. Memories of the past give way to thoughts of the
present.

Pompey is dead, so he no longer has a rival for the kingship
of Rome. But will it not increase his popularity in the capital
if he appears horrified at what the Egyptians have done? If
he dissimulates altogether the exultation he feels at the death
of Pompey?

He covers his face with his hands. He groans. As though unable to bear the sight of the head of his dead rival he turns his
face still further away, while motioning to a centurion to have
the bloody object removed. His body droops as though bowed
down by grief.

But suddenly he seems to recover. With angry glances at
the Egyptians he steps aside into a group of his officers, and
gives orders for the head to be buried, and a temple to Nemesis
to be built at the grave.

The signet ring he sends to Rome to prove that the civil war
is over—that Pompey the Great is really dead.

Pompey had been murdered not by an Egyptian but by a
Roman.

When the news of his defeat at Pharsalia reached Alexandria, and it was known that he was fleeing to Egypt—he had
unwisely chosen Egypt as his refuge because he hoped he

would be safe here on account of the services rendered by him in the past to the Flute-player, now dead three years—the Egyptians had seen their opportunity for revenge on the Roman tyrant whom they saw as the cause of all their miseries. It was Pompey who had murdered the Alexandrian deputation which went to Rome to protest against the reinstatement of Ptolemy. It was Pompey who had sent Gabinius with a Roman army to put the Flute-player back on the throne. It is to pay Pompey the enormous sum of 10,000 talents ($12,000,000), the price for reinstating Ptolemy, that for the last seven years the Egyptian people have been taxed to the point of starvation. At last the hour of retribution seems to have come. Shortly before Pompey's arrival Egypt had revolted against, and driven from the country, Cleopatra, who sixteen years old when her father, the Flute-player, died, had been left in his will joint ruler with her brother Ptolemy, aged ten. The Roman army of occupation left in Egypt by Gabinius has intermarried with the Egyptians, and goes over to the nationalists.

Pompey, unaware of the change in sentiment among the legionaries of the Roman garrison, but less sure of the loyalty of the Egyptians who come out in a boat to meet him off Alexandria, no longer hesitates about landing when he sees among them the military tribune Lucius Septimius, one of his own veterans. As he steps ashore Septimius stabs him in the back.

His head is cut off to be given to Cæsar, who will surely be grateful to the Alexandrians for killing his rival. Impatiently the Egyptian city awaits the arrival of Cæsar. In gratitude will he not lift from their shoulders the intolerable burden placed there by Pompey? Will he not put an end to the exploitation of Egypt by the greedy Roman Senate? Will he not as long as he lives be a friend of Egypt? The name of Rome's new ruler is on the lips of every Alexandrian. . . . Ships are sighted. . . . The population of the city rushes to the harbor. . . . Yes, it is he!

But he has frowned at the committee of welcome that

brought him Pompey's head and signet ring. And now. . . .

At first in dismay, then with anger, the citizens of Alexandria watch 3000 legionaries and 800 cavalry escort Cæsar in haughty state to the royal palace on the Lochias Promontory. In front of the Roman general march the lictors carrying their axes. Has Egypt got rid of one foreign tyrant merely to welcome another? Is the rule of the *fasces* to continue?

Street riots break out. A number of the legionaries are killed. But Cæsar reaches the palace. . . . He enters it, and disappears. . . . His soldiers are seen quartering themselves in the neighboring buildings. . . .

Rumors cause furious crowds to collect. . . . He has made the palace his home. . . . He has demanded the immediate payment of 1,600 talents ($2,000,000). . . . He has ordered the young king Ptolemy to obey his father's will, and allow Cleopatra to reign with him as joint ruler of Egypt. . . .

Pothinus, the leader of the nationalist party, is his prisoner. . . .

In the palace Cæsar is looking forward to the arrival of Cleopatra, expelled from Egypt because, true daughter of her father, she had been willing to sell Egypt into bondage to Rome.

She is a Macedonian Greek, not an Egyptian. Rome, during Cæsar's first consulship,—a fact forgotten by the Egyptians in their later hatred of Pompey,—had officially recognized her father, the Flute-player, when he usurped the throne of Egypt. Her older sister, Berenice, made queen when Ptolemy was driven from the country, had been murdered by Ptolemy on his return to Egypt with the army of Gabinius. At this time Cleopatra, a girl of fourteen, had been made love to by Mark Antony, in command of the Roman cavalry. A year before Cæsar's arrival she had had a second love affair with a Roman, her lover this time being Pompey's son Cnaeus, in Africa raising troops for his father. . . . Cæsar will be the third. . . .

He has been in Alexandria long enough to come to an understanding of the existing situation. Cleopatra, when expelled because of her Roman sympathies, had fled to Syria, from which in the past Gabinius and Mark Antony had come to reinstate her father. She is now returning with an army to take the throne away from her brother, the boy-king Ptolemy. Besides Cleopatra and the boy-king, there are two other royal children; a still younger Ptolemy, aged nine, and Cleopatra's younger sister, Arsinoe, fourteen. The boy-king and Arsinoe, with their guardian Pothinus, represent the patriot side of the family. Cleopatra is the Romanomaniac. The little Ptolemy is too small to care about either the Romans or the Egyptians.

Three of the four royal children are in the palace. When Cleopatra arrives—Cæsar has sent for her so that he can smooth out the difficulties between her and her brother—he will have them all with him. He intends to make Egypt safe for Romans by insisting that Ptolemy's will be not set aside—Cleopatra shall rule with her brother. If the nationalists refuse to tolerate his interference, it will be an excuse, in the name of justice and equity, to make war on Egypt.

He needs money to pay his soldiers. Before crossing the Rubicon his own private fortune had been used up bribing the Gauls to stay loyal, giving presents to his army, and buying Romans over to his party. The civil war has long since exhausted what he took from the treasury.

By forcing the Egyptians to pay him the amount still owed Pompey he will be able to recuperate his sadly depleted finances. And in Rome the war should be popular, as it will indicate that though in defense of the liberties of the Republic he reluctantly took up arms against Pompey he has not forgotten they are both Romans—Egypt is therefore paying dearly for the murder of the man whom he, had Pompey fallen into his power, would magnanimously have spared.

Cleopatra arrives.

Unable to come to the palace openly because of the nationalist army guarding the city, she makes her entry into the palace, and presents herself to Cæsar, according to Plutarch, in the following manner——

"She took a small boat, and one only of her confidants, Apollodorus, the Sicilian, along with her, and in the dusk of the evening landed near the palace. She was at a loss how to get in undiscovered, till she thought of putting herself into the coverlet of a bed and lying at length, while Apollodorus tied up the bedding and carried it on his back through the gates to Cæsar's apartment."

Whether she slips in in this way or not,—Plutarch, as previously stated, lived nearly a hundred and fifty years after Cæsar, and in an age when historians were greatly given to romancing—she does manage somehow to join Cæsar in the palace. He passes the night with her. By the time morning comes he is more determined than ever that she shall be queen of Egypt.

"Her charm of speech," says Dion Cassius, another historian, "was such that she won all who listened."

Dion Cassius lived more than two centuries after Cæsar. Cleopatra, small but voluptuously proportioned, and excessively amorous, doubtless possessed other charms than that of speech which made the most impression on her third Roman lover their first night together.

He is an aging sensualist of fifty-four. She is not yet twenty. He thrills at the thought of playing at war, with Cleopatra for his audience. While his soldiers loot the temples of Alexandria of their gold and silver ornaments, which will be melted down to coin the money he needs to pay his army, he dallies amorously with Cleopatra in the palace.

He holds a solemn meeting at which Ptolemy and Cleopatra are both present. In a fatherly manner he rebukes the boy-king for the wrong thing he has done in permitting Pothinus to banish his sister, who from now on, he says, will again rule as queen. He generously gives Cyprus to Arsinoe and the little Ptolemy, so that they too may have a people to govern.

His vanity expands enormously under Cleopatra's flatteries. She never seems to tire of asking him questions about his great victories in Gaul. She not only believes he is descended from the goddess of love, Venus, but tells him he is also the earthly impersonation of the Egyptian god, Jupiter-Amon. She assures him that his epileptic fits are not any ordinary mortal sickness, but divine seizures.

Rome—the civil war—the urgent need for his presence in the capital if the survivors of Pharsalia are not to rally again (though the twenty thousand unslaughtered soldiers of the Pompeian army had surrendered after the battle, all the leaders with the exception of the consul Lentulus killed in Egypt with Pompey, have made good their escape) have no longer a place in his thoughts. To his officers he gives as his excuse for staying on in Alexandria not Cleopatra but—unfavorable winds.

Though he has only four thousand men with him, and the city seethes with resentment at the arbitrary manner in which he has occupied the palace and taken over the government of Egypt, he knows he has nothing to fear from the Alexandrians. Has he not the royal children and Pothinus as hostages? Has he not sent to Asia for reinforcements? Has he not lying in the harbor close by the palace his fleet which he can board at any time in order to escape serious danger?

For six months now the Alexandrians, a brave and industrious people, fight in their turn for liberty against this greatest pirate-general of all ages.

Unknown to Cæsar, the boy-king and Pothinus have communicated with the Roman army of occupation stationed on the Nile near Alexandria. And this army, on hearing that the Alexandrians have risen to drive out the invader, makes a decision which, when Cæsar hears of it, startles him out of his sense of security. The soldiers left by Gabinius have been denationalized by their eight years' residence in Egypt to the extent that they now voluntarily renounce their rights as Roman citizens and under the Egyptian general Achillas march on Alexandria to help the townspeople in their fight against Cæsar.

Pothinus, held a prisoner in the palace, prays that the army of occupation may arrive before Cæsar's reinforcements. Cæsar's assurances that what he is doing is all for the good of Egypt the minister listens to with scorn.

For as an Egyptian he feels himself immeasurably superior to the Roman. Is the dirty sprawling city of Rome to be compared with stately Alexandria with its great pharos, its splendid theatre, its large library? Of what value, indeed, is this Roman civilization that is being forced on the world? Has Rome ever been a truly cosmopolitan metropolis as was Carthage, as now is Alexandria?

What industries has it developed, what large-scale commerce, other than the slave traffic, has it encouraged? What handicrafts can it show to be compared with those of the busy Phœnicians? What taste has it for art or science?

No, Rome has created nothing, but has always destroyed. It is the Romans, so quick to call foreigners Barbarians, who are themselves the Barbarians.

To the monstrous treachery and greed of the Republic have been sacrificed Carthage and Corinth. The isles of Greece are littered with the ruins of the once prosperous and beautiful towns destroyed by these Italian vandals. And what Rome does not destroy it steals. Are not the palaces of the Roman millionaries adorned with columns plundered from Grecian temples? Do not the writings of the great Greek philosophers lie buried in the private libraries of these vulgar collectors of antiques, who themselves cannot read? Are not yearly more and more of the incomparable statuaries of Praxiteles and Phidias dragged from Greece to swell the stolen glories of the robber city by the Tiber?

Do not the Romans still go to Rhodes to study oratory? Has there ever been a Roman scientist to be ranked with the great Archimedes, brutally hacked to pieces by a Roman legionary at the siege of Syracuse? Are not all the physicians in Rome Greek and Egyptian slaves? Where is the Roman astronomer to be mentioned in the same breath as the Egyptian, Sosigenes?

And the grandeur of Rome as a great engineering nation, its pride in its military highway, bridges and aqueducts— Were not the first paved roads in Italy copied from those of Car-

thage? Was not the principle of the arch known to Greece before the Trojan War? Had it not been made use of in the
tombs of the Pharoahs fifteen hundred years ago? Is there a
city built by Romans which possesses the intricate system of
aqueducts by which Alexandria draws its water from the Nile?

In the art of ship-building it has been the same. Was not
the first large Roman ship modelled on a Carthaginian vessel
wrecked on the coast of Italy, which fell into the hands of the
Romans?

For years the mailed fist of Rome has darkened the sky
over Alexandria. Will it fall now and crush the Egyptian city
as it crushed Carthage and Corinth?

The noise of a great shouting rises to the roof of the palace on which Pothinus stands staring out over the city. His thin
face lights up with triumph, for he knows it is made by the
army of occupation arriving in Alexandria.

Cæsar, too, has heard the shouting.

When he learns that the army of occupation has come to
fight not for but against him he feels momentarily uneasy. He
sends messengers to the nearest subject countries, to Syria,
Crete, and Rhodes, ordering these to furnish him with troops
and ships. He contemplates leaving the palace with Cleopatra
and going on board one of the vessels of his fleet.

But he quickly recovers his assurance. Shall he, the conqueror
of Gaul, the victor over Pompey the Great, flee before the
petty forces of the Alexandrians? To impress Cleopatra must
he not stay in character as the descendant of Venus, the earthly
impersonation of the great god, Jupiter-Amon?

So he laughs at the fears of his officers. Around the palace
and the neighboring theatre seethe the angry Alexandrians.
Can four thousand legionaries hold out against the population
of a city as large as Rome, reinforced by several thousand of
their own former comrades? He smiles, and refuses to be
alarmed. What have the legionaries to fear when he, CÆSAR,
is with them?

He is confident because he still has the children and Pothinus as hostages, and because he knows that, as in Gaul, he can always win the advantage by burning and destroying, when the Alexandrians from love of their city will hesitate to take similar drastic measures against him. If he destroys Alexandria he will win the good-will of the Roman capitalists who have long hated Alexandria as a commercial rival. So he sets fire to the great library, and to the granaries and docks along the waterfront. . . . While the Alexandrians are fighting the fire to keep it from spreading throughout the city he captures the lighthouse at the entrance to the harbor.

The Pharos stands on an island—it is connected with the city by a mole which divides the harbor into two parts, arched openings in the mole allowing passage from the east to the west harbor. The palace faces the west harbor, in which lies his fleet. With the lighthouse in his possession, and his fleet drawn up near the palace need he any longer worry? He returns to the embraces of Cleopatra.

But the Alexandrians fight on grimly. Having extinguished the fire, they try to destroy the Roman fleet by sending fireships through the arched openings in the mole, from the west harbor which they control. They storm the palace, only to be repulsed by the legionaries. They make undrinkable the palace water by pumping the sea into the conduits from the Nile which go to the quarter of the town held by Cæsar—the legionaries find fresh water by sinking wells. Their fleet has been destroyed in the conflagration on the waterfront—they start building a new one, while assembling all the vessels lying in the canals along the river. They continue the uneven struggle after the first of Cæsar's reinforcements have arrived—a legion sent by Calvinus from Asia Minor. And one day they recover the lighthouse.

In the fighting Cæsar has lost several hundred legionaries. His soldiers, who want to return to Rome, begin to grumble at this petty war which is keeping them in Egypt. The loss of the island controlling the entrance to the harbor has put their commander in a bad temper. Is Cleopatra to see him worsted by the motley forces of the Egyptians? To avenge the slur on

his reputation as an invincible general, and to restore the
confidence of the legionaries, he will immediately regain possession of the lighthouse. He orders it to be attacked simultaneously by his war vessels on the seaboard and the fleet inside the harbor.

He himself directs the assault. The island is taken, the
Egyptians being driven back along the mole as far as the second
arch-opening. At this point he orders the mole to be closed towards the city by a transverse wall.

He stands in his scarlet cloak looking triumphantly towards
the palace. Cleopatra must already know that her Cæsar has
been victorious! But suddenly all around him is confusion. The
Alexandrians have unexpectedly landed a body of soldiers on
the mole near the island. These come charging down on the
legionaries at work on the wall. A panic seizes the Romans who
buffet Cæsar to right and left in their mad scramble to escape
by boarding the ships lying alongside the mole.

He becomes one of the crowd fighting to reach the ships. He
pushes his officers and soldiers aside with his long arms while
shouting to them to turn and face the enemy. He heaves a
sigh of relief as at last he feels his feet treading the deck of
one of the ships.

But the legionaries are still crowding after him. The crew
though they hear his furious cries to push off from the mole
are powerless to move their oars. The ship, overloaded, cap-
sizes, throwing him into the water with the common soldiers.

He rises sputtering to the surface and has to swim for his
life until picked up by one of the other ships which recognizes
his bald head bobbing up and down.

Furious at his narrow and ignominious escape he returns to
the palace. Here a messenger who has come through the Alexandrian lines is waiting for him with the news that the relief
army from Syria is nearing the city.

He smiles triumphantly. *Alexandria, which has imperiled
the life of Cæsar, will soon be at his feet.* But before the war

ends there are three who shall die—the boy-king Ptolemy, the minister Pothinus, and the general Achillas. In Egypt as in Gaul he will pursue the policy of putting to death the patriots who refuse to submit to Roman rule. Pothinus he will have murdered here in the palace. In the camp of Achillas there are undoubtedly officers jealous of their general—one of these he will bribe to kill the Egyptian commander. And the boy-king——?

Cæsar reflects. On account of Ptolemy's youth would it be politic to kill him? Would it not be better, after Achillas is out of the way, to affect admiration for the young king's courage in opposing him—to magnanimously release him, and encourage him to take command of the Egyptians now that the general is dead—to let him perish with his army?

For he himself has resolved not to allow his military reputation to suffer by seeming to have been in desperate straits before the arrival of the relief army—he intends to leave Alexandria and meet it on the way—led by their boy-king, the Egyptians should fall an easy prey to the Roman eagles.

And for the murder of Pothinus he will make his soldiers responsible—himself generous and forgiving, he will seem deeply grieved at the minister's death—he will give out that "contrary to his natural humanity" he has been forced by the clamors of his legionaries to punish Pothinus, as the instigator of all the treacheries of the Egyptians, in the same way that in Gaul he had been obliged to have Guturvatus whipped to death, and other Gallic chiefs similarly tortured, because of his soldiers' impatience with the perfidiousness of the Barbarians.

He sends a messenger to a eunuch named Ganymede in the Egyptian camp, with whom he has already held secret negotiations. Then he orders Pothinus and the boy-king to be brought to him, and reprimands them for inciting their countrymen to the treacherous actions committed by the Alexandrians since his arrival—first the street riots when he marched to the palace, in which many of the legionaries were killed, then the bringing to Alexandria of the army of occupation, last of all the recent outrage on the mole, in which, though the lighthouse is still in his possession, he has lost four hundred soldiers.

He dwells sternly on their ingratitude to Rome, which in the past has done so much for the royal family, saying that since they are his hostages for the good behavior of the city he would be entitled by all the rules of civilized warfare to put them to death as a retaliation for the killing of his soldiers.

Now he raises his hand in a gesture of benevolence. A kindly smile plays on his lips as he says that he intends to let them go free. If he cannot make them his friends, he prefers to have them as open rather than secret enemies. They may both therefore leave the palace and go to the Egyptian camp.

It is the same smile, and the same tone of voice, that he used to the German chiefs, detained in his camp during the massacre on the isthmus between the Meuse and the Rhine.

When the boy and the man have left his presence Cæsar goes to Cleopatra.

The palace rings with the cry of a man in mortal agony, repeated once, and followed by silence.

A centurion brings Cæsar the news that the soldiers, furious at the disaster on the mole, have fallen on the minister Pothinus as he was leaving the palace with the young king, and stabbed him to death.

Intense agitation crosses his face. He hurries with Cleopatra to the scene of the murder. He orders the soldiers who have killed Pothinus to be placed under arrest.

Beside the body of the minister, lying in its pool of blood, stands the boy-king, white and trembling. The Roman general puts an arm around his shoulder and leads him to one side. He talks to Ptolemy long and earnestly as though he were his son. Deeply, indeed, does he regret the accident that has happened to Ptolemy's guardian. But the legionaries have become unmanageable, he insinuates, because of the treacherous mode of fighting adopted by the rabble in the city. Let Ptolemy hasten to the Egyptian camp, and oppose Cæsar in open and honest warfare, as befits a king. He presses the boy-king's hand as he adds the hope that some day, instead of being enemies, they may be friends. After doubling the escort of Ptolemy, he himself accompanies him to the edge of the quarter of the town occupied by the legionaries.

The boy-king arrives in the Egyptian camp, pitched on the bank of the Nile, facing that of the relief army. A crowd of soldiers surging around the tent of Achillas parts to let him through. He sees Achillas sprawled on the floor of the tent with a dagger in his side.

Dazed with horror, he stares. Superimposed on the body at his feet he still sees that other one in the palace, hacked by the swords of the legionaries, lying in its pool of blood. His lips quiver, he is on the verge of bursting into tears. With his guardian and general both dead, what hope is there of resisting mighty Cæsar?

A pathetic and lonely little figure the Egyptian boy-king stands a moment facing the murdered general in trembling indecision, then pushing back his fears as he remembers he is king, and making a desperate attempt to live up to his royal dignity, he turns to the Egyptian officer and announces that since Achillas is dead he himself will command the nationalist army in the coming battle with the Romans.

So the stage is set for the battle between the Roman of fifty-four and the frail Egyptian boy of fourteen.

Cæsar takes his three legions by ship from Alexandria to the delta of the Nile, west of the city. He marches into the delta and joins forces with the relief army from Syria, coming to meet him.

He has determined not merely to defeat the nationalist army, but utterly to destroy it. Behind the Egyptian camp is the Nile.

Attacked on three sides by the Roman army, the Egyptians waver—their lines of defense break—their retreat becomes a mad flight towards the river. Those that escape being cut to pieces by the pursuing Roman cavalry drown in the Nile.

Among the latter is the boy-king Ptolemy. The boat on
which he has taken refuge sinks overladen with struggling soldiers. The world vanishes from his vision a nightmare of
screams and blood—faces hideously contorted in death-agonies
and with lust of killing—the monstrous bellows of a Roman
bucina—red swords rising and falling—Cæsar in his scarlet
cloak. . . .

Alexandria surrenders when Cæsar, after the battle of the
Nile, marches on the town. He warns the inhabitants never
again to depart from their peace occupations to engage in war
with Rome. He points to their burnt library, granaries and
docks as an example of the calamity that always befalls the
people which attempts to overpower him by treachery. He will
not destroy the city as he has destroyed others for lesser crimes,
but the 1600 talents must be paid, and a large indemnity also
for bringing about the war. Now that the older Ptolemy is
dead, Cleopatra shall reign jointly with the little Ptolemy.
Arsinoe he sends to Rome to be led in his triumph.

Cleopatra is pregnant. He celebrates a mock marriage with
her—then they make a trip up the Nile together in a floating
palace with a roof garden, sumptuous dining apartments, col-
onnaded walks, and shrines dedicated to Venus and Dionysos.
Four hundred ships carrying his army and Cleopatra's attendants accompany them through the Nile-land. They visit Mem-
phis and Thebes, going as far as the first Cataract.

He lives in a voluptuous paradise. From either bank of the
Nile stretches away the desert, overhead blazes the tropical
sun. Slaves fan them with palm leaves as Cleopatra, reclining
at his side, tells him she wishes to be queen of the world.

Cæsar dreams of future conquests. In this strangely silent
Nile-land, over which eternity seems to brood, a change has
stolen over him. He believes now what he has always wanted
others to believe. Caius Julius Cæsar is no more—*Cæsar the
God-King has been born.*

But the legionaries, at the first Cataract, five hundred miles
from the mouth of the Nile, refuse to go further. Victorious

though they have been under Cæsar, they are weary of his end-
less wars. They want the peace he has promised them for years.
They have come to believe the story that he is descended from
Venus and therefore bears a charmed life—but are not they,
his soldiers, only mortal? Do not a few more of them fall in
every battle? In the end will any of the veterans be left alive
to enjoy the rewards promised them? They refuse to follow
their commander into Ethiopia, and he has to turn back.

He returns to Alexandria. Reluctantly, at the news that the
Pompeian leaders, because of his year's absence, have managed
to arm against him again, he decides to leave Cleopatra and
return to Rome. She is to follow him to the capital to be present when he celebrates his triumph, bringing with her the son
that has been born to them—Cæsarion.

But what has Cæsar, the God-King, to fear from the sons
of Pompey, or petty Asiatic chiefs? Before embarking for
Italy he proceeds against Pharnaces, the son of Mithridates,
who is attempting to over-run Asia Minor, and after defeating
Pharnaces he sends to Rome his historic message——

"I came, I saw, I conquered!"

9

There have been rumors in Rome that he has been killed
by the Alexandrians, that the interior of Africa has swallowed
him, that his whole army has been cut to pieces by Pharnaces.
Cicero, daily more fearful of the growing strength of the Pompeians, hears at last the glad news that he is coming home. To
Terentia, on August the 11th, Cicero writes——

"I have not yet heard any news of Cæsar's arrival, or of his
letter which Philotimus I was informed had in charge to deliver
to me. . . . Take care of your health."

On August the 12th,

"I have at last received a letter from Cæsar and written in
no unfavorable terms. It is now said that he will be in Italy
much sooner than was expected. I have not yet resolved whether
to wait for him here, or to meet him on his way; but as soon as
I shall have determined that point I will let you know. . . .

Let me conjure you to take all possible care of your health."

On September the 1st,
"I am in daily expectation of my couriers whose return will perhaps render me less doubtful what course to pursue. As soon as they shall arrive, I shall give you immediate notice. Meanwhile be careful of your health."

On October the 1st—Cæsar has landed at Tarentum, and Cicero, hurrying to this town, has had an interview with him that ended much to his satisfaction—now he is following Cæsar to Rome——

"I purpose to be at my Tusculan villa about the 7th or 8th of this month. I beg that everything may be ready for my reception, as I shall perhaps bring several friends with me; and I may probably too continue there some time. . . . If a vase is wanting in the bath, let it be supplied with one."

Suddenly he is in Rome. He is scornful of the fears in the capital that the Pompeians, because of his prolonged absence in Egypt, may yet win back to power. He orders his army to prepare for another campaign in Africa, where Cato and Labienus, with King Juba as their ally, have concentrated their forces.

The legions mutiny. The soldiers of his own favorite Tenth legion march on Rome, and demand their discharges. . . . Once again he makes the gesture of indifference. He calls them not *commilitones*, "comrades—brothers-in-arms," but *quirites* "citizens." Those who wish to leave him may do so. They shall be given the land in Italy he has promised them—the money also; but having disobeyed their general's orders, they need not expect to be allowed to participate in his triumph. . . . The soldiers agree to follow him on one more campaign. . . . He again calls them *commilitones*, and seems to graciously overlook the mutiny. . . . But he has the leaders secretly put to death later.

He stays in Rome only a few weeks, then sails for Africa.

It is midwinter—he expects to be in the capital again before spring. But the civil war, instead of ending at Pharsalia, is just beginning. The Pompeian army has fewer leaders now. Labienus has more authority. For months victory hangs in the balance. Labienus, imitating the methods used by Vercingetorix in Gaul and the Parthians in Asia, opposes Cæsar with an army consisting almost entirely of mounted troops and light-armed infantry which will not engage in a fixed battle. His supplies are cut off. His foraging parties are harassed by the Pompeian cavalry. Three of his legions, sent out for supplies, are surrounded, and almost annihilated.

In the end it is not superior generalship, but the same quarreling among the leaders of the Pompeian army which existed before Pharsalia that brings him victory. Now that Cæsar's defeat seems a certainty, the Pompeians are contending bitterly with each other for the honor of commanding the army that is to destroy him. Varus, as governor of the province in which the war is taking place, claims the right of leading the legions. Scipio, because his daughter is Pompey's widow, insists upon being ranking general. The legionaries clamor for Labienus. The senators want Cato. King Juba, the native monarch of Mauretania, threatens to withdraw his 2000 cavalry and 120 elephants unless, as the only king in the camp, he is allowed to take precedence in the councils of war.

Cato, elected to settle the dispute, gives the command to the consul, Scipio, who, against the advice of the others, chooses to abandon the plan of guerilla warfare, and to lead a disorganized army against Cæsar, repeating the mistake of Pharsalia.

At the battle of Thapsus the Pompeian army again goes down to defeat. This time the Cæsarians give no quarter. Furious at how narrowly he has escaped losing the war in Africa, Cæsar drops his mask of clemency—now that he is at last victorious he will end the civil war as he ended his Gallic wars by exterminating the enemy. For days the fleeing Pompeians are pursued, until fifty thousand corpses are scattered over the plain around Thapsus. With few exceptions the captured leaders are executed—Cæsar sparing, however, his own kinsman

Lucius Cæsar, in order to have him privately assassinated later.

At the battle itself Cæsar was not present. Foaming at the
mouth, he fell down in an epileptic fit before the attack. When
he revives his legionaries have won the victory for him.

Standing beside the body of Cato, who has committed suicide at Utica, he wears the mask again. His glance sweeps the
faces of his officers, grouped around him. He looks down at
the body. He exclaims slowly and sorrowfully——

"Cato, I grudge you your death—as you have grudged me
the preservation of your life!"

He is in Rome again, triumphing for the great victories
won by him during the fourteen years that have elapsed since
his first consulship. Cleopatra has arrived in the capital with
Cæsarion, and is lodged in his magnificent palace in the Ti-
berine gardens. The celebration, to which she has been invited
as an honored guest, lasts four days. There is a day for Africa,
a day for Egypt, and a day for Greece. But the biggest day of
the festival is the day for Gaul, which has Vercingetorix as its
main feature.

The triumphal procession is led by the senators who have
gone over to Cæsar. Next come trumpeters. Then follows a
pictorial history of the Gallic wars crudely painted on boards
erected on platforms high enough for the crowds to see—lurid
battle scenes showing Cæsar leading his army to victory over
the Helvetii, the Belgian confederacy, the Germans—pictures
of the naval battle in the bay of Quiberon, of the Rhine, of
the cliffs of Britain . . . of the sieges of Avaricum, Gergovia
and Alesia—with, in huge letters, the names of the vanquished
nations; this exhibit also contains Gallic coins, samples of Barbarian armor, and several of the British chariots. More music
follows—a body of flute-players. Now appear the sacrificial
bulls—white, their horns gilded and draped with garlands of
flowers and fruit, accompanied by the slaughtering priests.
Next comes a small menagerie of the animals native to Gaul,
Germany and Britain—the lack of spectacular creatures such as

elephants and giraffes is made up for by immense pictures, resembling those of a modern circus side-show, showing the mythical monsters said to inhabit the vast Hercynian forest beyond the Rhine.

Shouts of *Hail Cæsar!* rise from the mob as the general is seen approaching. He stands in a circular chariot drawn by four white horses. Before him are the Gallic captives, and lictors walking in single file, their fasces wreathed in laurel. Behind come his generals mounted, and the legionaries on foot waving their spears likewise wreathed in laurel.

Vercingetorix, the captive of greatest distinction, walks alone in chains so that he may be the more readily recognized. He has spent nine years in Roman prisons.

The leering brutish faces of the mob, jeering and spitting at him, stream by. Dragging his chains, he walks proudly between the two lines of hostile faces.

But his thoughts? Is he to die when the triumphal procession reaches the base of the Capitoline hills? His wife has begged Cæsar for his life—the Roman has magnanimously promised it to her. Cæsar himself has visited him in prison and protested friendship. By reputation in Italy, Cæsar is great-hearted, forgiving. But what of his cruel murders in Gaul?

The Capitol appears. And though he has steeled himself to expect not life but death a sudden mist blurs the eyes of Vercingetorix as nearer and nearer approaches the temple on the hill-top. Haughtily as he walks, his heart is torn by memories of faraway Gaul.

Once he glances back. He sees Cæsar bowing and smiling from the triumphal car to the crowds thronging the steps of the public buildings in the Forum.

Now the procession has reached the foot of the Capitol. And as a centurion leads him aside Vercingetorix turns. For an instant his eyes meet those of Cæsar as the conqueror rides by. The eyes of the Roman look quickly and furtively away.

The walls of the dungeon close around Vercingetorix.

A fierce yell of triumph rises from the Roman mob as one of the executioners who has strangled the Barbarian appears in the doorway of the dungeon and shouts that he is dead. The crowd rushes forward to fling insults at the body that comes rolling down the long flight of steps leading to the Forum.

On the summit of the Capitol, Cæsar, standing before a smoking altar, raises his eyes heavenwards and commences the customary sacrifices to the Gods.

PART 5

The Invincible God

I

"I HAVE hopes that Cæsar intends, and indeed that he actually has it under his consideration, to establish a republican form of government of some kind."

Thus writes Cicero to a friend shortly after Cæsar's return from Africa.

The orator is for the moment breathing easily. Thapsus has ended his fears that he will fall a victim to the revenge of the Pompeians. Cæsar, when they met at Tarentum, had promised him that after the campaign in Africa all his efforts would be directed towards the task of organization which his year's stay in Egypt has delayed. In the new government Marcus Tullius Cicero is to be a conspicuous figure.

Pompey the Great, the consuls Lentulus and Scipio, Domitius Ahenobarbus, Cato, and three-fourths of the Senate which had left Italy with Pompey when Cæsar crossed the Rubicon—all are dead. Of the Pompeian leaders there remain alive only Pompey's two sons, in Spain when the battle of Thapsus was fought, and Labienus, one of the few survivors of the battle, who had escaped to Spain. Two of the Pompeian armies have been cut to pieces—can a third ever be raised? Cicero is no longer tormented by doubts as to which is the safe side. In his relief at being forgiven for having at the commencement of the civil war thrown in his lot with Pompey he forgets for a brief period his life-long jealousy of Cæsar.

But gradually it returns. Can he, once officially recognized as the Saviour of his Country, and called by Cato the Father of his Fatherland, be satisfied to help further the ambitions of Caius Cæsar? Can he be a spectator of Cæsar's four-day triumph without brooding over the injustice of being awarded none himself for his exploits in Cilicia?

The gnawings of envy increase as the celebrations in the capital continue. The great gladiatorial combats, and public banquets, with which Cæsar is entertaining the populace so that they will forget the misery brought on the country by the civil war—already over two hundred thousand Italians have lost their lives in it—fill him with brooding resentment. Is there in Rome today a single reveller who remembers the noble part played by the consul Cicero in suppressing the Catiline conspiracy?

While Cæsar was in Africa his mood had been more carefree. Rejoicing that his life had been spared he had still had visions of a glorious future. Even the lurking dread that the Pompeians might be victorious had not been sufficient to dampen the high spirits coming as a reaction to the despondency in which he was wrapped during the year's waiting at Brundisium. With his friend Marcus Terentius Varro, the writer, who had likewise served under Pompey and with the same prudence resolved to remain neutral after Pharsalia, he plans a trip to the gay pleasure resort of Baiae on the Bay of Naples.

"But will it be altogether decent to appear in so gay a scene, at a time when Rome is in such a general flame? and shall we not furnish an occasion of censure to those who do not know that we observe the same philosophic life in all seasons and in every place?"

He overcomes his scruples. Let the world—and Terentia—think what they please, he intends to go.

"For, after all, what imports it? since the world will talk of us in spite of our utmost caution. And, indeed, whilst our censurers are immersed in every kind of flagitious debauchery, it is much worth our concern, truly, what they say of our innocent relaxations: in just contempt, therefore, of these illiterate barbarians, it is my resolution to join you very speedily."

But a letter written to Varro shortly afterwards shows the

philosopher less fearless of public opinion. The battle of Thapsus is about to be fought. He is worrying over the outcome. He decides to put off the pleasure trip for awhile.

"Much will depend on the general result of this battle, and the temper in which Cæsar will return. . . . I should be glad if you would postpone your journey to Baiæ till the first transports of this clamorous joy are subsided; as it will have a better appearance to meet you at those waters, when I may seem to go thither rather to join with you in lamenting the public misfortunes, than to participate in the pleasures of the place."

He becomes nervous in the extreme on hearing how Cæsar has dropped the mask of clemency at Thapsus. The fate of Lucius Cæsar—pardoned, and then killed—particularly disturbs him. Is Marcus Tullius Cicero to meet the same fate?

"When I heard of the fate that has attended Lucius Cæsar, I could not forbear saying to myself with the old man in play 'what *tenderness* then may not I expect!' For this reason I am a constant guest at the tables of our present potentates; and what can I do better, you know, then prudently swim with the current of the times? . . . I am unable to answer your question, when Cæsar will arrive, or where he proposes to land. Some, I find, doubt whether it will be at Baiæ; and they now talk of his coming home by the way of Sardinia. It is certain, at least, that he has not yet visited this part of his *demesnes;* and though he has not a worse *farm* upon all his *estate,* he is far, however, from holding it in contempt."

His resentment deepens when after Cæsar's return to Rome he finds that the latter treats him coolly because his tongue has been wagging too freely in derision of the coming monarchy. Cæsar's favorites, particularly Mark Antony, are openly antagonistic. More and more embittered by the revelry in Rome he retires at last to sulk on one of his estates. Night and day the thought that Cæsar—who has allowed himself to be appointed Dictator—will soon be king, torments him.

Slowly there grows in his mind the thought that perhaps

where armed opposition has failed flattery may succeed. If in a burst of oratory he eulogizes Cæsar as the greatest of all Romans, and praises him as a Liberator, may he not renounce his intention of destroying the constitution?

His opportunity comes when the Senate petitions Cæsar to pardon, and allow to return from exile, Marcus Marcellus, who, consul during Cæsar's last year in Gaul, had agitated strenuously to have him recalled from his command. Many of the other Romans who had gone with Pompey at the beginning of the war, and had retired into Greece or Asia after his death in Egypt, to let future events shape themselves, Cæsar has permitted to return to Rome, but against Marcellus he nourishes a bitter hatred. Cicero is present in the senate-house when the Dictator humiliates the senators by forcing them, one by one, to come to him and beg that he pardon Marcellus. . . . Unwilling to make himself unpopular by refusing, Cæsar still cannot smother his resentment against the man who tried to take his army away from him. His dark eyes smouldering, he stares at the floor. . . . Suddenly a thought comes to him. . . . He looks up—he smiles—he tells the senators their petition is granted—Marcellus may return.

Whereupon Cicero rises and delivers himself of his famous speech in behalf of Marcus Claudius Marcellus. (Appendix, p. 305) in which he extols Cæsar to the skies for his merciful disposition, applauds his unselfish interest in the welfare of the Republic, and bids him dismiss any fears he may have that he is in danger of being assassinated.

The senate-house rings with applause. Cicero has not failed to notice that his speech seems to have made a deep impression upon the Dictator. A feeling of triumph surges through him as he reflects that after all he is still Cicero, the greatest orator of his age, whose eloquence not even Cæsar can resist.

But Cæsar has smiled. Before many weeks have passed Cicero receives a letter from a friend in Greece telling him how Marcellus, on the point of returning from exile, has been mysteriously assassinated.

Again he is in the depths of despondency, his pride revolting at the thought that he has been tricked by Cæsar's treacherous clemency. He resolves that his oration for Marcellus shall have been his farewell to Roman politics. Nothing will ever induce him to take part in the affairs of the Republic again. From now on he will shun all human society, bury himself in the country with his books. In a letter to his friend Papirius Paetus he hints indeed at an act of renunciation even sterner than that of becoming a hermit.

"Cato's death," he writes, "must be acknowledged to have been truly, and I can still follow his example," but here he pauses, and when he resumes his letter it is to qualify his desperate resolution with the prudent afterthought, "whenever I shall be so disposed."

2

But not yet is the civil war over. Rumors come to Rome of the army that the two sons of Pompey, and Labienus, are collecting in Spain. The Pompeians, whom Cæsar had reported as completely crushed at Thapsus, are again active on the peninsula to the west. For months Cæsar affects to ignore their activities, but at last he has to take them seriously. The whole peninsula has revolted against the troops left by him there after the campaign preceding the one in Macedonia, and gone over to the Pompeians. Pamphlets and satirical poems secretly circulated by his enemies in the capital show that hope is reviving that he may yet be thwarted of his desire to be king.

Black rage in his heart, he prepares for another campaign. Such persistent opposition fills him with baffled fury similar to that which he felt when Gaul, which he had thought subdued, continued to rise against him. He longs, by some act of unparalleled ferocity, as that at Uxellodum, to forever terrorize the Pompeians into submission. His bitter resentment, which as usual he covers with unconcern, is aggravated by the thought that it is not any of his old enemies in the Senate, but Labienus, his own favorite general, whose hatred is the most implacable.

Cicero, who, for all his resolutions, has not been able to bring himself to the point of retiring from public life, and still less to that of committing suicide, is once again torn by conflicting desires. He longs to see Cæsar destroyed in the coming Spanish campaign, but dreads the vengeance of the Pompeians should they be victorious. He is posing in the rôle of a Roman who thoroughly disapproves of all Cæsar's actions, yet is resigned to non-resistance. To raise money the Dictator is busy selling seats in the Senate to Gauls, and bestowing the title of "friend of Rome" on Asiatic princes. He has put a heavy tax on luxuries, and to further humiliate the wealthy aristocrats who still favor the oligarchy has organized a special police who—like modern prohibition agents—force their way into banquets and snatch the forbidden dishes from the tables. These measures Cicero, smarting under Cæsar's neglect, and the cavalier manner in which he is treated by his favorites, brings his most biting wit to bear upon whenever he feels safe among friends; while at the same time not omitting to lament the sad state of public affairs which has pushed him into the background. To Papirius Paetus, who with other members of the old senatorial party has urged him not to abandon the cause, even though it appears a lost one, brooding over past glories and present injustices he writes——

"I then sat at the helm of the commonwealth . . . but now I can scare claim the privilege to officiate even in the lowest functions of the State. Were I to reside at Naples, would there be a single decree of the Senate the less by my absence? On the contrary, though I live in Rome, and appear publicly in the Forum, they are settled by our friend in his own house, entirely without my participation. If I happen, however, to occur to his memory, he sometimes does me the honor to prefix my name. Accordingly, I am often informed, from Syria and Armenia, that a decree of the Senate is published in those provinces, and published too as made on my motion, of which I had never heard the least mention before. You will suspect, perhaps, that I am not serious; but be assured I speak the literal truth. I have at this instant letters in my possession from the remotest

*In the senate-house he lies . . . a huddled heap of
lifeless flesh and purple rags.*

potentates of the globe, returning me thanks for having procured them an acknowledgment of their regal title from the Senate; when I was so far from knowing they were honored with that appellation, that I was utterly ignorant there were any such persons existing. Nevertheless, as long as this *superintendent of our manners* shall continue in Rome, I will comply with your request; but the moment he leaves us I shall certainly set out to join you over a plate of mushrooms."

Cæsar leaves for Spain, riding out of Rome in a carriage containing besides himself his general Decimus Brutus, who now holds the position of trust once occupied by Labienus, and his grand-nephew, Octavius, a youth of seventeen, whom, as he has had no son by Calphurnia, he has chosen to be his heir. When he departs he gives the capital the assurance that the war in Spain will be over in a few weeks.

Months pass, during which the suspense in Rome is reflected in Cicero's letters to his friends.

To Cassius——

"We are in great expectation of the news from Spain, having as yet received no certain intelligence from that quarter. Some flying reports, indeed, have been spread, that things do not go well there; but they are reports without authority."

To Cassius again——

"We have hitherto received no certain intelligence from Spain. . . ."

To Lepta——

"We have no news from Spain; all that we know with certainty is, that the young Pompey[1] has drawn together a very considerable army. This we learn from a letter of Paciaccus to Cæsar, a copy whereof Cæsar himself has transmitted to us; in which it is affirmed that he is the head of eleven legions. Messala, in a letter he lately wrote to Quintus Salassus, in-

---

[1] The older brother, Cnaeus.

forms him that his brother, Publius Curtius, has been executed by the command of Pompey in the presence of his whole army. This man had entered, it seems, into a consipracy with some Spaniards, by which it was agreed in case Pompey should march into a certain village for provisions, to seize upon his person, and deliver him into the hands of Cæsar."

To Aulus Torquatus——

"Various and contradictory reports are every day propagated amongst us concerning affairs in Spain. . . . No one can determine what will be the event of the approaching battle; but as to that of the war in general, I have no manner of doubt; at least, none with respect to its consequences. For one side or the other must certainly be victorious; and I am well convinced of the use that either party will make of their success: such a use, indeed, that I had rather suffer what is generally esteemed the most terrible of all evils, than live to be a spectator of so dreadful a scene.

To Torquatus again——

"One of these three events must neccessarily take place; either we shall never see an end of our civil wars, or they will one day subside and give the Republic an opportunity of recovering its vigor, or they will terminate in its utter extinction."

In Spain Cæsar is fighting not for victory but for life. This last of his campaigns is the most desperate he has ever engaged in. He has had to discard the illusion that once again, as after his quick defeat of the "paltry Pharnaces," he will be able to send to the Senate the message, *Veni, vidi, vici!* His hope of descending on the Pompeians like a thunderbolt out of a clear sky has fallen far short of realization. He has found the entire peninsula hostile, his own garrisons lined up with Labienus, and the towns everywhere fortified against him.

What the Pompeians have lost in numbers through past defeats they have gained in increased unity of command. Their headquarters is no longer cluttered with consuls and senators wrangling over formalities of rank. Cnaeus Pompey the Younger, nominally commander-in-chief, has agreed to relinquish to Labienus the supreme authority in the conducting of the war. And in Spain, as in Africa, Labienus opposes to Cæsar the tactics of Vercingetorix by refusing to come to an engagement. He intends to prolong the war until the halo of military greatness around the name of Cæsar begins to dim. The longer he can keep Cæsar in Spain the more opportunity will there be for the Dictator's enemies in Rome to organize a revolution. From town to town he lures Cæsar on, satisfied with cutting off his supplies, and harassing his dwindling army with cavalry and mounted archers.

But once again, as at Pharsalia and Thapsus, victory in the end is Cæsar's because of division of leadership in the Pompeian camp. Pompey's sons, eager to revenge the death of their father, though willing to defer to Labienus at the beginning of the campaign, insist on a battle now that Cæsar's situation seems to have become desperate. They accuse Labienus of over-cautiousness, and of wishing to avoid a battle only because he is reluctant to have victory deprive him of the special powers with which he has been invested by the Pompeys. Are not the two armies now equal in numbers? May not delay mean that Cæsar will receive reinforcements from Italy? What dread can the Cæsarian forces inspire when the Spanish army is more than half composed of Cæsar's own veterans now fighting against him?

So on the 17th of March in the year 45 is fought the battle of Munda which ends the civil war. With the odds even, should not Cæsar, who has astounded Rome by leading his legions to victory over almost limitless hordes of Barbarians, who conquered Egypt with a handful of soldiers, who boasts that his mere presence on the battlefield is worth an army, overcome this last stand of the Pompeians almost at the first trumpet-sound?

To inspire his soldiers with confidence in a quick and easy victory, he has played on their supernatural fears to the utmost. Meteors that fall the night before the battle, the roll of distant thunder, are interpreted by him as auguries showing that the gods are with Cæsar. He reports to the legionaries at an assembly that letters just arrived from Rome mention all the marble images in the capital as sweating, another favorable omen.

He goes further—he tells them that many of the silver eagles of the enemy legions have been seen leaving the standards and flying away from the Pompeian camp.

But for hours the battle rages with no indication of victory. The Spanish and Moorish auxiliaries on either side, anticipating a desperate struggle, have refused to take part in the fighting until they know who is going to be the victor—overshadowing the inducements which have allied them to Cæsar or Pompey is their general hatred of all Romans—they stand by watching with grim satisfaction the legionaries slaughtering one another, and wait to fall on the vanquished with the conqueror.

At one moment the Cæsarians are seen to give way. Furiously the Pompeians press them back. The flight is only checked by Cæsar, who, believing the day is lost, leaps from his horse and seizes a standard—his praetorian guard closes around him, the standard moves back towards the enemy, and the panic is stayed. The auxiliaries, who have begun to advance, stand silently by again. The battle resumes its aspect of a carnage which will end only with the annihilation of both armies.

When victory comes to Cæsar eventually it is through an accident. While the two armies are at a deadlock, Labienus, noticing a suspicious movement among the auxiliaries, and fearing that they have decided to enter the battle in support of Cæsar, gallops diagonally across the battlefield in their direction. Conspicuous in his general's cloak, he attracts the attention of the soldiers. It is the psychological moment when a mere nothing is enough to decide the issue of the battle. The spark of doubt lit by a soldier crying, "He flies—he flies!" spreads like wildfire through the ranks of the Pompeians—the cry is repeated with a roar by a thousand throats in the Cæsarian army, the Pompeians give way in a panic—with that cry, FEAR, the dread and omnipresent phantom of battlefields, crouching ever watchful of its opportunity, has leaped into their midst—in an instant it has converted them from resolute soldiers into two lines of frenzied fugitives, the one fleeing towards the town of Munda, the other in the direction of Cordova, with the Cæsarian cavalry, joined by the auxiliaries, thundering in pursuit.

On the plain of Munda is repeated with even greater ferocity the massacres of Pharsalia and Thapsus, Cæsar throwing aside all that pretense of affection for the Pompeian soldiers as old "brothers-in-arms," by which he had hoped to encourage desertion before the battle. With diabolical fury, when he finds the gates of Munda closed against him, he blockades the town within an enclosing wall built of thousands of dead bodies pinned together with lances, and surmounted by a fringe of heads on swords' points with the faces turned toward the town so that the besieged may readily recognize their former comrades. The town, on its surrender, is given over to plunder by the legionaries, and in Cordova where the resistance is more determined, besides the Pompeian fugitives, the whole Spanish population of twenty thousand is put to the sword.

He stays in Spain until the last survivors of the battle of Munda have been rounded up and killed. Of the Pompeian rank and file thirty thousand have perished on the field of battle, and an equal number in Munda and Cordova. Of the leaders, Labienus was killed early in the retreat, while the head of the elder Pompey, who managed to escape to the mountains, is brought to Cæsar later by captains of his pursuing cavalry.

3

His life has six months to run after his return from Spain. He arrives in Rome toward the end of September, 45, he will be assassinated in the senate-house on the 15th of March of the year following.

There no longer exists an opposition army. Rome is at the feet of Cæsar. He can at last give free rein to the egotism flattered by Cleopatra, who is still in the capital.

He celebrates a fifth triumph—for Munda. . . .

He has himself appointed Dictator for life, *praefectus morum*, or "superintendent of manners and morals," for life, and Imperator for life. The title Imperator is to be hereditary—with Cæsar it loses its previous sense of a purely military honor conferred on a victorious general by his soldiers, to be laid aside when the general surrenders his command to return to civil life. Afraid of the popular prejudice against the name of king, he makes use of *Imperator* as a synonym for *Rex*, the title to give him in reality all the royal prerogatives. He takes it as his prænomen, instead of writing it *after* his name. He is no longer Cæsar Imperator, but Imperator Cæsar, and thus the first of the line of Roman emperors.

He forces the Senate to pass decrees giving him the right of deciding on war and peace without consulting either it or the people, of nominating new patricians, of conducting elections, of nominating the provincial governors, of taking personal charge of the keys of the state-chest, and disposing as he may see fit of treasures and armies.

His image is placed on all new coins struck. The name of the month he was born in—Quintilis—is changed to Julius. His birthday is made a perpetual holiday. The *Genius of Cæsar* is added to the constitutional oath.[1] He is voted the name of Liberator; also—most cruel blow of all to Cicero—that of *Pater Patriæ*, Father of his Fatherland.

The colonies in Africa and Greece, which he plans to settle on the sites of destroyed Carthage and Corinth with thousands of his discharged soldiers, are to be named, the first "The Venus Colony," the second, *Laus Julius*, "Honor to Julius." . . . He builds an immense temple to Venus in the Forum, and in it places a statue of Cleopatra. . . . He builds another huge temple to Mars, and in this places a statue of himself. . . .

He appears publicly in the costume of the old kings of Rome—an all-purple toga. . . . He sits on a golden chair, placed between the two stools of the consuls, in the senate-house, and receives the Senate in kingly fashion, without rising. . . .

To commemorate his clemency, a third temple, dedicated to

[1] Today it is the genius of Mussolini

Concord, is built. . . . And the foundations of a fourth are laid—here Cæsar himself is to be worshipped . . . with Mark Antony as his priest. . . .

He is no longer Caius Julius—mortal; but Divus Julius—divine. . . .

He has images of himself made, which bear the inscription, Θεὸς ἀνίνητος, the *Invincible God.*

In the Capitol there have stood from ancient times the statues of the seven kings of Rome—he has his own erected beside them as the eighth. . . .

On the 15th of February, Antony formally offers him the crown.

But it is only the swords of his soldiers that are keeping Rome quiet. He has aroused the bitter resentment of the whole capital by allowing his desire to parade once again before Cleopatra to lead him into triumphing for his victory at Munda. For, since the beginnings of the Republic, triumphs have only been given generals for conquests over foreign foes, never for those over Roman citizens. In the civil war three hundred thousand Italians have lost their lives. Some of the oldest families in Rome have been wiped out; there is none which has not lost a father or several sons. The war has brought Rome no rich booty, such as Pompey plundered from the East, and Cæsar himself sent back from Gaul. Its expenses have been enormous —to keep his soldiers loyal he has had, during the course of it, to increase the reward promised them on the Rubicon from $250 to $1000—to every citizen in Rome who has remained neutral he has had to pay $15. Though he has ground down the foreign nations to the utmost in order to finance the war, it is Rome, largely, through property confiscations, and money taken from the treasury each time he returned to the capital, that has had to shoulder the staggering weight of the cost.

Rome, mourning for its dead, recoils from the sight of Cæsar, bowing and smiling, being driven through the streets in his quadriga. It resents as an insult and a mockery his moral

prohibitions—his harsh laws against adultery and divorce—
when he is openly keeping Cleopatra in Rome as his mistress,
and the capital contains no one more dissipated than his own
general, Mark Antony.

He has won for himself the emnity of all artists and writers
by his attempted censorship of books and plays, and by his refusal to pardon the authors who fought him with their pens
as well as their swords during the civil war. His angry temper
towards the latter is revealed in a letter received at this time
by Cicero from the writer, Aulus Caecina, whom Cæsar is
keeping exiled from Rome. (Appendix, page 314.)

The censorship, like all censorships, does him more harm
than good. It becomes the fashion to write plays and satires in
which he is indirectly attacked. A dozen lives of Cato, eulogiz-
ing him as a martyr, appear—Cicero himself writes one. Cæsar exposes the insincerity of his own generous comment on
Cato's death at Utica when he attempts to counteract this tide
of disparagement by himself writing a venomous little volume
entitled, "Anti-Cato."

Busily as his staff of scribes labor to justify his actions, they
are impotent to influence in his favor a public opinion that has
grown hostile to him. Rome has not been deceived by his refusal of the crown. It is too well known that he himself in-
stigated Mark Antony to offer it. And the street demonstra-
tions whenever he appears—can it be doubted that he is likewise the instigator of these when, after a recent disturbance
caused by a crowd collecting and hailing him as king, the tribunes of the people who arrested the ring-leaders, were by his
orders in turn arrested and thrown into prison?

The Senate, shorn of all power, is satisfied to fight him—
for a while—with derision. Wall-placards burlesquing the new
military monarchy appear everywhere. Anonymous verses once
again ridiculing him as "queen" rather than king of Rome are
distributed. Obscene cartoons of Cæsar and Cleopatra pass from
hand to hand. His bitterest enemies, in order to make him the
more hated, are those most eager to shower empty honors upon
him. On a day when he is absent from the senate-house, one of

the senators rises, and solemnly proposes that every woman in Rome shall be at his disposal.

The humor grows more sinister. A week before the assassination, when the conspiracy to kill Cæsar is already well under way, the Senate passes a decree declaring his person to be sacred—whoever injures him by word or deed commits sacrilege!

Cæsar, I reflected, was but mortal; and there were many ways in which he might be got rid of!

Sixty senators are privy to the conspiracy. The active conspirators are Decimus Brutus, Trebonius, Cassius, Marcus Brutus, Casca, Ligarius, and Metullus Cimber—two of them his own trusted generals, and a third his reputed illegitimate son by Cato's sister, Servillia.

He intends to leave Rome shortly to make war on the Parthians. He is advertising a prophecy that the Parthians will never be defeated except by a king. Again, when he departs, Mark Antony is to have charge of Rome. And unless the conspirators act quickly they will not be able to act at all, as Decimus Brutus is being sent as governor to the north of Italy, Marcus Brutus to Macedonia, and Trebonius to Asia Minor.

His generals, like Labienus, have become embittered by his habit of taking to himself all credit for victories, by his change of manner towards them now that he has assumed regal honors, by his infatuation for Cleopatra which has made him desirous of extending his conquests until the whole world is at his feet. His former enemies, whom he thinks he has won over by clemency, resent his favors as patronage—if he has made them governors of provinces, and assigned them other important posts in his new government, is it not only that they may the better serve Cæsar? Even the humbler burgesses forget and forgive the corruption of the oligarchy now that Rome is in the power of this treacherous megalomaniac and epileptic whom they see issuing in haughty state from the apartments of the hated Egyptian queen, then to watch the wreath of bay, wrought in gold, tumble from his bald head, as, foaming at the mouth, he falls down in the market-place.

So approaches that memorable Ides of March of nearly two thousand years ago.

The evening before, the conspirators meet at the house of Cassius. The main subject of discussion is whether Antony shall be killed as well as Cæsar. Were Cicero present he would cast his vote in the affirmative, but because of his well-known habit of talking too freely, he is not being admitted to the details of the conspiracy. The decision arrived at is that Antony, much as he is hated, shall be allowed to live—were he killed with Cæsar, the motive for the assassination, the foiling of Cæsar's ambition to wear a crown, would stand out less clearly.

The Ides of March, the 15th of the month, has been chosen as the day, because on this date there is to be a meeting of the Senate, the last of importance before Cæsar leaves for Parthia, at which Antony will again offer him the crown—this time Cæsar, because of the Parthian prophecy, is to accept it.

Having agreed to let Antony live, the conspirators rehearse the assassination. Cæsar is to be killed while sitting in the golden chair which Republican eyes see already as his virtual throne. Antony, who will doubtless be with him when he comes to the senate-house, is to be detained at the door in conversation by Trebonius until Cæsar has been stabbed. As soon as Cæsar seats himself, the conspirators, their daggers ready under their togas, are to gather around him—Cimber, whose brother is one of the exiles whom the Imperator has refused to pardon, is to petition Cæsar that he be allowed to return from banishment—the others are to join him in this petition—when Cæsar refuses, as it is known he will, the signal shall be Cimber's seizing hold of his robe with both hands, and pulling it down from his neck. After Casca gives the first stab, in the neck, the rest of the conspirators are also to bury their daggers in Cæsar, so that he will not be the only one compromised—only in the event that Antony attempts to rescue the Imperator, is he to be cut down by a gang of gladiators, concealed in the adjoining temple. After the assassination the conspirators are to rush boldly out on to the street, waving their bloody daggers, while they cry out to the people that the tyrant is dead.

Around these last hours of Cæsar the legends cluster thick. There is the story of him signing papers at the house of Lepidus. The conversation around him turns on death, and the kind of death most to be desired. Cæsar looks up quietly, and says, "A sudden one!"

There is the story of the armor of Mars, which stands in a hall of his palace, trying to warn him against the morrow by wandering with clanking steps around the palace awhile and finally crashing down upon the floor. Of the door of his room, similarly watchful over his welfare, flying open of its own accord. Of Calpurnia dreaming she saw him murdered, and then ascending into heaven, where God stood with his hand out, ready to welcome Cæsar. Of the importunate old soothsayer who in a cracked voice bids Cæsar beware of the Ides of March, and is paid no attention to.

There is the story of the scared priests who hurry to Cæsar with the news that the results of the sacrifices have been most ominous, and of the Imperator's scornful reply, "Am I to be frightened because a sheep is without a heart?"

There are the tales of the prodigies which set all Rome quaking. The lion seen prowling around the Capitol but which annoys no one, only giving everyone it meets a surly look. The men "all in fire" who parade up and down the Forum. The bird of night which sits in the market-place hooting and shrieking.

The Ides of March have come.

In the senate-house the conspirators are assembled, the daggers under their robes. In the adjoining temple the gang of gladiators lies in waiting. The senators, many who know what is about to happen, some who do not, are in their places, waiting the arrival of Cæsar.

All eyes are fixed on that golden chair which an attendant

has just placed between the lower curule seats of the consuls. Trebonius stands ready at the door. Near the chair, a statue of Pompey, which Cæsar has magnanimously not had removed from its place in this new senate-house built by Pompey shortly after the Lucca Conference, faces the assembled Senate.

The minutes pass. Still he does not come.

And suddenly the attendants reappear, and begin taking out the chair, while it is announced that Cæsar is unwell, and will therefore not be able to be present at this meeting of the Senate.

But if he stays away all is lost. The conspirators, trembling for their own lives, gather together to discuss in low agitated tones how best to dispel any fears he may have. They send Decimus Brutus, in whom he is known to have implicit trust, to him, to make light of his suspicions and urge him to attend.

Will he come?

Yes, he is here.

His head, crowned with the gold bay leaf, has appeared at the entrance to the senate-house. Trebonius is drawing Antony aside.

He seats himself in the gold chair, hurriedly brought back by the attendants. The conspirators gather around him. Cimber makes his petition.

Cæsar refuses to grant it. The others join their entreaties to Cimber's. Angrily, he again refuses. Cimber puts both hands on his robe and drags it down from his neck.

Casca strikes—Cassius strikes—Decimus Brutus strikes—Marcus Brutus strikes—Cimber strikes—Ligarius strikes.

He has struggled to his feet after the first two blows. At the third he gasps, *"Et tu, Brute!"* [1] and falls.

Above the red swirl of knives flashing over him he sees Pompey looking down, first a tiny marble face leering at him from an infinite distance, then suddenly of such colossal proportions that it obliterates the whole world in darkness.

[1] "And you too, Brutus!" Cæsar's dying remark was made to his trusted general Decimus Brutus, and not, as commonly supposed, to Marcus Brutus.

After making sure he is dead by hacking the body until the blood gushes from thirty-five wounds, the conspirators push their way to the street through the crowd of senators scrambling to escape from the scene of the assassination, and hurry about the city crying the glad news that the Republic has been delivered of its tyrant, that the Constitution is once again safe.

In the empty senate-house he lies at the foot of Pompey's statue, the overturned golden chair and his gold bay-wreath beside him . . . a huddled heap of lifeless flesh . . . and purple rags.

Epilogue

THE assassination plunged Rome into another civil war. For three years it raged—first Antony and Octavius against the conspirators, then Antony against Octavius. One by one, the "tyrannicides," as they call themselves, come to violent ends, some dying on their own swords, others in battle. Antony has his second disastrous affair with Cleopatra. To please her, he murders her sister, Arsinoe. Later, defeated by Octavius, he kills himself. Cleopatra kills herself. Octavius murders Cæsarion. Then Octavius, taking to himself the title of Augustus, rules Rome as the second Imperator.

So the Republic changes into a military monarchy, and the line of Roman emperors, with powers more autocratic than ever had the ancient kings—but careful never to call themselves kings—picks up the coveted prize of world exploitation where the oligarchy had so unwillingly dropped it.

Cæsar's "reforms" may be dismissed with a few instances of the two classes into which they naturally fall. The first contains laws passed to remedy evils which he himself has created. In this class fall his marriage and divorce laws, designed to make the word *proletarius* "children-producer" a term of honor among Romans, so that the population of Italy into which the civil war with its attendant disease and famine has made such appalling inroads, may be again built up to the point where there will be, in the jargon of modern militarists, plenty of "human material" for future wars. In the second class are the reforms that attempt to lift Rome—which affects to have carried the banners of Progress into the dark hearts of Africa, Asia and Europe—not to any dizzy heights of enlightenment above the murdered nations, but to the same level of culture reached centuries before by the Greek, Phoenician, and Egyptian civilizations hacked to pieces by the swords of the legionaries. Cæsar has burnt the great library in Alexandria—on returning to Rome he has the foundations laid for a Roman public library which shall be modelled on this. He uplifts Roman law by abolishing the law that debtors who cannot pay shall become the slaves of their creditors—the more humane Greek and Egyptian codes need no such an improvement.

His most noted reform in this second class is that made to the Roman calendar. The Roman lunar year, based on infantile observations of the moon coupled with equally childish mathematics, was sixty-five days in advance of the sun, the Roman so-called winter being thus in reality the autumn, and the spring the winter. The basis of the Egyptian calendar, on the contrary, was the solar year of 365 days, 5 hours, 52 minutes, and 12 seconds, a calculation so exact that it varies from that of modern astronomers by only 3 minutes and 24 seconds. It was only by bringing to Italy the Alexandrian astronomer, Sosigenes, who promptly threw the moon into the discard and made the sun the basis for the new time system, as it already was in that of Egypt and of Greece, that Cæsar was able to give Rome its new calendar, which, in honor to himself, he promptly called the Julian calendar.

The golden age of peace and prosperity which he is supposed by his admirers to have ushered into the ancient world is seen, in a truer light, as a period of unparalleled development of Roman greed and brutality. It was under the Cæsars that the passion for the bloody gladiatorial combats and wild-beast shows rose to its greatest height. That these might have a setting more in keeping with the grandeur of Rome than the old wooden amphitheatres and circus, the great stone Colosseum was built, at the dedication of which 9000 animals, and almost as many gladiators were killed. Trajan, after his triumph over the Dacians, exhibited 10,000 gladiators. Satiated with seeing men kill each other, the Roman mob clamored for variety—women gladiators were now thrust out into the arena. These bigger and better butcheries under the Empire included also the well-known burning, crucifying, and hunting of Christians. Nor were they merely patronized by such diseased monsters as Nero and Caligula, on whom the spotlight of imperial infamy is usually centered—the "good" emperors were quite as thoroughly Roman in their tastes for this amusement. It was not until Rome began to "fall" that the shows and combats became less popular—and what more ironic commentary on Roman greatness can be found than the fact that it was the Goths and Vandals—those hated Barbarians from northern Europe who, long after Cæsar's death, finally swept away the Empire—who at last abolished them?

But if Cæsar died, the legend of his greatness lived after him, and thrived. He became a model for all ruthless adventurers of later ages, who cloaked their greed for power in high-mindedness and lofty patriotism. He established an overwhelming precedent for "right of conquest." His bloody campaigns in Gaul "to hold back the tide of Barbarian invasion" gave sanction to that insidious policy of extension of boundaries which goes by the name of "aggressive defense." In emulation of his exploits as an empire-builder in Gaul, other nations have likewise ravished new worlds with their expeditionary forces, committing the same enormities upon the "Barbarians." Like Cæsar, they have broken down resistance and won their victories largely through lies, false professions of friendship, and treacheries, and with the aid of that more modern military asset—the Bible. His name has been perpetuated in Tsar and Kaiser.

The apologists for his monstrous acts in Gaul attempt to whitewash these with the blithe catch-phrase that the end justifies the means. They would subordinate Cæsar, the adventurer-general, to Cæsar, the consummate statesman. They see him as a great dreamer, looking beyond the bloody battlefields in the foreground to the Utopia he is striving to create. He is organizer, administrator, reformer, before he is soldier.

But what of that greatest of all his buildings projected by him before his death—that immense temple of Mars which, to quote the German historian, Mommsen, most ardent of Cæsar-worshippers, was "to surpass all that had hitherto existed in riches and glory," and in which his own statue was to occupy the most conspicuous place?

Is not here if anywhere to be found the true expression of Cæsar as destroyer rather than creator—a silent testimony to the fact that, had he lived, it would have been to continue to exalt organized rapine and murder above productive industry, . . . the cut-throat above the worker . . . the crime of war above the arts of peace?

There remains to chronicle briefly the end, and the events leading up to it, of that other outstanding Roman of the period —Marcus Tullius Cicero.

His sick wife, Terentia, who worked night and day when he was in exile to obtain his pardon, has grown old. He divorces her on the score that she is too extravagant a housekeeper, and marries a girl under twenty.

His daughter Tullia dies. Once again his letters to his friends become so maudlin with self-pity that they lose all patience with him. Servius Sulpicius, after condoling with him over his loss, writes——

"Nevertheless, I think proper to suggest a few reflections, which have occurred to me upon this occasion; not as imagining they will be new to you, but believing that, in your present discomposure of mind, they may possibly have escaped your attention. . . . Do not forget that you are Cicero—the wise, the philosophical Cicero, who were wont to give advice to others; nor resemble those unskillful empirics, who, at the same time that they pretend to be furnished with remedies for other men's disorders, are altogether incapable of finding a cure for their own. On the contrary, apply to your private use those judicious precepts you have administered to the public. . . . But it would be ill-manners to dwell any longer upon this subject, as I should seem to question the efficacy of your own good sense. I will only add, therefore, that as we have often seen you bear prosperity in the noblest manner and with the highest applause, show us, likewise, that you are not sensible of adversity; but know how to support it with the same advantage to your character. In a word, let it not be said, that fortitude is the single virtue to which my friend is a stranger."

Lucius Lucceius, the historian requested by Cicero to make a separate volume of the Catiline conspiracy, writes in a similar vein——

"If you have withdrawn from the world in order to give free vent to those tears which you so immoderately indulged when you were here, I shall lament, indeed, your grief; but, if you will allow me to speak the truth, I can never excuse it. For tell me, my friend, is it possible that a man of your uncommon discernment should not perceive what is obvious to all mankind? Is it possible you can be ignorant that your perpetual complaints can profit nothing, and only serve to increase those disquietudes which your good sense requires you to subdue?"

Cicero is not an active member in the conspiracy, but once the assassination is an accomplished thing, does throw the whole weight of his oratory in favor of the conspirators. He delivers himself of his fourteen celebrated Philippics against Mark Antony, in the second of which his hatred for Antony makes him surpass all his previous efforts at personal invective.

Addressing himself directly to Antony, who is present in the senate-house, he thunders——

"Shall we, then, examine your conduct from the time you were a boy? I think so. Let us begin at the beginning. Do you recollect that, while you were still clad in the prætexta, you became a bankrupt? That was the fault of your father, you will say. I admit that. In truth, such a defense is full of filial affection. But it is peculiarly suited to your own audacity, that you sat among the fourteen rows of the knights, though by the Roscian law there was a place appointed for bankrupts, even if anyone had become such by the fault of fortune and not by his own. You assumed the manly gown, which you soon made a womanly one; at first a public prostitute, with a regular price for your wickedness, and that not a low one. But very soon Curio stepped in, who carried you off from your public trade, and, as if he had bestowed a matron's robe upon you, settled you in a steady and durable wedlock. No boy bought for the gratification of passion was ever so wholly in the power of his master as you were in Curio's. How often has his father turned you out of his house? How often has he placed guards to prevent you from entering? while you, with night for your accomplice, lust for your encourager, and wages for your compeller, were let down through the roof. . . . But let us say no more of your profligacy and debauchery. There are things which it is not possible for me to mention with honor; but you are all the more free for that, inasmuch as you have not scrupled to be an actor in scenes which a modest enemy cannot bring himself to mention."

For a short time, when Antony has fled the capital, Cicero is again the head of the State. But with the defeat of the armies of the conspirators by those of Antony and Octavius, he, in, turn, has to flee for his life to one of his country estates.

Hearing that Antony's cavalry is approaching, he gets into a litter, and orders his slaves to carry him to the sea-coast. . . . On a hilltop far behind the litter appear the tiny figures of mounted men. . . . Louder and louder grow the hoof-beats. The slaves drop Cicero and run.

Grown slightly deaf, he puts his huge head inquiringly out through the curtains to find out the cause of the delay. . . . And one of Antony's cavalrymen, thundering up beside the litter with drawn sword, promptly cuts it off.

APPENDIX

FIRST ORATION AGAINST CATILINE

When, O Catiline, do you mean to cease abusing our patience? How long is that madness of yours still to mock us? When is there to be an end of that unbridled audacity of yours, swaggering about as it does now? Do not the mighty guards placed on the Palatine Hill—do not the watches posted throughout the city—does not the alarm of the people, and the union of all good men—does not the precaution taken of assembling the Senate in this most defensible place—do not the looks and countenances of this venerable body here present, have any effect upon you? Do you not feel that your plans are detected? Do you not see that your conspiracy is already arrested and rendered powerless by the knowledge which everyone here possesses of it? What is there that you did last night, what the night before—where is it that you were—who was there that you summoned to meet you—what design was there which was adopted by you, with which you think that anyone of us is unacquainted?

Shame on the age and its principles! The Senate is aware of these things; the consul sees them; and yet this man lives. Lives! ay, he comes even into the Senate. He takes a part in the public deliberations; he is watching and marking down and checking off for slaughter every individual among us. And we, gallant men that we are, think that we are doing our duty to the Republic if we keep out of the way of his frenzied attacks.

You ought, O Catiline, long ago to have been led to execution by command of the consul. That destruction which you have been long plotting against us ought to have already fallen on your own head.

What? Did not that most illustrious man, Publius Scipio, the Pontifex Maximus, in his capacity of a private citizen, put to death Tiberius Gracchus, though but slightly undermining the constitution? And shall we, who are the consuls, tolerate Catiline, openly desirous to destroy the whole world with fire and slaughter? For I pass over older instances, such as how Caius Servilius Ahala with his own hand slew Spurius Maelius when plotting a revolution in the state. There was—there was once such virtue in this Republic, that brave men would repress mischievous citizens with severer chastisement than the most bitter enemy. For we have a resolution of the Senate, a formidable and authoritative decree against you, O Catiline; the wisdom of the Republic is not at fault, nor the dignity of this senatorial body. We, we alone—I say it openly—we, the consuls, are wanting in our duty.

The Senate once passed a decree that Lucius Opimius, the consul, should take care that the Republic suffered no injury. Not one night elapsed. There was put to death, on some mere suspicion of disaffection, Caius Gracchus, a man whose family had borne the most unblemished reputation for many generations. There were slain Marcus Fulvius, a man of consular rank, and all his children. By a like decree of the Senate the safety of the Republic was intrusted to Caius Marius and Lucius Valerius, the consuls. Did not the vengeance of the Republic, did not execution overtake Lucius Saturninus, a tribune of the people, and Caius Servilius, the praetor, without the delay of one single day? But we, for these twenty days, have been allowing the edge of the Senate's authority to grow blunt, as it were. For we are in possession of a similar decree of the Senate, but we keep it locked up in its parchment—buried, I may say, in the sheath; and according to this decree you ought, O Catiline, to be put to death this instant. You live—and you live, not to lay aside, but to persist in your audacity.

I wish, O conscript fathers, to be merciful; I wish not to appear negligent amid such danger to the state; but I do now accuse myself of remissness and culpable inactivity. A camp is pitched in Italy, at the entrance of Etruria, in hostility to the Republic; the number of the enemy increases every day; and yet the general of that camp, the leader of those enemies, we see within the walls—ay, and even in the Senate—planning every day some internal injury to the Republic. If, O Catiline, I should now order you to be arrested, to be put to death, I should, I suppose, have to fear lest all good men should say that I had acted tardily, rather than that anyone should affirm that I acted cruelly. But yet this, which ought to have been done long since, I have good reason for not doing as yet; I will put you to death, then, when there shall be not one person possible to be found so wicked, so abandoned, so like yourself, as not to allow that it has been rightly done. As long as one person exists who can dare to defend you, you shall live; but you shall live as you do now, surrounded by my many and trusted guards, so that you shall not be able to stir one finger against the Republic: many eyes and ears shall still observe and watch you, as they have hitherto done, though you shall not perceive them.

For what is there, O Catiline, that you can still expect, if night is not able to veil your nefarious meetings in darkness, and if private houses cannot conceal the voice of your conspiracy within their walls—if everything is seen and displayed? Change your mind: trust me: forget the slaughter and conflagration you are meditating.

You are hemmed in on all sides; all your plans are clearer than the day to us; let me remind you of them. Do you recollect that on the twenty-first of October I said in the Senate, that on a certain day, which was to be the twenty-seventh of October, Caius Manlius, the satellite and servant of your audacity, would be in arms? Was I mistaken, Catiline, not only in so important, so atrocious, so in-credible a fact, but, what is much more remarkable, in the very day? I said also in the Senate that you had fixed the massacre of the nobles for the twenty-eighth of October, when many chief men of the Senate had left Rome, not so much for the sake of saving themselves as of checking your designs. Can you deny that on that very day you were so hemmed in by my guards and my vigilance, that you were unable to stir one finger against the Republic; when you said that you would be content with the flight of the rest, and the slaughter of us who remained? What? when you made sure that you would be able to seize Praeneste on the first of November by a nocturnal attack, did you not find that that colony was fortified by my order, by my garrison, by my watchfulness and care? You do nothing, you plan nothing, think of nothing which I not only do not hear, but which I do not see and know every particular of.

Listen while I speak of the night before last. You shall now see that I watch far more actively for the safety than you do for the destruction of the Republic. I say that you came the night before last (I will say nothing obscurely) into the Scythe-dealers' street, to the house of Marcus Lecca; that many of your accomplices in the same insanity and wickedness came there too. Do you dare to deny it? Why are you silent? I will prove it if you deny it; *for I see here in the Senate some men who were there with you.*

O ye immortal gods, where on earth are we? in what city are we living? what constitution is ours? There are here—here in our body, O conscript fathers, in this the most holy and dignified as-sembly of the whole world, men who meditate my death, and the death of all of us, and the destruction of the city, and of the whole world! I, the consul, see them; I ask them their opinion about the Republic, and I do not yet attack, even by words, those who ought to be put to death by the sword. You were, then, O Catiline, at Lecca's that night; you divided Italy into sections; you settled where everyone was to go; you fixed whom you were to leave at Rome, whom you were to take with you to Manlius; you portioned out the divisions of the city for conflagration; you undertook that you your-self would at once leave the city, and said that there was then only this to delay you, that I was still alive. Two Roman knights were found to deliver you from this anxiety, and to promise that very night, before daybreak, to slay me in my bed. All this I knew almost before your meeting had broken up. I strengthened and fortified my house with a stronger guard; I refused admittance, when they came, to those whom you sent in the morning to salute me, and of whom I had foretold to many eminent men that they would come to me at that time.

As, then, this is the case, O Catiline, continue as you have begun. Leave the city at last: the gates are open; depart. That Manlian camp of yours has been waiting too long for you as its general. And lead forth with you all your friends, or at least as many as you can; purge the city of your presence; you will deliver me from a great fear, when there is a wall between me and you. Among us you can dwell no longer—I will not bear it, I will not permit it, I will not tolerate it. Great thanks are due to the immortal gods, and to this very Jupiter Stator, in whose temple we are, the most ancient protector of this city, that we have already so often escaped so foul, so horrible, and so deadly an enemy to the Republic. But the safety of the commonwealth must not be too often allowed to be risked on one man. As long as you, O Catiline, plotted against me while I was the consul-elect, I defended myself not with a public guard, but by my own private diligence. When, in the next consular comitia, you wished to slay me when I was actually consul, and your competitors also, in the Campus Martius, I checked your nefarious attempt by the assistance and resources of my own friends, without exciting any disturbance publicly. In short, as often as you attacked me, I by myself opposed you, and that, too, though I saw that my ruin was connected with great disaster to the Republic. But now you are openly attacking the entire Republic.

You are summoning to destruction and devastation the temples of the immortal gods, the houses of the city, the lives of all the citizens; in short, all Italy. Wherefore, since I do not yet venture to do that which is the best thing, and which belongs to my office and to the discipline of our ancestors, I will do that which is more merciful if we regard its rigor, and more expedient for the state. For if I order you to be put to death, the rest of the conspirators will still remain in the Republic; if, as I have long been exhorting you, you depart, your companions, these worthless dregs of the Republic, will be drawn off from the city too. What is the matter, Catiline? Do you hesitate to do that when I order you which you were already doing of your own accord? The consul orders an enemy to depart from the city. Do you ask me, Are you to go into banishment? I do not order it; but, if you consult me, I advise it.

For what is there, O Catiline, that can now afford you any pleasure in this city? for there is no one in it, except that band of profligate conspirators of yours, who does not fear you—no one who does not hate you. What band of domestic baseness is not stamped upon your life? What disgraceful circumstance is wanting to your infamy in your private affairs? From what licentiousness have your eyes, from what atrocity have your hands, from what iniquity has your whole body, ever abstained? Is there one youth, when you have once entangled him in the temptations of your corruption, to whom you have not held out a sword for audacious crime, or a torch for licentious wickedness?

What? when lately by the death of your former wife you had made your house empty and ready for a new bridal, did you not even add another incredible wickedness to this wickedness? But I pass that over, and willingly allow it to be buried in silence, that so horrible a crime may not be seen to have existed in this city, and not to have been chastised. I pass over the ruin of your fortune, which you know is hanging over you against the ides of the very next month; I come to those things which relate not to the infamy of your private vices, not to your domestic difficulties and baseness, but to the welfare of the Republic and to the lives and safety of us all.

Can the light of this life, O Catiline, can the breath of this atmosphere be pleasant to you, when you know that there is not one man of those here present who is ignorant that you, on the last day of the year, when Lepidus and Tullus were consuls, stood in the assembly armed; that you had prepared your hand for the slaughter of the consuls and chief men of the state, and that no reason or fear of yours hindered your crime and madness but the fortune of the Republic? And I say no more of these things, for they are not unknown to everyone. How often have you endeavored to slay me, both as consul-elect and as actual consul? how many shots of yours, so aimed that they seemed impossible to be escaped, have I avoided by some slight stooping aside, and some dodging, as it were, of my body? You attempt nothing, you execute nothing, you devise nothing that can be kept hid from me at the proper time; and yet you do not cease to attempt and to contrive. How often already has that dagger of yours been wrested from your hands? how often has it slipped through them by some chance, and dropped down? and yet you cannot any longer do without it; and to what sacred mysteries it is consecrated and devoted by you I know not, that you think it necessary to plunge it into the body of the consul.

But now, what is that life of yours that you are leading? For I will speak to you not so as to seem influenced by the hatred I ought to feel, but by pity, nothing of which is due to you. You came a little while ago into the Senate: in so numerous an assembly, who of so many friends and connections of yours saluted you? If this in the memory of man never happened to any one else, are you waiting for insults by word of mouth, when you are overwhelmed by the most irresistible condemnation of silence? Is it nothing that at your arrival all those seats were vacated? that all the men of consular rank, who had often been marked out by you for slaughter, the very moment you sat down, left that part of the benches bare and vacant? With what feelings do you think you ought to bear this? On my honor, if my slaves feared me as all your fellow-citizens fear you, I should think I must leave my house. Do not you think you should leave the city? If I saw that I was even undeservedly so suspected and hated by my fellow-citizens, I would rather flee from their sight than be gazed at by the hostile eyes of everyone. And do you, who, from the consciousness of your wickedness, know that the hatred of all men is just and has been long due to you, hesitate to avoid the sight and presence of those men whose minds and senses you offend? If your parents feared and hated you, and if you could by no means pacify them, you would, I think, depart somewhere out of their sight. Now your country, which is the common parent of all of us, hates and fears you, and has no other opinion of you, than that you are meditating parricide in her case; and will you neither feel awe of her authority, nor deference for her judgment, nor fear of her power?

And she, O Catiline, thus pleads with you, and after a manner silently speaks to you: There has now for many years been no crime committed but by you; no atrocity has taken place without you; you alone unpunished and unquestioned have murdered the citizens, have harassed and plundered the allies; you alone have had power not only to neglect all laws and investigations, but to overthrow and break through them. Your former actions, though they ought not to have been borne, yet I did bear as well as I could; but now that I should be wholly occupied with fear of you alone, that at every sound I should dread Catiline, that no design should seem possible to be entertained against me which does not proceed from your wickedness, this is no longer endurable. Depart, then, and deliver me from this fear; that, if it be a just one, I may not be destroyed; if an imaginary one, that at least I may at last cease to fear.

If, as I have said, your country were thus to address you, ought she not to obtain her request, even if she were not able to enforce it? What shall I say of your having given yourself into custody? what of your having said, for the sake of avoiding suspicion, that you were willing to dwell in the house of Marcus Lepidus? And when you were not received by him, you dared even to come to me, and begged me to keep you in my house; and when you had received answer from me that I could not possibly be safe in the same house with you, when I considered myself in great danger as long as we were in the same city, you came to Quintus Metullus, the praetor, and being rejected by him, you passed on to your associate, that most excellent man, Marcus Marcellus, who would be, I suppose you thought, most diligent in guarding you, most sagacious in suspecting you, and most bold in punishing you; but how far can we think that man ought to be from bonds and imprisonment who has already judged himself deserving of being given into custody?

Since, then, this is the case, do you hesitate, O Catiline, if you cannot remain here with tranquillity, to depart to some distant land, and to trust your life, saved from just and deserved punishment, to flight and solitude? Make a motion, say you, to the Senate (for that is what you demand), and if this body votes that you ought to go into banishment, you say that you will obey. I will not make such a motion, it is contrary to my principles, and yet I will let you see what these men think of you. Be gone from the city, O Catiline, deliver the Republic from fear; depart into banishment, if that is the word you are waiting for. What now, O Catiline? Do you not perceive, do you not see the silence of these men? they permit it, they say nothing; why wait you for the authority of their words, when you see their wishes in their silence?

But had I said the same to this excellent young man, Publius Sextius, or to that brave man, Marcus Marcellus, before this time the Senate would deservedly have laid violent hands on me, consul though I be, in this very temple. But as to you, Catiline, while they are quiet they approve, while they permit me to speak they vote, while they are silent they are loud and eloquent. And not they alone, whose authority forsooth is dear to you, though their lives are unimportant, but the Roman knights too, those most honorable and excellent men, and the other virtuous citizens who are now surrounding the Senate, whose numbers you could see, whose desires you could know, and whose voices you a few minutes ago could hear—ay, whose very hands and weapons I have for some time been scarcely able to keep off from you; but those, too, I will easily bring to attend you to the gates if you leave these places you have been long desiring to lay waste.

And yet, why am I speaking? that anything may change your purpose? that you may amend your life? that you may meditate flight or think of voluntary banishment? I wish the gods may give you such a mind; though I see, if alarmed at my words you bring your mind to go into banishment, what a storm of unpopularity hangs over me, if not at present, while the memory of your wickedness is fresh, at all events hereafter. But it is worth while to incur that, as long as that is but a private misfortune of my own, and is unconnected with the dangers of the Republic. But we cannot expect that you should be concerned at your own vices, that you should fear the

penalties of the laws, or that you should yield to the necessities of the
Republic, for you are not, O Catiline, one whom either shame can
recall from infamy, or fear from danger, or reason from madness.

Wherefore, as I have said before, go forth, and if you wish to
make me, your enemy as you call me, unpopular, go straight into
banishment. I shall scarcely be able to endure all that will be said if
you do so; I shall scarcely be able to support my load of unpopularity
if you do go into banishment at the command of the consul; but if
you wish to serve my credit and reputation, go forth with your ill-
omened band of profligates; betake yourself to Manlius, rouse up the
abandoned citizens, separate yourself from the good ones, wage war
against your country, exult in your impious banditti, so that you may
not seem to have been driven out by me and gone to strangers, but
to have gone invited to your own friends.

Though why should I invite you, by whom I know men have been
already sent on to wait in arms for you at the forum Aurelium; who I
know has fixed and agreed with Manlius upon a settled day; by whom
I know that that silver eagle,[1] which I trust will be ruinous and fatal
to you and to all your friends, and to which there was set up in your
house a shrine as it were of your crimes, has been already sent forward? Need I fear that you can long do without that which you used
to worship when going out to murder, and from whose altars you
have often transferred your impious hand to the slaughter of citizens?

You will go at last where your unbridled and mad desire has been
long hurrying you. And this causes you no grief, but an incredible
pleasure.[2] Nature has formed you, desire has trained you, fortune has
preserved you for this insanity. Not only did you never desire quiet,
but you never even desired any war but a criminal one; you have collected a band of profligates and worthless men, abandoned not only
by all fortune but even by hope.

Then what happiness will you enjoy! with what delight will you
exult! in what pleasure will you revel! when in so numerous a body
of friends, you neither hear nor see one good man. All the toils you
have gone through have always pointed to this sort of life; your lying
on the ground not merely to lie in wait to gratify your unclean desires, but even to accomplish crimes; your vigilance, not only when
plotting against the sleep of husbands, but also against the goods of
your murdered victims, have all been preparations for this. Now you
have an opportunity of displaying your splendid endurance of hunger, of cold, of want of everything; by which in a short time you

[1] A military ensign used by Marius when he defeated the Cimbri, which
Catiline keeps in his house for good luck.
[2] Catiline has been laughing uproariously.

will find yourself worn out. All this I effected when I procured your rejection from the consulship, that you should be reduced to make attempts on your country as an exile, instead of being able to distress it as consul, and that that which had been wickedly undertaken by you should be called piracy rather than war.

Now that I may remove and avert, O conscript fathers, any in the least reasonable complaint from myself, listen, I beseech you, carefully to what I say, and lay it up in your inmost hearts and minds. In truth, if my country, which is far dearer to me than my life—if all Italy—if the whole Republic were to address me, "Marcus Tullius, what are you doing? will you permit that man to depart whom you have ascertained to be an enemy? whom you see ready to become the general of the war? whom you know to be expected in the camp of the enemy as their chief, the author of all this wickedness, the head of the conspiracy, the instigator of the slaves and abandoned citizens, so that he shall seem not driven out of the city by you, but let loose by you against the city? Will you not order him to be thrown into prison, to be hurried off to execution, to be put to death with the most prompt severity? What hinders you? is it the customs of our ancestors? But even private men have often in this Republic slain mischievous citizens. Is it the laws which have been passed about the punishment of Roman citizens? [1] But in this city those who have rebelled against the Republic have never had the rights of citizens. Do you fear odium with posterity? You are showing fine gratitude to the Roman people, which has raised you, a man known only by your own actions, of no ancestral renown, through all the degrees of honor at so early an age to the very highest office, if from fear of unpopularity or of any danger you neglect the safety of your fellow-citizens. But if you have a fear of unpopularity, is that arising from the imputation of vigor and boldness, or that arising from that of inactivity and indecision most to be feared? When Italy is laid waste by war, when cities are attacked and houses in flames, do you not think that you will be then consumed by a perfect conflagration of hatred?"

To this holy address of the Republic, and to the feelings of those men who entertain the same opinion, I will make this short answer: If, O conscript fathers, I thought it best that Catiline should be punished with death, I would not have given the space of one hour to this gladiator to live in. If, forsooth, those excellent men and most illustrious cities not only did not pollute themselves, but even glorified themselves by the blood of Saturninus, and the Gracchi, and Flaccus, and many others of old time, surely I had no cause to fear lest for

---

[1] Every Roman citizen was supposed to have the right of "provocatio" cr appeal to the people before being put to death for a crime.

slaying this parricidal murderer of the citizens any unpopularity should accrue to me with posterity. And if it did threaten me to ever so great a degree, yet I have always been of the disposition to think unpopularity earned by virtue and glory, not unpopularity.

Though there are some men in this body who either do not see what threatens, or dissemble what they do see; who have fed the hope of Catiline by mild sentiments, and have strengthened the rising conspiracy by not believing it; influenced by whose authority many, and they not wicked, but only ignorant, if I punished him, would say that I had acted cruelly and tyrannically. But I know that if he arrives at the camp of Manlius to which he is going, there will be no one so stupid as not to see that there has been a conspiracy, no one so hardened as not to confess it. But if this man alone were put to death, I know that this disease of the Republic would be only checked for a while, not eradicated forever. But if he banishes himself, and takes with him all his friends, and collects at one point all the ruined men from every quarter, then not only will this full-grown plague of the Republic be extinguished and eradicated, but also the root and seed of all future evils.

We have now for a long time, O conscript fathers, lived among these dangers and machinations of conspiracy; but somehow or other, the ripeness of all wickedness, and of this long-standing madness and audacity, has come to a head at the time of my consulship. But if this man alone is removed from this piratical crew, we may appear, perhaps, for a short time relieved from fear and anxiety, but the danger will settle down and lie hid in the veins and bowels of the Republic. As it often happens that men afflicted with a severe disease, when they are tortured with heat and fever, if they drink cold water, seem at first to be relieved, but afterward suffer more and more severely; so this disease which is in the Republic, if relieved by the punishment of this man, will only get worse and worse, as the rest will be still alive.

Wherefore, O conscript fathers, let the worthless begone—let them separate themselves from the good—let them collect in one place—let them, as I have often said before, be separated from us by a wall; let them cease to plot against the consul in his own house—to surround the tribunal of the city praetor—to besiege the senate-house with swords—to prepare brands and torches to burn the city; let, it, in short, be written on the brow of every citizen, what are his sentiments about the Republic. I promise you this, O conscript fathers, that there shall be so much diligence in us the consuls, so much authority in you, so much virtue in the Roman knights, so much unanimity in all good men, that you shall see everything made plain and manifest by the departure of Catiline—everything checked and punished.

With these omens, O Catiline, begone to your impious and nefarious war, to the great safety of the Republic, to your own misfortune and injury, and to the destruction of those who have joined themselves to you in every wickedness and atrocity. Then do you, O Jupiter, who were consecrated by Romulus with the same auspices as this city, whom we rightly call the stay of this city and empire, repel this man and his companions from your altars and from the other temples—from the houses and walls of the city—from the lives and fortunes of all the citizens; and overwhelm all the enemies of good men, the foes of the Republic, the robbers of Italy, men bound together by a treaty and infamous alliance of crimes, dead and alive, with eternal punishments.

LETTER FROM CICERO TO LUCIUS LUCCEUIS

I have frequently had it in my intentions to talk with you upon the subject of this letter; but a certain awkward modesty has always restrained me from proposing in person, what I can with less scruple request at this distance; for a letter, you know, spares the confusion of a blush. I will own then, that I have a very strong, and, I trust, a very pardonable passion of being celebrated in your writings; and though you have more than once given me assurance of your intending me that honor, yet I hope you will excuse my impatience of seeing your design executed. . . . It is my ambition, I confess, not only to live forever in the praises of future ages, but to have the present satisfaction, likewise, of seeing myself stand approved in your authoritative records. As I perceive you have almost completed your account of the Italic and Marian civil wars, I cannot forbear recommending it to your consideration, whether it would be best to weave the relation of Catiline's conspiracy into the general texture of your performance, or cast it into a distinct work. It is certain, several of the Greek historians will justify you in this latter method. Thus Callisthenes wrote a narrative of the siege of Troy, as both Timaeus and Polybius did of the Pyrrhic and Numantine wars, in so many detached pieces from their larger histories. As to the honor that will arise to me, it will be much the same, I must own, upon whichever scheme you may determine to proceed; but I shall receive so much the earlier gratification of my wishes, if instead of waiting till you regularly advance to that period of our annals, you should enter upon it by this method of anticipation. Besides, by keeping your mind attentive to one principal scene and character, you will treat your subject, I am persuaded, so much the more in detail, as well as embellish it with higher graces.

I must acknowledge it is not extremely modest, thus to impose a task upon you which your occupations may well justify you in refusing; and then to add a further request, that you would honor my actions with your applause; an honor, after all, which you may not think, perhaps, they greatly deserve. However, when a man has once transgressed the bounds of decency, it is in vain to recede; and his wisest way is to push on boldly in the same confident course, to the end of his purpose. I will venture, then, earnestly to entreat you, not to confine yourself to the strict laws of history; but to give a greater latitude to your encomiums, than possibly you may think my actions can claim. I remember, indeed, you declare in one of your very elegant prefaces, that you are as inflexible to all the pleas of affection, as Xenophon represents Hercules to have been to those of pleasure. Let me hope, nevertheless, if friendship should too strongly recommend my actions to your approbation, you will not reject her generous partiality; but give somewhat more to affection, than rigorous truth, perhaps, can justly demand.

If I should prevail upon you to fall in with my proposal, you will find the subject, I persuade myself, not unworthy of your genius and your eloquence. The entire period from the rise of Catiline's conspiracy to my return from banishment, will furnish, I should imagine, a moderate volume. It will supply you likewise with a noble occasion of displaying your judgment in politics, by laying open the source of those civil disorders, and pointing out their proper remedies, as well as by giving your reasons for approving or condemning the several transactions which you relate. And should you be disposed to indulge your usual spirit of freedom, you will have an opportunity of pointing out at the same time, with all the severity of your indignation, the treachery and perfidiousness of those who laid their ungenerous snares for my destruction. I will add too, that this period of my life will furnish you with numberless incidents, which cannot but draw the reader's attention in a very agreeable manner; as nothing is more amusing to the mind than to contemplate the various vicissitudes of fortune. And though they were far, 'tis true, from being acceptable in experience, they cannot fail of giving me much entertainment in the description; as there is an inexpressible satisfaction in reflecting at one's ease, on distresses we have formerly suffered. There is something likewise in that compassion which arises from reading an account of the misfortunes which have attended others, that casts a most agreeable melancholy upon the mind. Who can peruse the relation of the last moments of Epaminondas at the battle of Mantinea, without finding himself touched with a pleasing commiseration? That glorious chief, you may remember, would not suffer the dart to be drawn out of his

side, till he was informed that his shield was safe from the hands
of his enemies; and all his concern amidst the anguish of his wound
was, to die with glory. What can be more interesting also than the
account of the flight and death of Themistocles! The truth of it
is, a mere narrative of general facts, affords little more entertainment
to the reader, than he might find in perusing one of our public
registers. Whereas in the history of any extraordinary person, our
fear and hope, our joy and sorrow, our astonishment and expectation, are each of them engaged by turns. And if the final result of all
should be concluded with some remarkable catastrophe, the mind of
the reader is filled with the highest possible gratification. For these
reasons I am the more desirous of persuading you to separate my story
from the general thread of your narration, and work it up into a
detached performance; as indeed it will exhibit a great variety of the
most interesting and affecting scenes.

When I tell you it is my ambition to be celebrated by your pen, I
am by no means apprehensive you will suspect me of flattery. The
consciousness of your merit must always incline you to believe, it is
envy alone that can be silent in your praise; as on the other side you
cannot imagine me so weak as to desire to be transmitted to posterity
by any hand, which could not secure to itself the same glory it bestowed. When Alexander chose to have his picture drawn by Apelles,
and his statue formed by Lysippus, it was not in order to ingratiate
himself with those distinguished artists; it was from a firm persuasion
that the works of these admired geniuses would do equal credit both
to his reputation and their own. The utmost, however, that their art
could perform, was to perpetuate the persons only of their celebrated
contemporaries: but merit needs not any such visible exhibitions to im-
mortalise its fame. Accordingly the Spartan Agesilaus, who would
never suffer any picture or statue of him to be taken, is not less uni-
versally known, than those who have been most fond of having their
persons copied out for posterity. The single treatise which Xenophon
has written in praise of that renowned general, is more to his glory,
than all the pictures and statues of all the artists in the universe. It
would be a much higher satisfaction to me, therefore, as it would be a
far greater honor, to be recorded by your hand than that of any
other; not only because your genius would raise and adorn my actions
with the same advantage as Timaeus has displayed those of Timoleon,
or Herodotus those of Themistocles; but because of the additional
credit I shall receive from the applause of so illustrious, so experienced,
and so approved a patriot. By this means I shall enjoy, not only the
same glorious privilege which, as Alexander observed when he was
at Sigeum, Achilles received from Homer; but what is still more im-

portant, the powerful testimony of a man, who is himself distinguished by the noblest and most uncommon virtues. Accordingly, I have been always wonderfully pleased with the sentiment which Naevius puts into the mouth of Hector, where that hero, speaking of the approbaion he had received from his illustrious father, adds, that it gave him so much the more satisfaction, as coming from one who was himself the great object of universal applause. But should want of leisure, (for it would be an injustice to our friendship to suppose it can be want of inclination), should your occupations then prevent your compliance with this my request, I may perhaps be obliged to take a method, which, though often condemned, is supported, nevertheless, by several considerable examples: I mean, to be the historian of my own transactions. But, you are sensible, there are two inconveniences which attend this scheme; for a man must necessarily be more reserved in setting forth those parts of his conduct which merit approbation, as he will be inclined entirely to pass over others which may deserve reproach. I must add likewise, that what a writer says to his own advantage, always carries with it a less degree of force and authority, than when it comes from any other pen. In a word, the world in general is little disposed to approve any attempt of this kind. On the contrary, one often hears the more modest method of the poets at the Olympic games, recommended upon such occasions, who, after they have crowned the several victors, and publicly called over their names, always employ some other person to perform the same office to themselves, that they may not be the heralds of their own applause. This imputation, therefore, I would willingly avoid; as I certainly shall, if you should comply with my request, and take this employment out of my hands.

You will be surprised, perhaps, that I spend so much time and pains in soliciting you for this purpose, after having so often heard you declare your intentions of giving the world a very accurate history of my administration. But you must remember the natural warmth of my temper, and that I am fired, as I told you in the beginning of my letter, with an impatient desire of seeing this your design carried into execution. To own the whole truth, I am ambitious of being known to the present generation by your writings, and to enjoy in my lifetime a foretaste of that share of glory which I may expect from future ages. If it be not too much trouble, therefore, I should be glad you would immediately let me know your resolution. And should it prove agreeable to my request, I will draw up some general memoirs of my transactions for your use: if otherwise, I will take an opportunity of discoursing further with you upon this affair in person. In the mean time, continue to polish the work you have begun, and to love me as usual. Farewell.

SPEECH IN BEHALF OF MARCUS CLAUDIUS MARCELLUS

This day, O conscript fathers, has brought with it an end to the long silence in which I have of late indulged; not out of any fear, but partly from sorrow, partly from modesty; and at the same time it has revived in me my ancient habit of saying what my wishes and opinions are. For I cannot by any means pass over in silence such great humanity, such unprecedented and unheard-of clemency, such moderation in the exercise of supreme and universal power, such incredible and almost godlike wisdom. For now that Marcus Marcellus, O conscript fathers, has been restored to you and the Republic, I think that not only his voice and authority are preserved and restored to you and to the Republic, but my own also.

For I was concerned, O conscript fathers, and most exceedingly grieved, when I saw such a man as he is, who had espoused the same cause which I myself had, not enjoying the same good fortune as myself; nor was I able to persuade myself to think it right or fair that I should be going on in my usual routine, while that rival and imitator of my zeal and labors, who had been a companion and comrade of mine throughout, was separated from me. Therefore, you, O Caius Cæsar, have reopened to me my former habits of life, which were closed up, and you have raised, as it were, a standard to all these men, as a sort of token to lead them to entertain hopes of the general welfare of the Republic. For it was seen by me before in many instances, and especially in my own, and now it is clearly understood by everybody, since you have granted Marcus Marcellus to the Senate and people of Rome, in spite of your recollection of all the injuries you have received at his hands, that you prefer the authority of this order and the dignity of the Republic to the indulgence of your own resentment or your own suspicions.

He, indeed, has this day reaped the greatest possible reward for the virtuous tenor of his previous life; in the great unanimity of the Senate in his favor, and also in your own most dignified and important opinion of him. And from this you, in truth, must perceive what great credit there is in conferring a kindness, when there is such glory to be got even by receiving one. And he, too, is fortunate whose safety is now the cause of scarcely less joy to all other men than it will be to himself when informed of it. And this honor has deservedly and most rightfully fallen to his lot. For who is superior to him either in nobleness of birth, or in honesty, or in zeal or virtuous studies, or in purity of life, or in any description whatever of excellence?

No one is blessed with such a stream of genius, no one is endowed with such vigor and richness of eloquence, either as a speaker, or as a writer, as to be able, I will not say to extol, but even, O Caius Cæsar, plainly to relate all your achievements. Nevertheless, I assert, and with your leave I maintain, that in all of them you never gained greater and truer glory than you have acquired this day. I am accustomed often to keep this idea before my eyes, and often to affirm in frequent conversations, that all the exploits of our own generals, all those of foreign nations and of most powerful states, all the mighty deeds of the most illustrious monarchs, can be compared with yours neither in the magnitude of your wars, nor in the number of your battles, nor in the variety of countries which you have conquered, nor in the rapidity of your conquests, nor in the great difference of character with which your wars have been marked; and that those countries the most remote from each other could not be travelled over more rapidly by anyone in a journey, than they have been visited by your, I will not say, journeys, but victories.

And if I were not to admit, that those actions are so great that scarcely any man's mind or comprehension is capable of doing justice to them, I should be very senseless. But there are other actions greater than those. For some people are in the habit of disparaging military glory, and of denying the whole of it to the generals, and of giving the multitude a share of it also, so that it may not be the peculiar property of the commanders. And, no doubt, in the affairs of war, the valor of the troops, the advantages of situation, the assistance of allies, fleets, and supplies, have great influence; and a most important share in all such transactions, Fortune claims for herself, as of her right; and whatever has been done successfully she considers almost entirely as her own work.

But in this glory, O Caius Cæsar, which you have just earned, you have no partner. The whole of this, however great it may be—and surely it is as great as possible—the whole of it, I say, is your own. The centurion can claim for himself no share of that praise, neither can the prefect, nor the battalion, nor the squadron. Nay, even that very mistress of all human affairs, Fortune herself, cannot thrust herself into any participation in that glory; she yields to you; she confesses that it is all your own, your peculiar private desert. For rashness is never united with wisdom, nor is chance ever admitted to regulate affairs conducted with prudence.

You have subdued nations, savage in their barbarism, countless in their numbers, boundless, if we regard the extent of country peopled by them, and rich in every kind of resource; but still you were only conquering things, the nature and condition of which was such that they could be overcome by force. For there is no strength so great that it cannot be weakened and broken by arms and violence. But to subdue one's inclinations, to master one's angry feelings, to be moderate in the hour of victory, to not merely raise from the ground a prostrate adversary, eminent for noble birth, for genius, and for virtue, but even to increase his previous dignity—they are actions of such a nature, that the man who does them, I do not compare to the most illustrious man, but I consider equal to God.

Therefore, O Caius Cæsar, those military glories of yours will be celebrated not only in our literature and language, but in those of almost all nations; nor is there any age which will ever be silent about your praises. But still, deeds of that sort, somehow or other, even when they are read, appear to be overwhelmed with the cries of soldiers and the sound of the trumpets. But when we hear or read of anything which has been done with clemency, with humanity, with justice, with moderation, and with wisdom, especially in a time of anger, which is very adverse to prudence, and in the hour of victory, which is naturally insolent and haughty, with what ardor are we then inflamed (even if the actions are not such as have really been performed, but are only fabulous), so as often to love those whom we have never seen! But as for you, whom we behold present among us, whose mind, and feelings, and countenance, we at this moment see to be such, that you wish to preserve everything which the fortune of war has left the Republic, oh, with what praises must we extol you? with what zeal must we follow you? with what affection must we devote ourselves to you? The very walls, I declare, the very walls of this senate-house appear to me eager to return you thanks; because, in a short time, you will have restored their ancient authority to this venerable abode of themselves and of their ancestors.

In truth, O conscript fathers, when I just now, in common with you, beheld the tears of Caius Marcellus, a most virtuous man, endowed with a never-to-be-forgotten affection for his brother, the recollection of all the Marcelli presented itself to my heart. For you, O Cæsar, have, by preserving Marcus Marcellus, restored their dignity even to those Marcelli who are dead, and you have saved that most noble family, now reduced to a small number, from perishing. You, therefore, justly prefer this day to all the splendid and innumerable congratulations which at different times have been addressed to you. For this exploit is your own alone; the other achievements which have been performed by you as general, were great indeed, but still they were performed by the agency of a great and numerous band of comrades. But in this exploit you are the general, and you are your own sole comrade: and the act itself is such that no lapse of time will ever put an end to your monuments and trophies; for there is nothing which is wrought by manual labor which time will not sometime or other impair or destroy; but this justice and lenity of yours will every day grow brighter and brighter, so that, in proportion as time takes away from the effect of your deed, in the same degree it will add to your glory. And you had already surpassed all other conquerors in civil wars, in equity, and clemency, but this day you have surpassed even yourself. I fear that this which I am saying cannot, when it is only heard, be understood as fully as I myself think and feel it; you appear to have surpassed victory itself, since you have remitted in favor of the conquered those things which victory had put in your power. For though by the conditions of the victory itself, we who were conquered were all ruined, we still have been preserved by the deliberate decision of your clemency. You, therefore, deserve to be the only man who is never conquered, since you conquer the conditions and the violent privileges of victory itself.

And, O conscript fathers, remark how widely this decision of Caius Cæsar extends. For by it, all of us who, under the compulsion of some miserable and fatal destiny of the Republic, were driven to take up arms as we did, though we are still not free from the fault of having erred as men may, are at all events released from all imputation of wickedness. For when, at your entreaty, he preserved Marcus Marcellus to the Republic, he, at the same time, restored me to myself and to the Republic though no one entreated him in my favor, and he restored all the other most honorable men who were in the same case to ourselves and to their country; whom you now behold in numbers and dignity present in this very assembly. He has not brought his enemies into the senate-house; but he has decided that the war was undertaken by most of them rather out of ignorance, and because of some ungrounded and empty fear, than out of either any depraved desires or cruelty.

And in that war, I always thought it right to listen to all proposals that gave any hope of peace, and I always grieved, that not only peace, but that even the language of those citizens who asked for peace, should be rejected. For I never approved of either that or any civil war whatever; and my counsels were always allied to peace and peaceful measures, not to war and arms. I followed Pompey from my own private feelings, not because of my judgment of his public conduct; and the faithful recollection of the grateful disposition which I cherish had so much influence with me, that though I had not only no desire for victory, but no hope even of it, I rushed on, knowingly, and with my eyes open, as it were, to a voluntary death. And, indeed, my sentiments in the matter were not at all concealed; for in this assembly, before any decisive steps were taken either way, I said many things in favor of peace, and even while the war was going on I retained the same opinions, even at the risk of my life. And from this fact, no one will form so unjust an opinion as to doubt what Cæsar's own inclination respecting the war was, when, the moment that it was in his power, he declared his opinion in favor of saving the advisers of peace, but showed his anger against the others. And, perhaps, that was not very strange at a time when the event of the war was still uncertain, and its fortune still undecided. But he who, when victorious, attaches himself to the advisers of peace, plainly declares that he would have preferred having no war at all even to conquering.

And in this matter I myself am a witness in favor of Marcus Marcellus. For as our opinions have at all times agreed in time of peace, so did they then in respect of that war. How often have I seen him affected with the deepest grief at the insolence of certain men, and dreading also the ferocity of victory! On which account your liberality, O Caius Cæsar, ought to be more acceptable to us who have seen those things. For now we may compare, not the causes of the two parties together, but the use which each would have made of victory. We have seen your victory terminate at once by the result of your battles; we have seen no sword unsheathed in the city. The citizens whom we have lost were stricken down by the force of Mars, not by evil feelings let loose by victory; so that no man can doubt that Caius Cæsar would even raise many from the dead if that were possible, since he does preserve all those of that army that he can.

But of the other party I will say no more than what we were all afraid of at the time, namely, that theirs would have been too angry a victory. For some of them were in the habit of indulging in threats not only against those of their enemies who were in arms, but even against those who remained quiet; and they used to say that the matter to be considered was not what each man had thought, but where he had been. So that it appears to me that the immortal gods, even if they were inflicting punishment on the Roman people for some offense, when they stirred up so serious and melancholy a civil war, are at length appeased, or at all events satiated, and have now made all our hopes of safety depend on the clemency and wisdom of the conqueror.

Rejoice, then, in that admirable and virtuous disposition of yours; and enjoy not only your fortune and glory, but also your own natural good qualities, and amiable inclinations and manners; for those are the things which produce the greatest fruit and pleasure to a wise man. When you call to mind your other achievements, although you will often congratulate yourself on your valor, still you will often have reason to thank your good fortune also. But as often as you think of us whom you have chosen to live safely in the Republic as well as yourself, you will be thinking at the same time of your own exceeding kindness, of your own incredible liberality, of your own unexampled wisdom; qualities which I will venture to call not only the greatest, but the only real blessings. For there is so much splendor in genuine glory, so much dignity in magnanimity and real practical wisdom, that these qualities appear to be given to a man by virtue, while all other advantages seem only lent to him by fortune.

Be not wearied then in the preservation of virtuous men; especially of those who have fallen, not from any evil desires, or depravity of disposition, but merely from an opinion of their duty—a foolish and erroneous one perhaps, but certainly not a wicked one—and because they were misled by imaginary claims which they fancied the Republic had on them. For it is no fault of yours if some people were afraid of you; and, on the other hand, it is your greatest praise that they have now felt that they had no reason to fear you.

But now I come to those severe complaints, and to those most terrible suspicions that you have given utterance to; of dangers which should be guarded against not more by you yourself than by all the citizens, and most especially by us who have been preserved by you. And although I trust that the suspicion is an ungrounded one, still I will not speak so as to make light of it. For, caution for you is caution for ourselves. So that, if we must err on one side or the other, I would rather appear too fearful, than not sufficiently prudent. But still, who is there so frantic? Anyone of your friends? And yet who are more your friends than those to whom you have restored safety which they did not venture to hope for? Anyone of that number who were with you? It is not credible that any man should be so insane as not to prefer the life of that man who was his general when he obtained the greatest advantages of all sorts, to his own. But if your friends have no thought of wickedness, need you take precautions lest your enemies may be entertaining such? Who are they? For all those men who were your enemies have either already lost their lives through their obstinacy, or else have preserved them through your mercy; so that either none of your enemies survive, or those who do survive are your most devoted friends.

But still, as there are so many hiding-places and so many dark corners in men's minds, let us increase your suspicions, for by so doing we shall at the same time increase your diligence. For who is there so ignorant of everything, so very new to the affairs of the Republic, so entirely destitute of thought either for his own or for the general safety, as not to understand that his own safety is bound up with yours? that the lives of all men depend on your single existence? I myself, in truth, while I think of you day and night—as I ought to do—fear only the chances to which all men are liable, and the uncertain events of health and the frail tenure of our common nature, and I grieve that, while the Republic ought to be immortal, it depends wholly on the life of one mortal man. But if to the chances of human life and the uncertain condition of man's health there were to be added also any conspiracy of wickedness and treachery, then what god should we think able to assist the Republic, even if he were to desire to do so?

All things, O Caius Cæsar, which you now see lying stricken and prostrate—as it was inevitable that they should be—through the violence of war, must now be raised up again by you alone. The courts of justice must be re-established, confidence must be restored, licentiousness must be repressed, the increase of population must be encouraged, everything which has become lax and disordered must be braced up and strengthened by strict laws. In so vast a civil war, when there was such ardor of feeling and of warlike preparation on both sides, it was impossible but that—whatever the ultimate result of the war might be—the Republic which had been violently shaken by it should lose many ornaments of its dignity and many bulwarks of its security, and that each general should do many things while in arms, which he would have forbidden to have been done while clad in the garb of peace. And all those wounds of war thus afflicted now require your attention, and there is no one except you who is able to heal them. Therefore, I was concerned when I heard that celebrated and wise saying of yours, "I have lived long enough to satisfy either nature or glory." Sufficiently long, if you please, for nature, and I will add, if you like, for glory; but, which is of the greatest consequence of all, certainly not long enough for your country.

Give up then, I entreat you, that wisdom of learned men shown in their contempt of death; do not be wise at our expense. For it has often come to my ears that you are in the habit of using that expression much too frequently—that you have lived long enough for yourself. I dare say you have; but I could only be willing to hear you say so if you lived for yourself alone, or if you had been born for yourself alone. But as it is, as your exploits have brought the safety of all the citizens and the entire Republic to a dependence on you, you are so far from having completed your greatest labors, that you have not even laid the foundations which you design to lay. And will you then limit your life, not by the welfare of the Republic, but by the tranquillity of your own mind? What will you do, if that is not even sufficient for your glory, of which—wise man though you be—you will not deny that you are exceedingly desirous? "Is it then," you will say, "but small glory that we shall leave behind us?" It may, indeed, be sufficient for others, however many they may be, and insufficient for you alone. For whatever it is, however ample it may be, it certainly is insufficient, as long as there is anything greater still. And if, O Caius Cæsar, this was to be the result of your immortal achievements, that after conquering all your enemies, you were to leave the Republic in the state in which it now is; then beware, I beg of you, lest your virtue should earn admiration rather than solid glory; since the glory which is illustrious and which is celebrated abroad, is the fame of many and great services done either to one's own friends, or to one's country, or to the whole race of mankind.

This, then, is the part which remains to you; this is the cause which you have before you; this is what you must now labor at—to settle the Republic, and to enjoy it yourself, as the first of its citizens, in the greatest tranquillity and peacefulness. And then, if you please, when you have discharged the obligations which you owe to your country, and when you have satisfied nature herself with the devotion of your life, then you may say that you have lived long enough. For what is the meaning of this very word "long" when applied to what has an end? And when the end comes, then all past pleasure is to be accounted as nothing, because there is none to come after it. Although that spirit of yours has never been content with this narrow space which nature has afforded us to live in; but has always been inflamed with a desire of immortality. Nor is this to be considered your life which is contained in your body and in your breath. That—that, I say, is your life, which will flourish in the memory of all ages; which posterity will cherish; which eternity itself will always preserve. This is what you must be subservient to; it is to this that you ought to display yourself; which indeed has long ago had many actions of yours to admire, and which now is expecting some which it may also praise.

Unquestionably, posterity will stand amazed when they hear and read of your military commands; of the provinces which you have added to the empire; of the Rhine, of the ocean, of the Nile, all made subject to us; of your countless battles, of your incredible victories, of your innumerable monuments and triumphs. But unless this city is now securely settled by your counsels and by your institutions, your name will indeed be talked about very extensively, but your glory will have no secure abode, no sure home in which to repose. There will be also among those who shall be born hereafter, as there has been among us, great disputes, when some with their praises will extol your exploits to the skies, and others, perhaps, will miss something in them—and that, too, the most important thing of all—unless you extinguish the conflagration of civil war by the safety of the country, so that the one shall appear to have been the effect of destiny and the other the work of your own practical wisdom. Have regard, then, to those judges who will judge you many ages afterward, and who will very likely judge you more honestly than we can. For their judgment will be unbiased by affection or by ambition, and at the same time it will be untainted by hatred or envy. And even if it will be incapable of affecting you at that time (which is the false opinion held by some men), at all events, it concerns you now to conduct yourself in such a manner that no oblivion shall ever be able to obscure your praises.

The inclinations of the citizens have been very diverse, and their opinions much distracted; for we showed our variance, not only by our counsels and desires, but by arms and warlike operations. And there was no obscurity in the designs of, and contention between, the most illustrious generals: many doubted which was the best side; many, what was expedient for themselves; many, what was becoming; some even felt uncertain as to what it was in their power to do. The Republic has at last come to the end of this miserable and fatal war; that man has been victorious who has not allowed his animosities to be inflamed by good fortune, but who has mitigated them by the goodness of his disposition; and who did not consider all those with whom he was displeased deserving on that account of exile or death. Arms were laid aside by some, were wrested from the hands of others. He is an ungrateful and an unjust citizen, who, when released from the danger of arms, still retains, as it were, an armed spirit, so that that man is better who fell in battle, who spent his life in the cause. For that which seems obstinacy to some people may appear constancy in others. But now all dissension is crushed by the arms and extinguished by the justice of the conqueror; it only remains for all men for the future to be animated by one wish, all at least who have not only any wisdom at all, but who are at all in their senses. Unless you, O Caius Cæsar, continue safe, and also in the same sentiments as you have displayed on previous occasions, and on this day most eminently, we cannot be safe either. Wherefore we all—we who wish this constitution and these things around us to be safe—exhort and entreat you to take care of your own life, to consult your own safety; and we all promise to you (that I may say also on behalf of others what I feel respecting myself), since you think that there is still something concealed, against which it is necessary to guard—we promise you, I say, not only our vigilance and our wariness also to assist in those precautions, but we promise to oppose our sides and our bodies as a shield against every danger which can threaten you.

But let my speech end with the same sentiment as it began. We all, O Caius Cæsar, render you the greatest thanks, and we feel even deeper gratitude than we express; for all feel the same thing, as you might have perceived from the entreaties and the tears of all. But because it is not necessary for all of them to stand up and say so, they wish it at all events that by me, who am forced in some degree to rise and speak, should be expressed both all that they feel, and all that is becoming, and all that I myself consider due to Marcus Marcellus, who is thus by you restored to this order, and to the Roman people, and to the Republic. For I feel that all men are exulting, not in the safety of one individual alone, but in the general safety of all. And as it becomes the greatest possible affection, such as I was always well known by all men to have toward him, so that I scarcely yielded to Caius Marcellus, his most excellent and affectionate brother, and certainly to no one except him, that love for him which I displayed by my solicitude, by my anxiety, and my exertions, as long as there was a doubt of his safety, I certainly ought to display at this present time, now that I am relieved from my great care and distress and misery on his account.

Therefore, O Caius Cæsar, I thank you, as if—though I have not only been preserved in every sort of manner, but also loaded with distinctions by you—still, by this action of yours, a crowning kindness of the greatest importance was added to the already innumerable benefits which you have heaped upon me, which I did not before believe were capable of any augmentation.

LETTER FROM AULUS CÆCINA TO CICERO

I hope you will not only pardon the fears, but pity the misfortunes, which prevented your receiving my performance as soon as I intended; but my son was apprehensive, I hear, that the publication of this piece might prove to my prejudice. And, indeed, as the effect of compositions of this kind depends more upon the temper in which they are read, than on that in which they are written, his fears were by no means irrational; especially as I am still a sufferer for the liberties of my pen. In this respect, my fate, surely, is somewhat singular: for the errors of an author are generally either reformed by a blot, or punished by the loss of his fame; whereas banishment, on the contrary, has been thought the more proper method of correcting mine. And yet the whole of my crime amounts only to this; that I poured forth my invectives against the man with whom I was openly at war. Now there was not a single person, I suppose, in the same party with myself, who was not in effect guilty of the same offense; as there was not one who did not send up his vows for success to our cause, or that offered a sacrifice, though upon an occasion ever so foreign to public affairs, without imploring the Gods that Cæsar might soon be defeated. If he imagines otherwise, he is extremely happy in his ignorance. But if he knows this to be fact, why am I marked out as the particular object of his wrath, for having written something which he did not approve; whilst he forgives every one of those, who were perpetually invoking heaven for his perdition!

But I was going to acquaint you with the reason of those fears, which I mentioned in the beginning of my letter. In the first place, then, I have taken notice of you in the piece in question; though at the same time, I have touched upon your conduct with great caution and reserve. Not that I have by any means changed my opinions concerning it, but as being afraid to say all that they dictated to me.— You will think yourself, perhaps, obliged to me: for as I was not at liberty to represent your actions in the manner they deserve, the next favor to being totally silent concerning them, was to mention them as little as possible. But difficult as it was to contain myself upon so copious a subject, I however forbore; and as there were various parts of your conduct I did not venture even to touch upon, so in the revisal of my work I not only found it necessary to strike out several circumstances I had inserted, but to place many of those which I suffered to remain, in a less advantageous point of view. But should an architect, in raising a flight of steps, omit some, cut away part of those he had fixed, and leave many of the rest loose and ill joined together, might he not more properly be said to erect a ruin, than an easy and regular ascent? In the same manner, where an author is constrained, by a thousand unhappy circumstances, to break the just coherence of his piece, and destroy its proper gradation, how can he hope to produce any thing that shall merit the applause of a refined and judicious ear? But I was still more embarrassed, where my subject led me to speak of Cæsar; and I will own that I trembled whenever I had occasion to mention his name. My fears, however, did not arise from any apprehension that what I wrote might draw upon me his farther chastisement; but lest it should not be agreeable to his particular sentiments, with which, indeed, I am by no means well acquainted. But with what spirit can a man compose, when he is obliged to ask himself at every sentence, "Will Cæsar approve of this? May not this expression appear of suspicious import! Or will he not think it still worse if I change it thus?" But besides these difficulties, I was perplexed, likewise, in regard to the applauses and censures which I dealt out to others; as I was afraid I might apply them where they would not, perhaps, be very agreeable to Cæsar, though they might not actually give him offense. I reflected, that if his vengeance pursued me for what I wrote, whilst I had my sword in my hand, what might be the consequence should I displease him now that I am a disarmed exile?

INDEX

INDEX